D1329916

A Light for Hope Renewed

The Diary of Paul Mayer

A Half-Jewish Young Man's Story of Survival in Nazi Germany
and of His New Life in the United States
1945-1951

In German and English

Virginia Wagner Mayer, Editor
Laura Mayer Kelley, Co-Editor

ISBN 978-1-62806-260-1

Library of Congress Control Number 2019918600

Published by Salt Water Media
29 Broad Street, Suite 104
Berlin, MD 21811
www.saltwatermedia.com

Interior illustrations by Paul Mayer
Cover design by Sean Kelley; painting by Laura Jeanne Mayer Kelley

Meinen Freunden,

vornehmlich meiner Mutter

gewidmet

Dedicated to my Friends,
Especially to my Mother

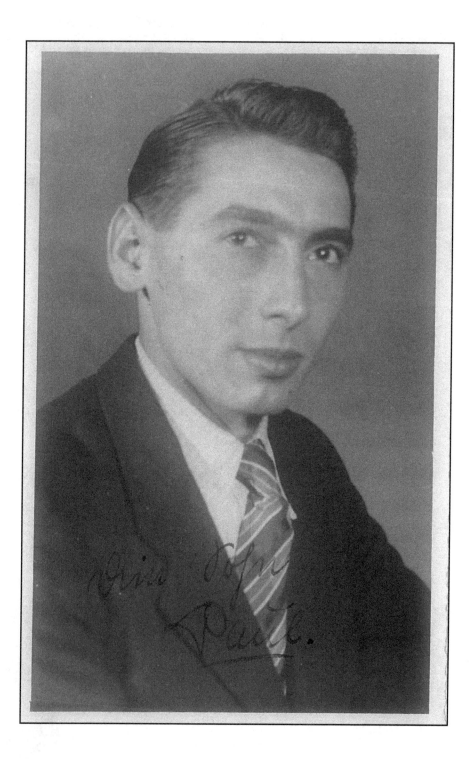

If I were ever privileged to fathom all the reasons, the causes, and the deeds committed in this war, I could still never grasp the consequences, much less condone them. It seems to me that what people have done and will yet do to one another in this struggle is entirely the product of human nature and its inadequate sense of responsibility. Generations to come will suffer the consequences; they will never be able to condone what was done with such boundless fanaticism to the dismay of all who have to live in these times or those yet to come. It's utterly useless for me as an individual to speculate about the future, but I certainly hope that each person's fate is determined by his acts and merits.

Paul Mayer, age 21
Excerpt from a diary entry on April 4, 1945
while in Derenberg Labor Camp.

TABLE OF CONTENTS

The original diaries as well as related documents and pictures are archived as "The Paul Mayer Papers" at the National Holocaust Museum in Washington, D.C. They can be accessed either on site by appointment at the Museum or through the website www.paulmayerpapers.org. Also accessible through www.daviddelaneymayer.com is David Delaney Mayer's documentary *Questions For My Grandfather*, a film that retraces the locations in Germany mentioned in the diary and reflects on the experience of being half Jewish during this time.

Acknowledgements

The transcription, translation and editing of this diary has been an ongoing project for many years and many people have been helpful along the way.

I would first like to thank Günther and Traute Eisenhauer for encouraging me to publish the diary. It was Günther who suggested that this should be done for family and friends and it was he who transcribed the parts of the diary which were written in old German script into typewritten German. Both he and his wife, Traute, were steadfast in helping at each step along the way. Together we explored the places mentioned in the diary and together we fine-tuned the translations on visits in Germany and the United States.

Thanks to Ulrike Guthrie, who translated the body of the diary; to her mother, Inge Heller, who translated the poetry, to many who made helpful suggestions, including Paul's brother, Heinz, as well as Cindy Runyan, Whitney Hostetler, Nadine Royal and Barbara Waldman. My appreciation to Mary O'Neal for her help with formatting and proofreading, to her husband, Klaus Schopmeier for producing a preliminary booklet, to Emily Wexler and David Glenn for high definition scanning and to Christophe Fricker for his contributions.

Special thanks to my family for their support; to son, Fritz Mayer, for his involvement in the preliminary preparation of the manuscript, to daughter, Marianne Pettis, for her help with technical aspects of the production, to daughter, Laura Kelley, for her contributions and encouragement in the completion of the diary, and to son, Donald Mayer, for his interest throughout the process.

Thanks to Katrin Huber, Benjamin and Beate Beck, and Dr. Adam Woodis of Salisbury University for proofreading the German version of the diary. Thanks to my Kelley grandchildren, Sean, Ian, Morgan and Aidan, for proofreading the English. Thanks also to the folks at Salt Water Media, Andrew Heller and Stephanie Fowler, who were willing to take on this somewhat unique project. I would also like to recognize the contributions of grandson David Delaney Mayer and nephew Dan Mayer who have continued to tell the stories through their art.

Finally, thanks to the people at the National Holocaust Museum in Washington, D.C., Becky Erbelding, Kara Shuster and Kassandra LaPrade Seuthe, whose interest in preserving our family story is much appreciated.

Virginia Wagner Mayer

Foreword

Paul Gustav Wilhelm Mayer wrote this diary during and immediately after World War II. It is in three parts, the first describing his life in Germany during the Nazi era as a young man with one Jewish parent, the second, his immigration to the United States, and the third, (written in English), his experiences in Cincinnati as a recent immigrant. Paul, who had been denied the opportunity to attend secondary school in Germany, was eventually to earn a PhD from Cornell University and to become a Regents Professor at the Georgia Institute of Technology. He was always grateful for the opportunities given to him by his adopted country.

Born in 1923, Paul was the fourth child and first son for Friedrich Wilhelm Mayer, a German Jewish merchant, and Alice Lucie Waeldin, a French Protestant Christian. His birth was closely followed by that of a second son, Heinz. He had three older sisters, Marianne, Gretel, and Helga.

Paul's parents had met and were married in Strasbourg at the time when Alsace was controlled by Germany. Friedrich served in the German army during World War I. Because of this, after the War, when Alsace had become a part of France, the family, now including a daughter, Marianne, was forced to leave and their business was confiscated. They settled in Fechenheim, a suburb of Frankfurt, where Friedrich and his brother opened a store selling household goods. By the time Gretel was born, they had established themselves. Helga, Paul and Heinz were born in rapid succession.

Home was a spacious flat occupying the third floor of a building on the Hanauer Landstrasse, a major highway between Frankfurt and Hanau. The business flourished. The Mayers were sponsors of local sports teams. The children had a happy life. Sundays were times for baking cakes, for walks in the woods, or for rides in a cart behind their pony. A kindermädchen helped with the busy household. The children, brought up as Christians, attended Sunday School and were confirmed in the Evangelische Kirche.

But this comfortable life began to change, first in small ways and then dramatically. For Friedrich was Jewish and this was Nazi Germany. The business was boycotted and to make ends meet, Alice went to work in a Frankfurt store which sold fine linens. The children were not permitted to attend secondary schools. The girls found jobs as household helpers, the boys as apprentices, Paul learned a trade as a locksmith and Heinz as a coppersmith and plumber.

In the Kristallnacht pogrom of November 9, 1938, the business was completely destroyed. Shortly after this, Friedrich was taken to the infamous concentration camp, Buchenwald. A year later he was released and sent back to Fechenheim, a broken man. He tried to make a living selling things from a pushcart. But this was only a temporary reprieve and in 1941, he was again arrested and taken to Auschwitz/Birkenau. This time he did not return.

Marianne, the beloved oldest sister, became ill, but because of her Jewish heritage, admittance to a hospital was delayed. Likely because of this, she died in 1942 of kidney disease. One year later, on August 8, 1943, the family received the official notice of Friedrich's death in Auschwitz.

The rest of the family continued with their work in Frankfurt. As this was a time of incessant bombing of the city, they began to fear for their lives in Fechenheim, where their house was so close to the I. G. Farben plant and to the main railway line between Frankfurt and Berlin. It was decided that they should move to a "safer" part of the city.

It would be this new residence which would be reduced to rubble, while I.G. Farben and the railway were never bombed and the home in Fechenheim stood until the late 1960's. In the apartment at the time were sister, Helga, and her little son, Christian. They had fortunately taken refuge in the basement during the bombing and were able to escape through the adjacent building.

But now, the family had to find a safer place to stay. The young people had often gone hiking and skiing in the Taunus Mountains and they knew the little town of Wüstems, a small farming community. They went to investigate and found a family, the Molls, who were willing to take them in, in spite of the risk to them of doing this.

Wüstems is approximately 60 kilometers from Frankfurt. Helga and Christian lived there full time. Christian's father was in the German navy and, although as an Aryan he was forbidden to marry his half Jewish sweetheart, he was able to visit occasionally.

Heinz found work in a nearby village. Alice. Gretel and Paul continued with their jobs in Frankfurt where Alice and Gretel lived in a rented room, Paul with the family of his employer, Herr Thielemann, the master locksmith from whom he learned his trade. All made frequent trips to Wüstems on the weekends. Paul also played soccer with Kickers Offenbach during this time. This was the situation on January 1, 1945, when he started to write this diary.

Friend's Note
by Günther Eisenhauer, Educator & Theologian
Bremen, Germany

It was a day in August of 1979. My oldest daughter, Christine, and I were with Virginia and Paul in order to get to know their home and their family who were so welcoming as to invite Christine to spend the last two weeks of her vacation with them. I would have to fly back to Germany a few days later.

Over a cup of tea, we had already had a long conversation – in English of course- and were getting ready to leave when Virginia proposed that we should look at the room on the second floor where Christine would be staying. We went up the stairs and there on the wall, close enough to touch, were pictures of familiar buildings in Frankfurt, some of which had been destroyed by bombs during the war. I pointed out the pictures to Christine. "Christine, that is Frankfurt, where I was born!"

Paul, who was behind me, said in unmistakable Hessian dialect, "I also. I also was born in Frankfurt and I lived there until 1947."

We then stayed much longer, and Paul and I, in German and English, talked about those years which we, separated by only six years in age and ten kilometers, had experienced so differently. I could, of course, remember the soccer teams with whom or against whom Paul played and the names of some of the players.

Of greater significance was what Paul told me when I asked him the reason for his emigrating. During the conversation that followed, he also showed me his diary. His trusting frankness was surprising to me. Even 35 years after the end of the war, persons who were persecuted during the Nazi years were seldom willing to recall those painful experiences, let alone speak about them to a contemporary (German of the same age) who had not been persecuted. Until that time, Paul had spoken seldom and mostly only to Virginia about his experiences during the war. She, too, was surprised at the animated and intense way he shared his story with me.

Afterwards, during the remaining days before my flight to Germany, Virginia and Paul took us on an auto tour of the Atlanta area. A further discussion of the times that we had lived through together and yet so differently did not take place. I hesitated to ask him for his diary and to continue our discussion through correspondence from a distance.

Not until some years after Paul's death and after I was retired, did I speak with Virginia about the diary, and I was happy that she immediately agreed that it should not be lost and should be accessible at least to the children and grandchildren. For the years 1945 and 1946, the diary was written on poor quality paper with pencil and in Sütterlin (old German script). I, too, had learned this type of writing during my school years. I could read and transcribe it and that is what I did.

In this way, I have become so well acquainted with Paul, or should I say his life story, that even today I can hardly believe that I spoke with him only that one time on a level so direct, intense and personal. How I would like to have asked him about many things, always seeking the common threads by which we as individuals are at one and the same time both bound together and separated, woven into the political fabric of society with our feelings, thoughts and actions.

Zwei Brüder

Two Brothers

Two Brothers

Paul Mayer, Cincinnati, Ohio, July 18, 1947

Written by Paul Mayer as an introduction to From the Main to the Ohio, the part of the diary which Paul sent to his mother in Germany from his new home on the Ohio River

"Mama! Mama!", Little Heinze cries, fit to break one's heart, as he stumbles up the stairs. Tears course ceaselessly down his rosy cheeks; his frost-reddened fists are clenched defiantly and are dug deep into the pocket of his blue apron, which is embroidered with a little flock of ducks.

"Mama, Paul won't let me join in the game!" he now whimpers, letting the door slam shut behind him. But then he can see into the kitchen, where mother is busy baking cakes for the approaching Christmas festivities, and his pretty, boyish face lights up remarkably quickly.

"Oh, Mama, may I help?" Of course he may, so he eagerly gets the little rolling pin from his toy cupboard, and starts working on a lump of dough. Yet he never seems satisfied with the shapes he fashions, for he keeps on kneading the dough again and again, asks for more flour, and adds it to his pastry just as mother does. Untiringly, he starts over again. The fact that the dough has become first grey, then almost black, doesn't bother him, and then finally everything is put on mother's last cookie tray and put in the oven.

"Mama, when can I get them back?" His trophies have to stay in the black hole far too long. And yet he waits patiently, happily anticipating that, when his father returns from his work, he will be able to offer him some of his baked goods from his little store.

A quiet, sunny smile spreads on her face as she watches the efforts of her little Heinzelmännchen, as she endearingly refers to him at times. She need not worry about him. He wants to become a pastry chef one day. Well, there's still a way to go with that. For now he's still her dear, good little boy and as handy as a little housewife.

Zwei Brüder

Paul Mayer, Cincinnati, Ohio, den 18 Juli 1947

Von Paul Mayer als Einleitung geschrieben zu „Vom Main zum Ohio", dem Teil des Tagebuches, den Paul seiner Mutter in Deutschland schickte von seinem neuen Zuhause am Ohio Fluss.

"Mama! Mama!" Herzzerbrechend weint der kleine Heinze, während er die Treppen heraufstolpert. Über seine Apfelbäckchen kullern unaufhörlich die Tränen, seine frostroten Fäuste sind trotzig geballt und graben sich fest in die Tasche der blauen Schürze, auf die eine kleine Entenschar gestickt ist.

"Mama, der Paul läßt mich nicht mitspielen!", greint er jetzt, indem er die Tür hart hinter sich zuschlagen lässt. Nun sieht er aber in die Küche, wo Mutter mit Kuchenbacken für das nahende Christfest beschäftigt ist und merkwürdig schnell erhellt sich sein hübsches Bubengesicht.

"Oh Mama, darf ich auch!" Natürlich darf er und holt emsig aus seinem Spielschrank das kleine Kuchenholz hervor und bearbeitet damit einen Teigklumpen. Jedoch er scheint nicht endgültig mit den erzielten Formen zufrieden, denn immer wieder knetet er den Teig zusammen, verlangt noch Mehl und mengt es bei, grad so wie es Mutter auch macht. Unermüdlich beginnt er von neuem; selbst dass inzwischen der Teig erst grau, dann fast schwarz wird, stört ihn nicht und dann auf Mutters letztem Kuchenblech kommt alles mit in den Backofen.

"Mama, wann kann ich sie wiederhaben?" Schier zu lange müssen ihm seine Erzeugnisse in dem schwarzen Loch bleiben. Doch wartet er geduldig und freut sich jetzt schon, dass er seinem Papa, wenn dieser von der Arbeit kommt, das Backwerk in seinem Kaufladen anbieten kann.

Ein sonnig stilles Lächeln begleitet die Anstrengungen ihres "Heinzelmännchens", wie sie ihn zuweilen liebkosend nennt. Über ihn braucht sie sich keine Sorgen zu machen. Konditor will er einmal lernen. Nun ja, da geht noch eine geraume Zeit dahin. Jetzt ist er noch ihr lieber, braver Bub und geschickt wie ein kleines Hausmütterchen.

But as for Paul! Of course she doesn't love him any less, but she worries more about him, though the two boys are separated by only a year. He's a veritable little rascal, a daredevil and contrary so-and-so. No doubt he has those traits from his father. No doubt he's downstairs at the moment playing with his ball, from which he's inseparable. Or maybe he's in the neighbor's garden, where he can be found from time to time.

In the meantime, father has come home with a not exactly friendly "Good Evening" greeting. After he's hung up his lined great coat and put on his carefully pre-warmed slippers, he sits down at the ready-laid table. It was pretty cold today and even at work there had been some frustrations. But certainly he can't complain at home. It was always cozy and comfortable, and his children were always clean and obedient.

He likes Paul best; he's his firstborn son, and his pride. But where is he? Now he misses him and his wife can only tell him that once again he's nowhere to be found. "Then I'll....I'll teach him a lesson. He knows it's mealtime. And it's already dark outside!" Father grumbles and leaves the room. He stands and surveys the scene at the front of the house. And just one short whistle; that's the final warning, as Paul knows.

And truly, not long after this Paul does arrive, but not alone. He peers anxiously from behind the wide apron of the ample neighbor woman. He's totally filthy. Father's energetic questions and mother's concerned appeals are met with only a whimpering response, so that the neighbor is forced to narrate the events she witnessed.

Aber der Paul! Gewiß hat sie ihn nicht minder gern, nur macht ihr der mehr Sorgen, obwohl die beiden nur ein Jahr trennt. Ein rechter Wildfang ist der, ein kleiner Tollkopf und Trotzkopf. Das hat er wohl von seinem Vater. Jetzt ist er wohl drunten und spielt mit seinem Ball, von dem er unzertrennlich ist. Oder ist er wieder in Nachbars Garten, man kann ihn zuweilen suchen.

Inzwischen kommt der Vater mit nicht gerade freundlichem "Guten Abend" Gruß herein und nachdem er seinen gefütterten Wegrock aufgehängt und seine vorsorglich angewärmten Hausschuhe angezogen hat, setzt er sich an den gedeckten Tisch. Heute war es recht kalt gewesen, und auch im Geschäft gab es manchen Verdruss. Zu Hause darf er sich aber nicht beklagen, gewiss nicht. Immer behaglich und gemütlich, seine Kinder sauber und gehorsam.

Ihm ist der Paul der Liebste; der Erste und sein Stolz. Aber wo steckt denn er Jetzt vermisst er ihn und seine Frau kann ihm nur sagen, dass er wieder nicht aufzufinden sei. "Den soll doch ……, ich will ihn lehren. Er weiß doch, dass es Essenszeit ist. Und draußen schon Nacht!", so grollte der Vater und verlässt das Zimmer. Von der Rückfront des Hauses hält er Ausschau. Und nun ein kurzer Pfiff: Das war die letzte Mahnung! Das weiß auch Paul.

Und wirklich nicht lange hernach kommt er an; doch nicht allein. Hinter der breiten Schürze der rundlichen Nachbarin lugt er ängstlich hervor, über und über beschmutzt. Auf des Vaters energische wie auf der Mutter besorgte Fragen kommt nur ein weinerliches Gedruckse als Antwort, sodass die Nachbarsfrau den von ihr beobachteten Vorgang erzählen kann.

5

"It's a miracle," she begins, "that nothing happened to the boy. I'd just finished carrying in the groceries and saw a ball flying into the street from your gateway, and the boy running right after it without regard for the heavy traffic. Well, and then everything happened so quickly! A car braked, people screamed, and I saw his red apron disappearing beneath the car!" It's obvious that the woman is truly in shock from the events, and even the parents are at a loss for words for a while. So Paul got away without the feared disciplinary sermon only because his mother led him away to undertake his execution with soap and water.

Long after the delayed consumption of the evening meal the parents were still discussing the event, while the boy had long since left behind the events for a dream world. When mother, on going to bed herself, casts another glance into the children's bedroom, she sees two identical shocks of brown hair peeking out from under the blanket.

*   *   *

This story is not completely fictional, but, as you might expect, it's only the retelling of an event such as might have taken place at that time. Among other things, the story shows what differences became, or rather, were, evident between the two of us brothers.

Now we're both adults, and we're dependent on one another for many things through our shared experience of emigration. Our way, however, remains fundamentally different. For this reason I suppose it's quite understandable if I say little about him in these journals, for after all, I am writing about experiences as I've seen them through my own lenses (which I don't literally possess)] and on which I report from my perspective.

„Es ist wie ein Wunder", so beginnt sie, „dass dem Jungen nichts passiert ist. Ich kam gerade vom Einholen und sah, wie ein Ball aus euerm Torbogen auf die Straße flog und ungeachtet des starken Verkehrs rannte der Bub hinterher. Ja und dann ging alles so schnell. Ein Auto bremste, die Leute schrieen und ich sah eben noch, wie seine rote Schürze unter dem Auto verschwand!" Man merkt der guten Frau den ausgestandenen Schrecken wirklich an, auch den Eltern verschlägt es zunächst die Stimme und so entgeht Paul der gefürchteten Strafpredigt nur dadurch, weil ihn die Mutter abführt, um in der Küche eine Exekution mit Wasser und Seife vorzunehmen.

Noch lange nach der verspäteten Einnahme des Nachtmahls besprachen die Eltern den Vorfall, während den Buben längst in Träumen die Ereignisse entfallen sind. Zum Verwechseln ähnlich ragen zwei braune Haarbüschel aus der Bettdecke, als die Mutter vor dem Schlafengehen nochmals einen Blick in das Kinderzimmer wirft.

*   *   *

Diese Geschichte ist nicht frei erfunden, aber auch logischerweise nicht nur die Nacherzählung einer tatsächlichen Begebenheit, so wie sie sich damals zugetragen haben mag. Sie zeigt unter anderem auch, welche Gegensätze zwischen uns beiden Brüdern schon während unserer Kindheit zutage getreten sind oder besser waren.

Nun sind wir erwachsene Menschen und durch die gemeinsame Auswanderung in vielen Dingen aufeinander angewiesen. Unsere Art jedoch blieb grundverschieden. Deshalb ist es auch wohl verständlich, wenn hier wenig die Rede von ihm sein wird, denn es sind ja Erlebnisse, die ich durch meine Brille (die ich wörtlich gar nicht besitze) gesehen und in meiner Anschauungsweise wiedergegeben habe.

Part One

January 1945-January 1947

Jahre von Schwierigkeit und Überleben

Years of Hardship and Survival

Original in German with English Translation

Happy New Year!

January 1

A new year! A new fight to be fought! Go, Torero! Enjoying jolly company at Gustav's in Oberems. Happy, carefree youth.

I tried to ski today for the first time this winter. There's still a real lack of snow but the exercise in such clean air did me good.

January 2

I had to get up early today, at 3:15 a.m. Despite a terrible sore throat, I stumbled my way to Königstein. I arrived at Frankfurt am Main on schedule, but the streetcar lost power halfway there, so the trip ended with a brisk walk.

On arriving in Fechenheim, I found Mr. (*Kurt*) Thielemann in a shockingly weak and apparently sick state. It seems the poor devil has been vegetating like this for over a week. Dr. Hain, called upon for counsel, thought a hospital stay advisable, especially since without care and given his unbelievable messiness, Thielemann would stand almost no chance of recovering.

January 3

After a few difficulties, Mr. Thielemann was admitted to the Deaconess Hospital. A rare specimen, this Thielemann.

January 4

The attack came surprisingly fast today. I was doing the useful task of splitting wood when, with a mighty droning sound, both the bomber and the antiaircraft guns began firing. Sensing nothing good was going to happen, I immediately went into the street. Shortly thereafter, the sound of falling bombs announced impending disaster. I was still undecided about what to do, as bombs began falling further afield. Facing no immediate personal danger, I thus continued to observe where the bombs fell and the direction of the bomber's flight until it disappeared. A four-engine plane was shot down.

Prosit Neujahr!

1. Januar

Ein neues Jahr! Ein neuer Kampf! Auf, Torero! In lustiger Gesellschaft beim „Gustav" in Oberems. Glückliche, unbesorgte Jugend.

Heute habe ich den ersten Versuch in diesem Winter auf Brettern angestellt. Es mangelt noch sehr an Schnee, doch die Bewegung in gereinigter Atmosphäre hat mir gut getan.

2. Januar

Heute hieß es früh aufstehen, um 3.15 Uhr. Trotz schrecklicher Halsschmerzen nach Königstein getippelt. Zwar kam ich planmäßig nach Frankfurt am Main, doch versagte auf halbem Weg der Straßenbahn der Strom, sodass ein tüchtiger Fußmarsch diese Fahrepisode beschloß.

In Fechenheim angekommen, fand ich Herrn (*Kurt*) Thieleman in erschreckend schwachem augenscheinlich krankem Zustand. Und so will der arme Tropf schon über eine Woche vegetiert haben. Dr. Hain zu Rate gezogen, hielt der den Krankenhausaufenthalt für zweckmäßig, zumal Thieleman ohne Pflege und in seiner unglaublichen Unordnung kaum je wieder auf die Beine käme.

3. Januar

Nach mancherlei Schwierigkeiten konnte Herr Thielemann ins Diakonissenhaus aufgenommen werden. Ein seltenes Exemplar, dieser Thielemann.

4. Januar

Überraschend schnell kam heute der Angriff. Ich war noch mit der nützlichen Mühe des Holzspaltens beschäftigt, als mit mächtigem Gebrumm der Flieger auch zugleich die Flak zu schießen begann. Nichts Gutes ahnend, begab ich mich sofort auf die Straße. Kurz darauf kündete das Rauschen fallender Bomben nahendes Unheil. Noch unschlüssig, welches Verhalten richtig, fielen die Bomben in weiterer Umgebung. Demnach befürchtete ich keine unmittelbare Gefahr für mich und beobachtete bis zum Ende die Flugrichtung der Bomber and die Einschläge der Bomben. Ein viermotoriges Flugzeug wurde abgeschossen.

January 6

Today's trip home was complicated. Having done the house cleaning yesterday with great vigor, there was nothing standing in the way of an early departure today.

Here it should be noted that, thanks to my athletic activity, I have developed a certain skill at jumping onto moving trucks. Despite my knapsack, I managed to climb onto the deck of a milk van, which brought me to Daimlerstrasse and the no easier job of jumping off. This is how it's done: let yourself down, hold on, run alongside the vehicle, then let go and run till you slow down! Super!

Having arrived at Königstein, I had the good fortune of being able to ride to Wüstems on a horse-drawn sled as a fare dodger. That was a lovely drive!

January 7

Snow fell this week and skiing went much better today, as numerous falls into the soft stuff could testify. Mrs. Steinmetz brought us a big helping of salted meat. A portion of it will enrich my menus this week.

January 11

Mr. Thielemann was released from the hospital today. So was he really all that sick? I almost believe that he's a bit too soft.

6. Januar

Das war heute eine komplizierte Heimfahrt. Nachdem ich gestern schon mit großem Elan Hausputz gehalten hatte, stand dem heutigen Frühstart nichts im Wege.

Hier will vermerkt sein, dass ich dank meiner sportlichen Betätigung eine gewisse Geschicklichkeit im Aufspringen auf fahrende Lastautos entwickelt habe. Trotz des Tornisters konnte ich das Verdeck eines Milchautos erklimmen, das mich an der Daimlerstrasse vor die keinesfalls leichtere Aufgabe des Abspringens stellte. Solches geht folgendermaßen vor sich: runterlassen, festhalten, mitlaufen, dann loslassen und auslaufen! Prima!!!

In Königstein angekommen, hatte ich das persönliche Glück, als Schwarzfahrer auf einem Pferdeschlitten nach Wüstems reisen zu dürfen. Dies war eine schöne Fahrt!

7. Januar

Nachdem diese Woche neuer Schnee gefallen war, ging heute der Skisport schon viel besser vonstatten, wovon zahlreiche Stürze ins weiche Element zeugten. Frau Steinmetz brachte uns eine große Portion „Gesalzenes". Ein Teil davon wird diese Woche meinen Küchenzettel bereichern.

11. Januar

Herr (Kurt) Thielemann wurde heute schon aus dem Krankenhaus entlassen. War er denn wirklich so krank? Ich glaube fast, dass der ein bisschen viel „matschig" ist.

January 12

Three Reichsmarks can be the price of haste. I learned this lesson today when, for lack of time, I went through the barrier at the Mainkur Station without a ticket. On attempting to pay on arrival at the East Station, I discovered that the deal - as I've already told you - cost me three RM. Of course, I never told the master anything about this!

At the moment no trams are running in Frankfurt between 9:00 a.m. and 4:00 p.m., to save energy. I discovered this myself when I wanted to go to Fechenheim again. So once again a delivery van had to serve as transportation, which carried me to Schwedlerstrasse. After a short walk, for lack of a better option I made do with a horse and cart which took me on to my doorstep.

January 15

Today Heinz and I went to the employment office for a health exam. As we learned there, it's expected that we'll be ordered out to Central Germany to work by next Sunday. Since I again had to get to Fechenheim on foot, it was 2:30 a.m. by the time I got there.

January 16

I explained the situation to the master, who agreed that I could pack up my things and move them to Wüstems. So I spent the whole day packing and getting things in order. My last official duty was to make myself a pair of new taps for the heels of my shoes. In the evening I sought out Georg (Hornes) once more and took my leave of him.

12. Januar

Drei Reichsmark kann der Übereifer kosten. Solches musste ich heute erfahren, als ich mangels Zeit ohne Billet durch die Sperre auf dem Bahnhof Mainkur ging. Als ich am Ostbahnhof nachlösen wollte, kostete der Spaß, wie schon berichtet, 3 RM!! Davon habe ich dem Meister nie berichtet, natürlich!

Zur Zeit fahren in Frankfurt während der Zeit von 9 bis 16 Uhr keine Straßenbahnen, zwecks Stromersparnis. Dies musste ich am eigenen Leib erfahren, als ich wieder nach Fechenheim fahren wollte. So musste halt wieder so ein Lastauto herhalten, das mich bis zur Schwedlerstraße beförderte. Nach kurzem Fußmarsch nahm ich, mangels besserer Gelegenheit, mit einem Fuhrwerk vorlieb, das mich bis vors Haus spedierte.

15. Januar

Heinz und ich waren heute auf dem Arbeitsamt wegen einer Untersuchung. Wie man da hören konnte, sollen wir schon kommenden Sonntag nach Mitteldeutschland zur Arbeit hinbeordert werden. Da ich außerdem noch nach Fechenheim laufen musste, kam ich erst um 2.30 Uhr dort an.

16. Januar

Ich habe dem Meister die Situation klargelegt, worauf er sich damit einverstanden erklärte, dass ich meine Sachen zusammenpacke und sie nach Wüstems transportieren kann. So habe ich heute den ganzen Tag gepackt and gerichtet. Als letzte Amtshandlung gewissermaßen habe ich mir ein Paar Absatzeisen angefertigt. Am Abend habe ich nochmals Georg (Hornes) aufgesucht und mich von ihm verabschiedet.

January 17

Today I moved out of Fechenheim gripping two suitcases, the bulging knapsack and my briefcase. A tedious and arduous ride to Frankfurt was followed by a similar trip from Königstein to Wüstems. Heinz met me at the station. Our luggage was stowed onto a sled, which Mrs. Scherer had kindly lent us. On the way, we jumped onto a truck which brought us as far as Eselseck. The sled scooted along behind us like a loyal dog. After Eselseck we had to go by foot again.

But this episode doesn't end here. I really wanted to return the sled today and so I set off after a bite to eat. Luckily a suitable car chanced by in Oberems. So up I jumped and stayed put until Königstein. I was lucky. Then I returned the sled and later rode back on the mail bus. By 8:00 p.m. I was back in Wüstems.

January 18

I checked my shoes today and repaired the heels. Also got the anticipated word from the mayor, according to which we're to meet on Sunday, January 21 at 3:30 p.m. on Platform Nine of the Central Train Station in Frankfurt.

January 20

Departure from Wüstems. Letter to Gertrud Heep. Knapsack ready for action.

January 21

Set off at 6:00 am. Fresh snow. Luggage on sleds.

Despite a great expenditure of energy, we arrived in Königstein too late and therefore had to walk to Frankfurt. It took us eight hours. And the bombshell was that at 3:30 there wasn't a soul to be seen, and, on asking at the police station, we learned that we should have been there at 3:30 in the morning; in short, that we were twelve hours too late. We also ascertained there that we were to report to a Mr. Dilcher on Linnestrasse. We spent the evening and night at Mrs. Neff's.

17. Januar

Mit zwei Koffern, dem vollbepackten Tornister und meiner Aktentasche bepackt, bin ich heute aus Fechenheim abgewandert. Auf eine umständliche und beschwerliche Fahrt nach Frankfurt folgte eine ebensolche von Königstein nach Wüstems. Heinz traf ich im Bahnhof. Unser Gepäck wurde auf einem Schlitten, den uns Frau Scherer freundlicherweise lieh, verwahrt. Unterwegs sprangen wir auf ein Lastauto, das uns bis zum Eselseck dienlich war. Der Schlitten lief wie ein treuer Hund hinterher. Vom Eselseck aus mußten wir wieder laufen.

Doch damit ist diese Episode nicht zu Ende. Ich wollte den Schlitten zu gern auch heute wieder hinbringen und habe mich darum auch nach beendeter Mahlzeit in Marsch gesetzt. Zum Glück kam schon in Oberems ein passendes Auto. Also drauf und erst in Königstein wieder runter. Also Glück gehabt. Dann habe ich den Schlitten abgeliefert und bin später mit dem Postomnibus zurückgefahren. Um 8 Uhr war ich wieder in Wüstems.

18. Januar

Heute habe ich meine Schuhe nachgesehen und die Absätze repariert. Auch kam der erwartete Bescheid durch den Bürgermeister, nach dem wir uns am Sonntag, dem 21. Januar, im Frankfurter Hauptbahnhof, 3.30 Uhr nachmittags, Bahnsteig 9 einzufinden haben.

20. Januar

Abschied von Wüstems. Brief an Gertrud Heep. Tornister feldmarschmäßig.

21. Januar

Start um 6 Uhr. Neuschnee. Gepäck auf Schlitten.

Trotz größter Kraftentfaltung kamen wir zu spät nach Königstein und mussten darum bis nach Frankfurt laufen. Dazu haben wir etwa 8 Stunden gebraucht. Und der Knalleffekt war, um 15.30 Uhr war kein Mensch zu sehen und auf Rücksprache bei der Kriminalwache im Bahnhof erfuhren wir, dass wir schon um 3.30 Uhr morgens hätten da sein sollen, somit also 12 Stunden zu spät seien. Da erfuhren wir noch, dass wir uns bei einem Herrn Dilcher in der Linne-Straße zu melden hätten. Den Abend und die Nacht haben wir bei Frau Neff zugebracht.

January 22

All we learned from Mr. Dilcher was that we were to report to the Gestapo on Lindenstrasse. And there, surprisingly, we were told that we could go back home until about March 1.

So I went straight to the station and bought a ticket to Idstein. The train left at 4 p.m. I reached Idstein sometime after 6 p.m. and was in Wüstems, totally exhausted, by about 10 p.m.

January 23

Since I basically had nothing to do, Galsworthy's novel, *The Patrician*, was a welcome way of passing the time.

January 25

Today I'm once again wearing shoes. While taking a spontaneous walk, I was overtaken by the horse-drawn sled belonging to Scharf, the village farm leader. I rode with him to Wallsdorf via Esch. On the return trip we were joined at Esch by "Carpenter" Willi who in the meantime had been drafted into the RAD (Reich Work Service.)

That evening I went skiing by moonlight. Fantastic!

January 26

Today it stormed and snowed so badly, you wouldn't have sent a dog out. Yet, for all that, mother came stumbling over from Königstein in this weather. She arrived quite exhausted but glad that we hadn't had to leave yet.

Hannelore wrote with news of Horst'l. I replied immediately because I was so happy to hear from her.

February 3

I don't even want to mention any more how difficult it has become to get to Wüstems. Today I was en route from 10 a.m. until 6:30 p.m.

February 4

Acquiring a few phrases of English is a lot of fun, but not even the gods know how long this ambition of mine will last.

22. Januar

Bei dem Herrn Dilcher konnten wir uns wiederum nur den Bescheid holen, dass wir uns bei der Gestapo in der Lindenstraße zu melden hätten. Und dort wurde uns überraschenderweise gesagt, dass wir wieder nach Hause durften, bis etwa zum 1. März.

Da bin ich denn auch gleich zum Bahnhof und hab mir ein Billet nach Idstein gelöst. Um 16.00 Uhr ging der Zug. Nach 18.00 Uhr war ich in Idstein and etwa um 22.00 Uhr in Wüstems, aber marode.

23. Januar

Bei gründlicher Ruhe war mir Galsworthys Roman „Der Patrizier" ein willkommener Zeitvertreib.

25. Januar

Heute habe ich erstmals wieder Schuhe an. Bei einem kurz gedachten Spaziergang wurde ich vom Pferdeschlitten des Bauernführers Scharf eingeholt, mit dem ich bis nach Wallsdorf über Esch gefahren bin. Auf dem Heimweg kam bei Esch der „Schreiner" Willi noch mit, der inzwischen seinen Einruf zum RAD (Reichsarbeitsdienst) erhaltem hat.

Am Abend, im Mondschein bin ich noch Ski gelaufen. Prima!

26. Januar

Heute hat's gestürmt und geschneit, dass man keinen Hund vor die Tür gejagt hätte. Und bei diesem Wetter kam die Mutter von Königstein rübergetippelt, ganz erschöpft kam sie an, jedoch glücklich, dass wir noch nicht weg gemusst hatten.

Hannelore hat geschrieben und vom Horst'l berichtet. Ich hab gleich gedankt, weil ich mich so sehr darüber gefreut habe.

3. Februar

Ich will jetzt gar nicht mehr erwähnen, wie beschwerlich der Weg nach Wüstems geworden ist. Heute war ich von 10.00 bis 18.30 Uhr unterwegs.

4. Februar

Der Erwerb einiger Brocken aus der englischen Sprache macht mir eben schon Spaß, doch wie lange dieser Ehrgeiz anhält, wissen auch die Götter nicht.

February 6

The name, Laber, has had a special ring for me for quite some time. Whether it's in reference to the now deceased Mr. Laber, his wife, Günther, Margot, or "Deli" it's all the same, although I don't know exactly why it's so.

Visiting them is always a holiday for me. I had dinner at their house tonight. Mrs. Laber and Odele were present. I am deeply interested in the fortunes of this family. At the moment, Günther is in the infirmary in Voralberg.

February 10

Since Mrs. Laber has little or no firewood, I've resolved to give her a small pleasure. Using various resources, I was able to deliver quite a nice wagonload of wood to her this evening. In return for a few cigarettes, Mr. Heger spared me a tedious and time-consuming task and split the wood for me with his power saw.

For Heinz Ebert, I had a wooden box made for an electric hotplate, while I fashioned a matching tin lid for it.

February 11

The ski boots had to be repaired yet again. Today for the first time in quite a while I did not go to Wüstems. For lunch, I made myself a couple of potato pancakes that helped somewhat to reconcile me with this unfortunate Sunday.

I was in Frankfurt in the afternoon. After dinner at the Börsenkeller, I went to visit mother in Querstrasse, since she had also stayed in Frankfurt.

February 12

Gretel has brought me all kinds of foragings from Wüstems, for which I'm most grateful. The only problem was that what was intended to be a stockpile of groceries became merely provisions for the return journey to Fechenheim. Nonetheless, everything – apples, potato dumplings, sausage and cheesecake – tasted glorious.

6. Februar

Der Name Laber hat für mich schon seither einen besonderen Klang. Sei es nun der verewigte Herr Laber, seine Frau, Günther, Margot oder „Deli" ist ganz gleich, obwohl ein stichhaltiger Grund mir selbst unbekannt ist.

Ein Besuch bei ihnen ist mir stets ein Feiertag. Heute habe ich da mit zu Nacht gegessen. Frau Laber und Odele waren anwesend. Für die Geschicke dieser Familie habe ich regste Anteilnahme. Günther liegt zurzeit in Vorarlberg in einem Lazarett.

10. Februar

Da Frau Laber keinen oder ungenügenden Brand besitzt, habe ich mich entschlossen, ihr eine kleine Freude zu bereiten. Durch Anwendung verschiedener Hilfsmittel konnte ich bis zum Abend einen schönen Wagen voll Holz bei ihr abliefern. Für einige Zigaretten hat mir Herr Heger auf seiner Kreissäge eine mühselige und zeitraubende Arbeit abgenommen und das Holz zersägt.

Für Heinz Ebert habe ich einen Holzkasten für eine elektrische Kochplatte anfertigen lassen, dazu noch selbst einen passenden Blechdeckel angefertigt.

11. Februar

Wieder einmal mußten die Skischuhe repariert werden. Heute bin ich seit längerer Zeit einmal nicht in Wüstems. Zum Mittagessen habe ich mir ein paar Kartoffelpfannkuchen gemacht, die mich einigermaßen mit diesem mißlichen Sonntag ausgesöhnt haben.

Am Nachmittag war ich in Frankfurt. Nachdem ich im Börsenkeller zu Nacht gegessen hatte, ging ich zur Mutter in der Querstraße, weil sie ja auch in Frankfurt geblieben war.

12. Februar

Gretel hat mir aus Wüstems allerhand Furage mitgebracht, für die ich recht dankbar bin. Nur wurde aus der gedachten Vorratsbereicherung nur eine Wegzehrung für die Rückkehr nach Fechenheim. Alles aber: Äpfel, Kartoffelklöße, Wurst und Käsekuchen haben prächtig geschmeckt.

February 17

There must be such a thing as having a premonition; otherwise I would surely not have set off at 4:30 in the morning. I met mother and Gretel at the station and together we took the 6:43 train to Königstein. After a truly lovely walk, we arrived in Wüstems at 11:00.

Not long thereafter, bomber squadrons flew to Frankfurt ... and to Fechenheim. But no one could have anticipated that, and I only became aware of the whole mess on Monday, February 18.

February 18

Yesterday I fixed the light at Mrs. Schwarz's, and today at the former mayor's. In the afternoon, I fixed two locks for the people who, besides a good dinner, gave me three eggs and a quarter pound of butter.

February 19

Today is Deli Laber's birthday. I would so much have liked to have found her a radio set, but unfortunately nothing came of it. The damage done here by the bombers is quite considerable. And still, one must faithfully act like a good fellow and do menial work while others throw up their hands and don't know how to deal with the situation.

February 22

Georg is such a poor devil – now he is suffering from rheumatism. During the alarm, I brought his mother a few pieces of coal so that he could at least have a warm room. He also received an egg.

February 23

Today I had great good fortune. The loot was 125 grams of butter, 900 grams of bread, four cigars and three ham sandwiches.

An undoubtedly entirely new stage of my life has begun with my being drafted by the Stapo (*State Police*) into OT (*Organization Todt*).

17. Februar

Es muss doch so etwas wie Vorahnung geben, sonst wäre ich wohl kaum um 4.30 Uhr früh losgewandert. Im Bahnhof traf ich Mutter und Gretel und wir sind gemeinsam um 6.43 Uhr, nach Königstein gefahren. Nach wirklich schönem Fußmarsch waren wir schon um 11 Uhr in Wüstems.

Nicht lange danach flogen Bombengeschwader nach Frankfurt … und nach Fechenheim. Doch das konnte ja niemand ahnen und ich selbst wurde der Bescherung erst am Montag, dem 18.2. gewahr.

18. Februar

Gestern habe ich das Licht bei der Frau Schwarz repariert and heute bei „Alt-Bürgermeisters". Dazu kamen am Nachmittag zwei Schlösser bei den Leuten, von denen ich neben gutem Nachtessen noch 3 Eier und ¼ Butter bekam.

19. Februar

Heute hat „Deli" Laber Geburtstag. Zu gerne hätte ich ihr einen Radioapparat besorgt, doch leider ist nichts daraus geworden. Die Fliegerschäden hier sind ganz beträchtlich. Und da muss man noch brav den Gesellen spielen und unwichtige Arbeit leisten, wo andere die Hände überm Kopf zusammenschlagen und sich nicht zu helfen wissen.

22. Februar

Der Georg ist doch ein armer Tropf – jetzt wird er auch noch vom Rheumatismus geplagt. Seiner Mutter hab ich heut während des Alarms ein paar Kohlen gebracht, damit er wenigstens ein gewärmtes Zimmer hat. Ein Ei hat er auch bekommen.

23. Februar

Heute hab ich massig Glück gehabt. 125 Gramm Butter, 900 Gramm Brot, 4 Zigarren und 3 Butterbrote mit Schinken waren die Beute.

Eine wohl gänzlich neue Episode meines Lebens beginnt mit der Heranziehung zur OT (Organisation Todt) durch die Stapo.

March 9

Armed with all sorts of things for life and good wishes for our future, and carrying our orders, we (*Paul and his brother, Heinz*) set off for Königstein. That morning is particularly memorable because of the first bombs and the first victims which the war has visited on Wüstems. This happened because enemy planes, attracted by the fire of some forest workers, dropped a bomb resulting in five casualties among the workers.

My heartiest thanks to Huber, the cobbler, for working on my shoes until 11:00 p.m. so that at least in this respect I will not have any unpleasant surprises in store for me.

March 10

Three o'clock in the morning at the Central Station in Frankfurt. Departure was delayed until a later date – the same time on March 14 was the time set – because the previous day's air raid had damaged the trains. Of course this delay was most welcome and we hoped the railroad would be similarly devastated on the later date.

But first we made the return trip to Wüstems where we were, of course, welcomed with open arms.

March 14

The stay of execution is over and the departure can't be postponed any longer because the railroad has now been repaired.

9. März

Ausgerüstet mit allem Möglichen zum Leben und guten Wünschen für unsere Zukunft nebst dem bewußten Befehl ziehen wir (*Paul und sein Bruder, Heinz*) nach Königstein. Der Morgen ist besonders erinnerungswert wegen der ersten Bomben und der ersten Opfer, die der Luftkrieg dem Ort Wüstems auferlegte, insofern als die Feindflieger, angelockt durch ein Feuer der Waldarbeiter, unter jenen durch Bombenwurf 5 Verletzte forderten.

Dem Schuster Huber meinen herzlichen Dank, weil er bis um 23.00 Uhr an den Schuhen arbeitete, damit in dieser Beziehung keine unangenehme Überraschung entstehe.

10. März

Drei Uhr morgens im Hauptbahnhof in Frankfurt. Durch den am Vortag erfolgten Angriff und Schaden bedingten Ausfall der Züge verlegte sich die Abreise auf ein späteres Datum, welches auf den 14. März auf die gleiche Stunde festgesetzt wurde. Das war natürlich sehr willkommen und erwünscht, daß dann die Bahn ebenso zerstört sein möge.

Doch wurde zunächst die Rückkehr nach Wüstems beschlossen, wo uns natürlich ein begeisterter Empfang zuteil wurde.

14. März

Die Galgenfrist ist abgelaufen und die Abreise nicht mehr zu verschieben, weil auch inzwischen die Bahn wieder repariert wurde.

March 16

We arrived here today after many difficulties and interminable stopovers. Via Fulda, Bebra, Kreiensen, Ringelheim and Halberstadt to Blankenburg. It's not possible yet to get a clear picture of my fellow sufferers, but there will be the usual high and low. So far, the person who seems the most compatible to me is Erich Fl. whose calm disposition I like. After all, these young people have had to deal with all kinds of hardships, and in general the mood echoes this fact.

Heinz has found a nice friend who seems to complement well his own spiritual interests.

We hear from the sufferers from Berlin, Pomerania and Frankfurt am Main, who have been here quite a while already, that we will be used for labor or to guard concentration camp inmates. What an honor!

We're housed in a hut, really more a cattle barn, where we camp on bare planks. Our provisions are meager and lack any loving preparation.

We pass the time making music, playing cards, writing, or just doing nothing. All these activities, along with our football games in sight of the barbed wire fences and the people living behind them, bear witness to our unbroken human spirit.

The fortunes of people always define their habits, and beyond all material treasures our greatest assets are our health and an unbroken courage. And these treasures are worth guarding.

To what can we appeal if we know we also must bear a part of the guilt of the world?

What makes me most bitter is the realization that in the world's conflict over its shell, the kernel and the meaning are never discovered.

I lack not so much the knowledge as the strength and the means to draw nearer to the universe.

I wonder sometimes whether the right religion is not in fact deep awe in the presence of elemental power, instead of the weak perception that many have of a God before whom one will stand repentant of vice at the end, if one has, in "faithful" trust in mercy, gotten away with crimes all one's life. But that is only my opinion and not a universal doctrine.

16. März

Erst heute kamen wir hier an, nach mancherlei Schwierigkeiten und langwierigen Zwischenaufenthalten. Über Fulda, Bebra, Kreiensen, Ringelheim, Halberstadt nach Blankenburg. Von den Schicksalsgefährten lässt sich jetzt noch kein rechtes Bild machen, doch wird auch dabei das übliche Hoch und Tief zu verzeichnen sein. Die sympathischste Figur ist mir bis jetzt der Erich Fl., dessen ruhige Haltung mir gut gefällt. Die durchweg jungen Leute mussten ja mit allen entstehenden Schwierigkeiten fertig werden und dementsprechend ist auch die Stimmung im allgemeinen.

Heinz hat einen netten Kameraden gefunden, der ihn in seinen Geistesinteressen am besten zu ergänzen scheint.

Wir hören hier von den Schicksalsgefährten aus Berlin, Pommern und auch aus Frankfurt am Main, die schon länger hier sind, dass wir zur Arbeit oder zum Bewachen von KZ-Insassen verwendet werden. Welche Ehre!

Untergebracht sind wir in einer Baracke, mehr einem Stall, wo wir auf bloßen Planken kampieren. Die Verpflegung ist wenig umfangreich und entbehrt jeder liebevollen Zubereitung.

Die Zeit vertreiben wir uns mit Musizieren, Karten spielen, Schreiben, gar mit Nichtstun. Vom ungebrochenen Lebensgeist zeugen all diese Begebenheiten und auch das Fußballspiel angesichts der Stacheldrahtzäune und der dahinter lebenden Menschen!

Das Vermögen der Menschen ist ja immer maßgebend für die Gewohnheiten, und bei allen materiellen Schätzen ist unser größtes Vermögen allzeit die Gesundheit und ein ungebrochener Mut. Und darüber gilt es zu wachen.

Was kann uns denn anfechten, wenn wir im Wissen um die Schuld der Welt auch einen Teil tragen müssen?

Die größte Bitterkeit bereitet mir immer die Vorstellung, dass durch den Streit der Welt um deren Schale nie der Kern und Sinn gefunden wird.

Mir mangelt's weniger an der Erkenntnis als vielmehr an der Kraft und den Mitteln, dem Universum näher zu treten.

Ich schwanke zuweilen, ob die rechte Religion nicht doch die tiefe Ehrfurcht vor der Urkraft ist, als etwa die schwächliche Vorstellung der Allgemeinheit von einem Gott, dem man nach allerlei Laster am Ende doch bußfertig gegenübersteht, wenn man im "gläubigen" Vertrauen auf Gnade lebenslang ungestraft Frevel übt. Das ist aber nur meine Ansicht und nicht eine allgemeingültige Lehre.

March 17

Even though the disturbing specter of hunger plays a dominant role at times, it nonetheless doesn't alter the fact that the royal presence of humor from every corner greets and encourages us and helps to disguise our situation. And I can't seriously participate in the constant guessing games over what is to come because, after all, nothing will change by virtue of guessing, nor will my own wishes be fulfilled through it. By contrast, what does move all of us here is concern over the well-being of our loved ones at home, who seem so close and yet so terribly far away.

The letters HBE were written ornately on the windows of the clean cars of the train from Halberstadt to Blankenburg, and so we christened the freight wagon in which we delivered chopped wood to the barracks yesterday also the HBE. The former initials stood for Halberstädter Blankenburger Eisenbahn (*Halberstadt Blankenburg Railroad*); the latter is meant to denote Halbjuden Bahn Express. (*Half Jewish Express Train*).

While we were busy with tree felling, the church bells from a nearby village reminded us it was Sunday, a day which we can do little to honor in this place.

The afternoon remains in my memory as an example of one of those refreshing experiences that really seemed to reconcile me with the bad circumstances.

We have with us a fellow sufferer who can reproduce or imitate quite remarkably all kinds of sounds, as well as music or funny stories. Other comrades supplemented his offerings with their vocal or comedic acts, while a borrowed guitar provided various musical accompaniments.

March 18

This morning we had a checkup. As a result, I'm now deemed fit for action. We were in the process of playing a game when the orders to report for a checkup came down, and we were interrupted a second time because some comrades infuriatingly ate some others' lunches, with the result that ten comrades got no food at all and Ust. (*Unterstormführer*) Schaluppa mustered the work force and made it aware of the reprehensible action.

By the way, this Schaluppa is a decent fellow and I was able to do him a favor by repairing and cleaning his bicycle.

The universal mood was excited today by several rumors, which, however, all turned out to be outhouse talk.

17. März

Wenn die störende Anwesenheit Schmalhansens als dominierende Persönlichkeit zuweilen ins Gewicht fällt, so ändert das jedoch nichts an der Tatsache, dass die königliche Gestalt des Humors aus allen Ecken grüßt und ermuntert und uns unsere Lage gar nicht recht erkennen lässt. Und um das viele Rätselraten über Kommendes kann ich mich nicht ernstlich beteiligen, weil dadurch eine Änderung nie stattfinden wird, noch also meine eigenen Wünsche Erfüllung finden werden, dadurch nie! Dagegen bewegt uns hier alle die Sorge um das Wohlergehen der Lieben in der Heimat, die uns ja nah und wiederum so unendlich fern sind.

HBE stand in wunderlichen Schnörkeln an den Scheiben der sauberen Wagen der Eisenbahn von Halberstadt nach Blankenburg, und HBE haben wir den Lorewagen getauft, auf dem wir gestern das gefällte Holz vor die Baracken gefahren haben. Hieß das erstere HBE „Halberstädter Blankenburger Eisenbahn", soll das letztere „Halbjuden Bahn Express" bedeuten.

Als wir gerade mit dem Holzfällen beschäftigt waren, riefen aus dem nahen Ort die Glocken den Sonntag ins Gedächtnis, dem wir allerdings hier wenig huldigen können.

Der Nachmittag stand dann im Zeichen herzerfrischender Erlebnisse, die mich mit den Missständen wirklich versöhnten.

Wir haben unter uns einen Leidensgefährten, der in bewundernswerter Weise allerlei Geräusche wie auch Musik oder die lustigsten Geschichten wiedergeben und imitieren kann. Einige weitere Kameraden ergänzten mit ihrem gesanglichen oder komischen Können die Darbietungen, während eine geliehene Gitarre das Gebotene verschiedentlich musikalisch begleitete.

18. März

Heute morgen wurden wir untersucht. Ich selbst bin demnach einsatzfähig. Wir waren gerade beim Spiel, als uns der Befehl zur Untersuchung rief und ein zweites Mal wurde der Sport gestört, weil in gemeiner Weise einige Kameraden das Mittagessen von anderen mit aufaßen, sodass zehn Kameraden keine Mahlzeit mehr erhielten und Ust. (*Untersturmführer*) Schaluppa die Belegschaft antreten ließ und ihr das Verwerfliche vor Augen hielt.

Dieser Schaluppa ist übrigens ein anständiger Kerl und ich konnte ihm ebenfalls eine Gefälligkeit erweisen, indem ich sein Fahrrad repariert und gereinigt habe.

Die Gemüter der Allgemeinheit wurden heute verschiedentlich erregt und zwar durch Gerüchte, die sich jedoch allesamt als Scheißhausparolen erwiesen haben.

March 19

But then the actual truth and fact came faster than anyone expected. In light of this order, our sports group was quartered and my newly spun threads of friendship ripped apart.

And thus my dear comrades Kurt and Erich are off to Hadersleben, other comrades to Braunlage, and we ourselves to Derenburg, and only a small remnant now remains in Blankenburg, although these comrades were given accommodations more fit for human habitation than we had. Heinz's friend, Gerhard H. is also among this group.

The last evening in Blankenburg there was once again an expression of unbroken courage. The local cobbler repaired my defective shoes at 9:30 p.m. because we had to head out next morning at four a.m.

At first, Heinz and I were separated, but our complaint about this paid off, because we're together again today.

It's a real pity that I was separated from my friends, Erich and Kurt, because they were decent and easy-going companions. It's strange; I still hear their voices and think they're close by. Today, the first day of spring, our life and assignment in Derenburg begin. Early in the morning at 4 a.m. we had to say goodbye. A march in the gray predawn light was followed by a short train ride, then again by foot in the rising sun, to Derenburg.

We reached our destination at about 9:30 am and found accommodations in the hall of the Hotel zum Weißen Adler. Wooden army cots stand in a long row where perhaps a thankful public not so long ago applauded actors and actresses; at least we assumed so from the way the stage looked, still bedecked with flags today. No doubt some gay young people must have danced a waltz or two on the parquet floors, accompanied by wine and music.

Before lunch, which, by the way, was very good and plentiful, each man received two blankets that, together with one's own, promised to provide a warm bed for the night.

19. März

Die einzige Wahrheit und Tatsache kam dann schneller denn je erwartet. Durch diesen Befehl wurde unser Trimsport gevierteilt und mein angesponnener Freundschaftsfaden abgerissen.

So kommen nun meine lieben Kameraden Kurt und Erich nach Hadersleben, weitere Kameraden kommen nach Braunlage, wir selbst kommen nach Derenburg und nur ein kleiner Rest verbleibt in Blankenburg, allerdings erhalten jene Kameraden eine menschenwürdigere Unterkunft, als sie uns dort zuteil wurde. Unter jenen befindet sich auch Heinzens Kamerad, Gerhard H.

Der letzte Abend in Blankenburg wurde nochmals eine Kundgebung ungebrochenen Lebensmuts. Meine defekten Schuhe hat mir der Schuhmacher aus der Siedlung noch um 21.30 Uhr abends repariert, weil wir doch am nächsten Morgen um 4 Uhr ausrücken sollten.

Heinz und ich waren zunächst getrennt, doch lohnte sich die Reklamation, sodass wir heute wieder zusammen sind.

Es ist zu schade, dass ich von den Kameraden Erich und Kurt getrennt wurde, denn die zwei waren einmal anständige und zum andern ruhige Gefährten. Es ist so seltsam, immer noch höre ich ihre Stimmen und glaube sie in meiner nächsten Umgebung. Heut am Tag des Frühlingsbeginns fängt auch unser Leben und der Einsatzbeginn in Derenburg an. Schon am frühen Morgen um 4 Uhr hieß es Abschied nehmen, und nach einem Marsch im Morgengrauen folgte eine kurze Bahnfahrt und danach wieder auf Schustersrappen in die aufgehende Sonne, nach Derenburg.

Etwa um 9.30 Uhr erreichten wir unser Ziel und fanden Quartier im Saale des Hotels „Zum Weißen Adler". Da stehen hölzerne Feldbetten in langer Reihe, wo ehedem vielleicht dankbareres Publikum den Schauspielkünstlern ihren Applaus spendete, wie die noch heute fahnengeschmückte Bühne vermuten lässt. Auch dürfte junges und munteres Volk beim Wein und Musik manchen Walzer über den Parkett gebracht haben.

Noch vor dem Mittagessen, das übrigens sehr gut und reichlich war, erhielt ein jeder zwei Koltern (Decken), die mit der einen eigenen ein warmes Nachtlager zu werden versprechen.

March 22

Now things have gotten serious. This morning, after a good night's rest, our company went to work where we received our assignments. By and large, all comrades were designated as unskilled laborers, with a few exceptions, among them Fritz Reis and me as locksmiths and Fredy as a carpenter.

My first official task was to move a waterline, or rather pipes, which are intended someday to fulfill that purpose.

The site foremen are very crude and swear nonstop, although they should be aware that their workers include engineers, architects and industrialists and can't exactly be expected to be accustomed to this purely physical work of lifting and carrying.

The general contractor comes from Berlin (Kurt Eisenrieth und Co); the builder, Firma Fr. Prausse, on the other hand, is from Braunschweig. Access to the building site is by permit only; similarly, our work hours are noted precisely on forms. Work hours are from 7 a.m. until 6:30 p.m. In between, we have a one-hour meal break in which hot food is distributed. We get hot coffee mornings and evenings, along with 3,000 grams of bread per week and sufficient sandwich fixings.

Our washing facilities in our quarters are not so much pleasant as romantic. One pump in the courtyard and a stream running by the back side of the house serve the purpose.

Tomorrow, one of our friends is going home (to Friedberg) because he turned out to be M II (*a person with only one Jewish grandparent*). As a result of being discharged here, he will be drafted into the armed forces. He's taking mail with him to Frankfurt.

Once fighting begins around Mainz, this opportunity to write letters will soon disappear, and the hope of a quick reunion with loved ones is the only thing that helps pass the time.

22. März

Nun also ist es ernst geworden. Heut früh nach einer gut durchschlafenen Nacht ging unsere Kolonne zur Arbeit, wo sie eingeteilt wurde. Im großen Ganzen wurden sämtliche Kameraden zu Hilfsarbeitern erklärt, mit wenigen Ausnahmen, darunter Fritz Reis und ich als Schlosser und Fredy als Zimmermann.

Meine erste Amtshandlung war das Verlegen einer Wasserleitung, oder besser von Rohren, die einmal den Zweck erfüllen sollen.

Die Poliere sind sehr groß und schimpfen immerzu, obwohl sie wissen dürften, dass ihre Arbeiter mitunter Ingenieure, Architekten und gar Industrielle sind und diese rein körperliche Arbeit des Schippens und Bückens kaum gewöhnt sein können.

Der Bauunternehmer stammt aus Berlin (Kurt Eisenrieth und Co.), dagegen die ausführende Firma Fr. Prausse aus Braunschweig. Die Baustelle kann nur mit einem Ausweis betreten werden, ebenso werden die geleisteten Stunden auf Vordrucken genauestens vermerkt. Die Arbeitszeit läuft von morgens um 7 Uhr bis 18.30 Uhr abends. Dazwischen liegt 1 Stunde Essenszeit, in der warmes Essen verausgabt wird. Warmen Kaffee gibt es morgens und abends, daneben pro Woche 3000 g Brot und genügend Material zum Brotbelag.

Die Waschgelegenheit in unserem Quartier ist weniger angenehm denn romantisch. Dazu steht eine Pumpe im Hof und der vorbeifließende Bach an der hinteren Seite des Hauses zur Verfügung.

Morgen fährt ein Kamerad nach Hause (Friedberg), weil er sich als M II (*Eine Person mit nur einem jüdischen Großelternteil*) entpuppt hat. Die Einberufung zur Wehrmacht wird die Folge seiner hiesigen Entlassung sein. Nun, jener nimmt nochmals Post nach Frankfurt mit.

Nachdem um Mainz gekämpft wird, wird auch bald diese Gelegenheit des Briefschreibens erliegen müssen, und allein die Hoffnung auf ein baldiges Wiedersehen lässt einem die Zeit überstehen.

March 29

An entire week has already passed. Terribly boring, but in retrospect, it flew by quickly.

Heinz borrowed a guitar from the Russian girls, who work as hard as we do, so that we can enjoy some communal singing in the evenings. On Sunday, we worked until 12:30.

We can't get out of the dirt any more. The food, which at first seemed quite ample, no longer satisfies our hunger for long. The midday soup is very watery, and, together with the thin coffee, probably contributes to our equally thin bowel movements, in plain German, "Dünnschiss."

The food on Sunday was good. Alongside six boiled potatoes, we had a meat patty, yellow beets and gravy. We spent the afternoon cleaning. First our own bodies, then lots of laundry. There was even a barber present. With this, our masculine vanity was duly indulged.

An appeal by Krause, the camp leader, reminds us again not to send home any troublesome news, and also not to ask our folks for additional food or ration stamps, because we are amply supplied with everything here.

I picked the first violets today. It was like a greeting from home and a reminder of friendlier times.

I wonder if the Labers think of me as often as I think of them. With the front now knocking at their door, they could no doubt use a male protector. But God will protect them.

In fits of occasional sadness, I feel quite depressed, the more so since we can no longer expect news from home. How transforming the last fourteen days have been since our departure from Frankfurt. Who would have thought it?

And I wonder where mother is. With Gretel and Helga in Wüstems? Is the war passing over, leaving little, idyllic Wüstems unscathed? If only one could have just a little of what one unconsciously enjoyed then. I feel I'm being greedy with my desire for a white tablecloth and apple pancakes served by my mother on a pretty plate. Or have I become less demanding?

29. März

Eine ganze Woche ist nun schon vergangen. Furchtbar langweilig, doch im Rückblick rasch verflogen.

Heinz hat von Russenmädels, die gleich uns schippen müssen, eine Gitarre entliehen, sodass abends manches gemeinsame Lied steigen kann. Am Sonntag wurde bis um 12.30 Uhr gearbeitet.

Man kommt gar nicht mehr aus dem Dreck heraus. Das Essen, das erst so vollkommen ausreichend schien, langt nicht so weit, unseren Appetit längere Zeit zu stillen. Die Mittagssuppe ist sehr wässerig und mit dem dünnen Kaffee zusammen wohl auch die Ursache des ebenso dünnen Stuhlgangs, auf gut Deutsch „Dünnschiss".

Das Essen am Sonntag war gut. Neben 6 Pellmännern gab es eine Frikadelle, gelbe Rüben und Soße. Der Nachmittag war ausgefüllt mit Säuberungsaktionen. Einmal persönliche Körperreinigung, dann große Wäsche an Kleidungsstücken. Auch ein Friseur war anwesend. Damit wurde auch der eitlen Männlichkeit gehuldigt.

Ein Appell des Lagerführers Krause stellte uns nochmals anheim, keine irritierenden Nachrichten nach Hause zu senden, ebenso keine Bittgesuche um zusätzliche Lebensmittel bzw. -marken, weil wir alles hier in reichem Maße bekämen.

Die ersten Veilchen konnte ich ebenfalls schon pflücken. Das war mir ein Gruß aus der Heimat und der Erinnerung aus freundlicheren Zeiten.

Ob die Labers ebenso oft an mich denken wie ich an sie. Nachdem die Front an deren Haustür pocht, würden sie wohl einen männlichen Betreuer brauchen können. Aber Gott wird sie schon beschützen.

In zeitweilig traurigen Anwandlungen fühle ich mich recht bedrückt, zumal von zu Hause keine Nachrichten mehr zu erwarten sind. Wie umwandelnd waren doch die letzten 14 Tage seit unsrer Abreise aus Frankfurt. Wer hätte das geahnt?

Und wo wird die Mutter sein? Mit Gretel and Helga in Wüstems? Geht der Krieg spurlos an dem kleinen und idyllischen Wüstems vorüber? Hätte man doch nur jetzt manchmal einen Teil von dem, was man dort unbewusst genossen hat. Ich fühle mich recht unbescheiden in meinen Wünschen nach einem weißen Tischtuch und auf manierlichem Teller einen Apfelpfannkuchen von der Mutter dargereicht. Oder bin ich bescheiden geworden?

Today I went to Magdeburg for the firm. Seven other comrades came too, including Heinz and both Kosels. Our means of transportation was a truck with a trailer. We had to pick up a supply of bricks.

The work of loading by tossing the bricks to the next man was a difficult task and one we'd never before undertaken. Everyone's hands are blistered as a result. What I remember of the trip is a monotonous landscape and the sadly rather burned-down town of Magdeburg. I also saw the many unfamiliar windmills which characterize the region, along with fields that stretch far into the distance. By the way, let it also be noted that we were all really frozen and glad when we once again reached Derenburg, our point of departure.

Apparently another 6 men ran away from Blankenburg, including "Tintentod"!!! I wonder if they'll be able to reach Frankfurt?

March 30

So now I've been to Magdeburg twice. Well, what did I do there? Threw rocks! Come again? Yes, threw rocks. That seems better to me than shoveling stuff for days on end or building railroads.

We didn't pay much attention to the fact that it was Good Friday, and yet something celebratory did happen to us in that we were offered a hot meal in a restaurant there. We felt like we did in earlier times of freedom, except that we were embarrassed about our dirty hands and kept them hidden beneath the table. We had good red cabbage and lots of it. Of course, we mentioned several favorite dishes, but postponed their enjoyment till better times.

Easter Sunday, April 1

Today our deepest yearnings are at home with our loved ones, and our desire is to be reunited with them soon. The latter wish, however, is also the cause of some worry and some thoughts of escape. Although I deem the situation unsuited to it, both the Kosels and also Heinz are intrigued with this plan. May I succeed in preventing them from doing so or may the events themselves make them understand just how crazy it would be.

For starters, it's quite impossible to reach the goal without provisions, let alone on foot. In addition, it seems very questionable to me whether on reaching the enemy lines, we would be met with the reception they are imagining. Even Edmund Kr. shares my view that the Americans will not differentiate and will see us only as Germans.

Heute war ich für die Firma in Magdeburg. Mit dabei waren weitere 7 Kameraden, darunter Heinz und die beiden Kosels. Das Beförderungsmittel war ein LKW mit Anhänger. Abzuholen waren Backsteine.

Das Aufladen und Zuschocken war eine ebenso bisher unbekannte wie schwierige Arbeit. Allseits schwielige Hände ist das Resultat. Vom Erlebnis dieser Reise ist landschaftliche Eintönigkeit und eine leider sehr gebrandschatzte Stadt Magdeburg in Erinnerung geblieben. Auch sah ich öfters in unserer Heimat wenig bekannte Windmühlen, die neben weit ausgedehnten Ackerflächen das Charakteristikum der Gegend darstellen. Nebenbei bemerkt haben wir alle sehr gefroren und waren froh, als der Ausgangspunkt Derenburg wieder erreicht war.

In Blankenburg sollen wieder 6 Mann ausgekniffen sein, auch „Tintentod"!!! Ob sie noch nach Frankfurt kommen?

30. März

So, nun war ich schon zweimal in Magdeburg! Aha, und was tat ich da? Steine schocken! Wie bitte? Ja, Steine schocken. Und das dünkt mir noch angenehmer als etwa tagelang schippen oder Schienen zusammenbauen.

Vom heiligen Karfreitag haben wir zwar wenig gemerkt, doch etwas Feiertägliches ist uns begegnet, indem uns in einem Gasthaus dort eine warme Mahlzeit geboten wurde. Wie in ehemals freien Zeiten haben wir uns gefühlt, nur die schmutzigen Hände haben wir schamhaft unter den Tisch gehalten. Es gab guten Rotkohl und auch reichlich. Naturgemäß wurden einige Leibgerichte zitiert, der Genuß aber auf bessere Zeiten verschoben.

Ostersonntag, den 1. April

Unser aller sehnlichstes Gedenken ist heute in der Heimat bei den Lieben und die Wünsche gehen dahin, recht bald mit ihnen vereint zu sein. Letzterer Wunsch ist aber zugleich Ursache zu mancherlei Kopfzerbrechen und Fluchtgedanken. Während ich die Lage dafür ungeeignet halte, begeistern sich die beiden Kosels und auch Heinz an diesem Plan. Möge es mir gelingen, sie davon abzubringen, oder die Ereignisse mögen ihnen das Unsinnige selbst begreiflich machen.

Einmal ist es gänzlich unmöglich, ohne Proviant und evtl. sogar zu Fuß ans Ziel zu gelangen, Andererseits scheint mir es sehr fraglich, ob nach Erreichen der feindlichen Linien uns das Entgegenkommen zuteil wird, wie es in ihrer Fantasie herumspukt. Selbst Edmund Kr. teilt meine Ansicht, die darin besteht, dass die Amerikaner keinen Unterschied machen werden und auch in uns nur die Deutschen sehen.

The right thing to do seems to be to stay here and wait and see how the situation develops.

There is no trace of our comrades who fled, and no confirmation of whether their efforts were worthwhile. Even if they have succeeded in getting through to Frankfurt am Main, after a brief respite they'll soon have to start fighting again, principally for food, so as not to become a burden to their relatives.

Hopefully, mother is in Wüstems, together with Helga and Gretel, because then, in light of the circumstances, they might be spared some want. It is very distressing that we can no longer convey any news to each other. Only the hope of seeing each other again soon allows us to get through this time.

Today we had the day off. The Kosel brothers and Heinz used the time to visit Wernigerode. As for myself, I spent the day with ample relaxation and with what seemed to me to be a symbolic walk. What I mean is that when I joined a few comrades who were walking without any particular goal in mind, they gave up their walk half way and set off homeward out of sorts with the world. It seems to me that I shouldn't follow any path without a goal in mind, even less so with comrades who are not clear about their own wishes.

The walk in the fresh air did me a lot of good, and in addition to the aforementioned insight, I also brought home a little nosegay of sweet smelling violets.

The larks belong among my true friends, jubilantly singing their song everywhere, untiringly, in defiance of all the storms of life, and wonderfully sublime above all earthly burdens, very enviable, and for my part admired and welcome.

Richtig ist wohl hier zu bleiben und abwarten, wie sich die Lage entwickelt.

Von den geflüchteten Kameraden fehlt jede Spur und die Bestätigung, ob ihr Bemühen zweckvoll war. Selbst wenn es ihnen gelungen ist, nach Frankfurt am Main durchzukommen, werden sie nach kurzer Freude recht bald wieder kämpfen müssen, vor allem ums Brot, um den Angehörigen nicht zur Last zu fallen.

Hoffentlich ist Mutter in Wüstems, und zusammen mit Helga und Gretel, dann dürfte ihnen doch in Anbetracht der Gegebenheiten manche Not erspart bleiben. Dass wir einander keine Nachrichten mehr übermitteln können, ist sehr betrüblich, und allein die Hoffnung auf ein baldiges Wiedersehen lässt einen die Zeit überstehen.

Heute hatten wir einen arbeitsfreien Tag. Die Brüder Kosel und Heinz nutzten die Zeit zu einem Besuch nach Wernigerode. Ich selbst verbrachte den Tag mit reichlichem Ausruhen und einem wie mir scheint symbolischen Spaziergang. Solchermaßen, als ich mich einigen Kameraden anschloß, die ohne Ziel ihren Spaziergang auf halbem Wege wieder abbrachen und mit aller Welt unzufrieden den Rückmarsch antraten. Es will mir dünken, dass ich keinem Wege ohne Ziel folgen soll, noch weniger mit Kameraden, die sich im Unklaren mit ihren eigenen Wünschen befinden.

Mir tat der Gang durch die frische Luft denkbar gut und neben der Erkenntnis brachte ich mir noch ein Sträußchen duftender Veilchen mit.

Zu meinen erklärten Freunden gehören die Lerchen, die überall und unermüdlich ihr Lied jubilieren, allen Stürmen zum Trotz und zugleich herrlich erhaben über alle Erdenschwere, sehr beneidenswert und meinerseits bewundert und gegrüßt.

April 3

According to an old saying, new beginnings often happen unexpectedly. In this connection, I now think about our situation, which we view with so much discontent. And now the Allies are advancing relentlessly. How much further will they go? Will they reach us?

Heinz returned from his Easter excursion with potatoes, which will help to improve the food situation, but will also offer an opportunity for us to store up some supplies for a possible departure.

In addition, Heinz contacted Werner in Wernigerode. Because he wasn't there at the time, he sought us out today in Derenburg. But the biggest surprise was that Hilde arrived with Werner. The joy of seeing each other again was great, nor was a shadow cast on our joy when Werner learned the reason for our being here. Besides a loaf of bread which he was able to leave with us right then and there, he left us the promise that he would help us in whatever way and as soon as he could. For me, Hilde's presence was the surest guarantee of the sincerity of his intentions, especially now that he's been cured of his dreams of victory and fears only for Hilde's safety.

3. April

Oft kommt's unverhofft, sagt ein alter Spruch, ein ewig neuer! Damit denke ich jetzt an unsere so mißmutig aufgefaßte Lage. Und nun rücken die Alliierten unentwegt vor. Wie weit noch? Kommen sie bis zu uns?

Und von seiner Osterwanderung brachte Heinz Kartoffeln mit, die dazu beitragen werden, einmal die Essensfrage zu bessern, dann aber auch die Möglichkeit bieten, etwas Vorrat für eine eventuelle Abreise aufzusparen.

Außerdem hat Heinz in Wernigerode Verbindung mit Werner aufgenommen, der, weil selbst nicht anwesend, uns heute in Derenburg aufsuchte. Die größte Überraschung jedoch war, dass sich Hilde mit Werner einfand. Die Wiedersehensfreude war groß, auch dann noch ungetrübt, als Werner die Gründe unseres Hierseins erfuhr. Neben einem Laib Brot, den er gleich hier lassen konnte, hinterließ er das Versprechen, zu helfen, wie und sobald er kann. Die Anwesenheit Hildes ist mir die sicherste Gewähr für die Aufrichtigkeit seiner Absichten, zumal er von seiner Siegesutopie geheilt ist und nur noch Angst um seine Hilde hat.

April 4

I've had to stay in the camp since yesterday because of a blister on my right heel. In itself, it's an insignificant malady. But Dr. Vf. can't decide whether to operate or not, and I'm likewise in no hurry. I can quite capably manage a few small tasks, e.g., splitting wood or fetching coffee, and still have more than enough time left over to get to all kinds of personal matters. As a preventive measure against any unexpected eventualities, I'm toasting most of the bread, a ration I'd been keeping in a little bag. Like me, of course, Heinz nibbled a bit at the toast, but now we want to exercise our will power and, if possible, increase the advantage we have.

The hot topic of conversation is the military situation. The victory barometer, and with it, our mood, rises or falls depending on a wide variety of opinions, facts, and rumors. I must admit I'm only somewhat interested in the whole business, or only insofar as I long for a rapid end to the war and an early reunion with mother.

Besides this, or actually, first and foremost, the battle continues to be about managing to get by day to day, although it might seem as if that's not necessary, since our meals are prepared for us. Nevertheless, rationing oneself is not easy, and there's little use in consuming all your rations at once in an relentless attack of hunger, only next day, to eye someone else's saved-up delicacies with an empty stomach and craned neck. If you are lucky, you can occasionally acquire some extra food. For example, yesterday I bought a bowl of mixed pickles.

For this, I had to cough up eleven RM of good money, one mark per day. Still unpaid by the firm, I earned the money in a strange manner. To pass the time, Rolf, who is likewise ill, and I, were playing cards (17+4) when a third person showed up who suggested a game of poker. Just to keep the peace and against my general principles, I joined in and won almost ten RM. Nonetheless, I won't play again, especially not for money.

At noon the "jabos" (*Jagdbombers*) made the skies come alive and probably shot at the retreating vehicles that were crowding all the roads. Of the German airplanes, one could see only fleeing silhouettes. In the town itself, there are numerous garrisons. There's a field kitchen and a supply wagon in the Weissen Adler.

4. April

Seit gestern bin ich im Lager wegen einer Blase an der rechten Ferse. Eine an und für sich unbedeutende Krankheit. Da jedoch Dr. Vf. sich nicht zur Operation entschließen kann, habe ich ebenfalls gute Weile. Einige kleine Arbeiten, wie etwa Holz spalten oder Kaffee holen, kann ich ganz gut verrichten, um noch mehr als genug Zeit zu allerlei persönlichen Verrichtungen übrig zu haben. Vorbeugend gegen plötzlich eintreffende Eventualitäten, röste ich den größten Teil des Brotes, das in einem Säckchen verwahrt eine Ration darstellt. Genascht haben Heinz wie ich naturgemäß schon von dem Röstbrot, doch wollen wir nun eisern bleiben und möglicherweise den Vorsprung vergrößern.

Das aktuellste Thema ist die militärische Lage, und nach den mannigfaltigen Meinungen, Tatsachen und Gerüchten steigt oder fällt jeweils das Siegesbarometer und damit unsere Stimmung. Ich muss gestehen, mich interessiert das ganze Geschehen nur wenig oder nur insofern, als ich ein baldiges Kriegsende und somit auch ein baldiges Wiedersehen mit Mutter ersehne.

Und nebenher oder hauptsächlich geht der Kampf um das tägliche Auskommen weiter, obwohl es den Anschein haben könnte, dass solches nicht nötig sei, da ja die Mahlzeiten fertig sind. Trotzdem, das Einteilen ist auch nicht leicht und es nutzt wenig, durch irgendwelchen Hungerwutanfall die Ration auf einmal zu verzehren, um dann anderntags mit leerem Magen und langem Hals nach den ersparten Kostbarkeiten anderer zu schielen. Wenn man Glück hat, kann man auch ab und zu etwas zusätzliche Kost erwerben. So habe ich zum Beispiel gestern eine Schüssel mit Mix-Pickel erworben.

Elf Reichsmark Kostgeld musste ich blechen, pro Tag 1 Mark. Bei der Firma noch unentlohnt, habe ich mir das Geld auf kuriose Weise wiederverdient. Zum Zeitvertreib spielten Rolf, der ebenfalls krank ist, und ich Karten (17+4), als ein Dritter sich zugesellte mit dem Vorschlag einer Mauschelpartie. Nur um des Friedens willen und gegen meine Anschauung im allgemeinen spielte ich mit und gewann fast 10 RM. Trotzdem werde ich nicht mehr mitspielen, noch weniger um Geld.

Am Nachmittag belebten die „Jabos" (Jagdbomber) den Himmel und beschossen wahrscheinlich die Fahrzeuge, die auf dem Rückmarsch alle Straßen besiedelten. Von deutschen Flugzeugen sah man nur auskneifende Silhouetten. Im Ort selbst sind auch zahlreiche Einquartierungen. Im „Weißen Adler" steht eine Feldküche und ein Proviantwagen.

The day before yesterday, six of us had to help the Safety Division. Things are hidden in a former old people's home, things which, no doubt, have all kinds of illegal origins and make possible a profitable life for the beneficiaries. There are huge amounts of wine, champagne, dishes, and shoes around and also some things still in their original packaging. But does all this bring blessings?

I have the 10-11 p.m. watch now, which means I have to pay attention that no one is making any plans or preparations for escape, or is arranging such plans on someone else's behalf. The alarm sirens have just sounded! There's word of bomber squadrons advancing on Brandenburg and Braunschweig. Enemy planes roar noisily above us, and all the while the skat players continue their game until the light is turned off as a precautionary measure. After only a short interlude, both the skat players and I are able to resume our business. The card players are, by and large, the ones who don't have grueling jobs during the day and therefore try to balance out this deficit by keeping busy all night. Most of the others are fast asleep or are cleaning their clothes and shoes.

Announcements about the outcome of the enemy flights report action over Magdeburg and Dessau.

It's truly fortunate to know that our relatives are spared such madness for now.

If I were ever privileged to fathom all the reasons, the causes, and the deeds committed in this war, I could still never grasp the consequences, much less condone them. It seems to me that what people have done and will yet do to one another in this struggle is entirely the product of human nature and its inadequate sense of responsibility. Generations to come will suffer the consequences; they will never be able to condone what was done with such boundless fanaticism to the dismay of all who have to live in these times or those yet to come. It's utterly useless for me as an individual to speculate about the future, but I certainly hope that each person's fate is determined by his acts and merits.

Good night! My watch is over! Quickly off to bed!

Vorgestern mussten sechs Leute von uns dem Sicherheitsdienst helfen. In einem ehemaligen Altersheim sind Dinge untergebracht, die gewiß aus allerlei illegalen Quellen stammen und den Nutznießern ein schlaues Leben ermöglichen. Wein, Sekt, Geschirr und Schuhwerk, dazu noch manches Verpackte sind massig vorhanden. Aber ob es Segen bringt?

Von 22 bis 23 Uhr habe ich jetzt Wache, das heißt darauf zu achten, daß keiner irgendwelche Vorbereitungen zur Flucht oder diese selbst bewerkstelligen will. Eben ertönen die Alarmsirenen! Gemeldet sind Kampfverbände auf Brandenburg und Braunschweig. Mächtig brummen die Feindverbände über uns, der weil unberührt in der einen Ecke des Saales die Skatbrüder ihre Partie fortsetzen, bis vorsichtshalber das Licht abgedreht wird. Nach kurzer Pause können die Skatbrüder wie auch ich die Tätigkeit wiederaufnehmen. Jene sind durchweg solche, die tagsüber keine aufreibende Tätigkeit haben und durch allabendliche Aktion diesen Mangel auszugleichen suchen. Die übrigen sind größtenteils in tiefem Schlaf oder reinigen Kleider and Schuhe.

Die Meldungen über den Verlauf des Feindeinfluges künden Tätigkeit über Magdeburg und Dessau.

Ein wahres Glück ist es, nunmehr die Angehörigen vor solchem Wahnsinn verschont zu wissen.

Wenn es mir je vergönnt wäre, alle Gründe, Ursachen und vollendete Tatsachen dieses Krieges zu ergründen, könnte ich doch nie die Folgen begreifen, viel weniger aber gutheißen. Was sich die Menschen in diesem Ringen einander zugefügt haben und noch zufügen werden, das scheint mir auch ganz das Produkt menschlichen Geistes und seiner unzulänglichen Verantwortung anheim gestellt. An den Folgen werden Generationen kranken und nie gutheißen können, was da in grenzenlosem Fanatismus ausgetragen zum Leidwesen aller, die in dieser Zeit oder danach zu leben haben. Es ist gänzlich unnütz, meinerseits individuell über die Zukunft zu grübeln und ich hoffe bestimmt, dass einem jeden nach Tat und Verdienst sein Los beschieden ist.

Gute Nacht! Meine Wache ist vorbei! Nun rasch ins Bett!

May 1, in Wustems, Once Again

Since my last entry the ink in my pen had completely dried out and my memory is not in much better shape. I'll strain it now so that I can recall at least the most important events of this eventful time.

April 5-8: Derenburg

Life proceeds monotonously here, much work, even more thinking, but little to eat. Our food is supplemented by cold and warm boiled potatoes, whenever we can get them. Honestly procured onions help to fill the belly. Every evening and at other times too, the military reports are debated and the pros and cons considered.

A "senior council" was held due to the fact that the Osterode work camp, in the Harz Mountains south of here, has shut down operations and dismissed its inmates in an orderly fashion, complete with their identification papers. In order to be prepared for the possibility of a similar event here, the following decisions were reached:

If the camp is disbanded, the inmates will retreat from the Weissen Adler to the Schützenhof and there await the arrival of the Americans.

The strictest discipline is to be maintained, failing which vigilante justice will prevail, and

The camp leadership guarantees the best possible provisions and, if these above measures are implemented, predicts the fastest possible return home.

At first glance, this appears to be the most reasonable plan and also logically thought out, even if thousands of doubts were not undermining this assurance. It is mainly my own concerns, but also largely the behavior of the leadership, that shatters every illusion and provides quite a different picture of the situation.

It is not only the sanctimonious attitude of a Karry, Scheinberger, or whatever their names might be, that gives a foretaste of what they understand by comradeship in adversity.

While the dumb or dutiful have to toil at the worksite come rain or shine, these few pamper and gorge themselves due to their excessive free time and their black market dealings and schmoozing with foreigners. They do great honor to their racial ancestors, if such is a racially determined matter. I find their behavior offensive and draw my own conclusions.

1. Mai und in Wüstems geschrieben

Die Tinte im Federhalter war seit dem letzten Gebrauch gänzlich vertrocknet und wenig besser geht es mit meinem Gedächtnis. Mächtig will ich es jetzt anstrengen, damit ich wenigstens das Wichtigste dieser ereignisreichen Zeit wiederzugeben vermag.

5.-8. April, Derenburg

Eintönig geht das Leben hier weiter, viel arbeiten, noch mehr Gedanken, aber wenig zu essen. Zusätzlich essen wir eben kalte und warme Pellkartoffeln, wie und wo wir sie erreichen können. Ehrlich erworbene Zwiebeln ziehen den Schlund zusammen. Allabendlich und allgemein werden die militärischen Meldungen erörtert und sämtliche für und wieder erwogen.

Anlaß zu einer „Ältestenratsitzung" war die Tatsache, dass das Arbeitslager Osterode, südlich am Harz, die Arbeit eingestellt hat und die Insassen ordnungsgemäß und mit Papieren versehen entlassen wurden. Um nun im Falle einer gleichartigen Aktion gewappnet zu sein, wurden folgende Beschlüsse gefaßt:

Wenn das Lager aufgelöst wird, ziehen sich Insassen vom „Weißen Adler" nach „Schützenhof" zurück und erwarten dort die Ankunft der Amerikaner.

Es ist strengste Disziplin zu wahren, widrigenfalls wird exemplarische Selbstjustiz die Folge sein, und

Die Lagerführung garantiert bestmögliche Verpflegung und prophezeit durch Befolgung dieser Maßnahmen eine schnellstmögliche Heimkehr.

Im ersten Augenblick scheint dies nun auch die vernünftigste Sache zu sein und auch logisch gedacht, wenn nicht x-tausend Zweifel dieses Vertrauen untergraben würden. Zumeist selbstische Wünsche, zum großen Teil aber auch das Verhalten der Führenden zerstören jede Illusion und geben ein ganz anderes Bild der Tatsachen wieder.

Nicht nur die scheinheilige Haltung eines Karry, Scheinberger oder wie sie heißen mögen gibt einen Vorgeschmack von dem, was die sich in der Not unter Kameradschaft vorstellen.

Während sich die Dummen oder Braven bei Wind und Wetter auf der Arbeitsstelle plagen müssen, pflegen und mästen sich diese wenigen auf Grund der ihnen übermäßig zustehenden Freizeit und der von ihnen mit ihrem Schmus mit Ausländern und sonstigen Subjekten getätigten Schiebergeschichten. Sie machen ihren rassischen Vorfahren alle Ehre, wenn es eine solche wäre oder eine rassisch bedingte Angelegenheit. Mir ist das Gehabe widerlich und ich ziehe meine Konsequenzen.

April 9

A day like all the others. An icy-cold wind whistles around every corner and thick fog promises an uncomfortable day. Heinz stayed home today with toothache. Our work column marched through the streets in a very relaxed mood. Karry is at home; it's certainly far too cold for him in the mornings, as it is for many others.

In this situation, Rolf (*Kosel*) approaches me with a suggestion, and after brief resisting, I agree to it. Instead of going to work, we strike off sideways through the bushes, and set off on a hike to Wernigerode, where an aunt of Rolf's lives. Unwittingly, this jaunt begins a unique story that deserves a special chapter.

I have little memory of what problems we were preoccupied with that day or what tipped the scales to a determination, but by evening we were irrevocably decided: tomorrow morning we're making a run for it!

The plan's overall outline, which we'd discussed down to the last detail, was initially as follows:

Escape from the camp, get behind the front as quickly as possible, allow ourselves to be overrun, and finally get home with the aid of the Americans. My attitude about the last point had always been skeptical, and subsequent events confirmed my suspicions.

Our preparations were undertaken without much secrecy, which attracted little attention in the general chaotic mood of departure. First, two big pots of the remaining potatoes were cooked. We had one last really filling meal, and, once it had cooled, packed the other portion as travel provisions, supplemented with the obligatory onions and some toast. Quickly the things we had brought with us were packed. That was all for me, although Heinz managed to secure two camp blankets. Powdered peas also promise to supplement our rations.

Watching and waiting, the time for our departure draws near and soon we will be dragging ourselves through the dark night and the sleeping city. One after the other we leave the hall forever, and not even the loss of my gloves and Rolf's canteen, which we soon notice, causes anyone to turn around. The directors of the camp can reap the benefit.

9. April

Ein Tag wie alle anderen. Eiskalt pfeift der Wind aus allen Ecken, und dichter Nebel verheißt einen wenig angenehmen Tag. Heinz ist wegen eines Zahngeschwulstes heut zu Hause geblieben. Überhaupt reichlich aufgelockert marschiert unsere Kolonne über die Straßen. Karry ist zu Hause, dem ist's sicher zu kalt am Morgen, und mit ihm vielen anderen.

In dieser Situation kommt Rolf (*Kosel*) mit einem Vorschlag zu mir, dem ich nach kurzem Widerstreben dann beistimme. Statt auf die Arbeit zu gehen, schlagen wir uns seitlich durch die Büsche und unternehmen eine Wanderung nach Wernigerode, wo eine Tante von Rolf wohnt. Mit dieser Affäre beginnt unbewusst eine Geschichte, die in ihrer Einmaligkeit ein ganz besonderes Kapitel bildet.

Ich weiß auch nur noch wenig, was wir an diesem Tage für Probleme gewälzt haben oder was den Ausschlag zu dem Entschluß gab, der am Abend unwiderruflich feststand: Morgen früh hauen wir ab!

In allen Einzelheiten erörtert, bestand der Plan zunächst in großen Umrissen dergestalt:

Flucht aus dem Lager, dann schnellstens bis hinter die Front, dann überrollen lassen und dann endlich mit Hilfe der Amerikaner nach Hause. Im letzteren Punkte war meine Einstellung von jeher skeptisch und hat sich später in der Folge auch als richtig erwiesen.

Die Vorbereitungen werden unsererseits ohne große Heimlichkeiten vorgenommen, was in der allgemeinen Aufbruchspsychose auch weiter nicht auffiel. Zunächst wurden zwei große Töpfe mit dem Restbestand an Kartoffeln gekocht, noch einmal richtig sattgegessen und den andern Teil abgekühlt als Reiseproviant verpackt, dazu kamen die obligatorischen Zwiebeln und einiges Röstbrot. Fast sämtliche mitgebrachten Sachen wurden wieder eingepackt, bei mir aber auch nicht mehr; Heinz hat zwei Lagerdecken organisiert. Das Erbspulver verspricht ebenfalls eine Bereicherung unseres Küchenzettels.

So naht unter Ruhen und Wachen der Zeitpunkt unseres Aufbruchs und bald ziehen wir auch schon im Nachtdunkel durch die schlafende Stadt. Einer nach dem andern verließ auf Nimmerwiedersehen den Saal und selbst der rasch festgestellte Verlust meiner Handschuhe und von Rolfs Feldflasche kann keinen mehr zur Rückkehr bewegen. Soll sich die Lagerleitung damit beglücken.

Our first encounter was a curiosity! Four travelers pushing a cart in our direction. They are companions in misfortune, on their way from Blankenburg to Braunschweig.

We reach Heuteber in the first light of dawn, but the railroad station is deserted and the train that was scheduled to depart at 5:00 a.m. has been canceled.

So we continue on foot. Following the railroad tracks, our route leads past Langen and Wasserleben to Schauen, where a train to Goslar is supposed to depart about an hour later. And, in fact, the train does depart without much delay and we arrive in Goslar at 12:30 p.m. We are quite satisfied with the progress we've made, and though there is a possibility for traveling on to Haarhausen, nothing comes of it. What was at first only a rumor soon proves to be true: the Americans are advancing!

There's already shooting at the city limits. In a flash, the streets are empty and the last military cars depart the city from the opposite side. We also hurry from the train station and away from the downtown area. In a hollow on a hill, we lay down our packs and hunker down.

Soon we'll be out of Nazi hell; the Americans are coming. Tank after tank rolls into the city in an endless stream. But what's the meaning of the shooting coming from above us? Is it friend or foe? And now the Americans are responding to the fire. They must have discovered us and suspect we are the enemy. Machine guns and rifles hammer frantically; howling volleys from the tanks strike next to us and cover us with dirt and earth. The khaki-colored Yankees are swarming forwards, slowly and carefully, firing constantly.

And that we came through this danger-filled situation so well is a remarkable blessing, and that we travelers were able to make such a lovely and romantic journey through the spring, to arrive home safe and sound, allows us all, and especially me, to forget the hardships that we endured. Now, what I foresaw at the beginning of this episode has become reality: a new time for us.

(To view these events from a different perspective, see Heinz's Memoirs, Appendix A.)

Unsere erste Begegnung war ein Kuriosum! Vier Gesellen schieben eine Stoßkarre in eigener Richtung. Es sind Schicksalsgenossen aus Blankenburg auf dem Weg nach Braunschweig.

Im Morgengrauen erreichen wir Heuteber, jedoch liegt der Bahnhof verlassen und der planmäßige Zug um 5 Uhr fällt aus.

Also Fußmarsch. Immer den Bahngleisen entlang führt unser Marsch über Langen, Wasserleben nach Schauen, von wo nach etwa einstündiger Frist ein Zug nach Goslar gehen sollte. Tatsächlich fährt der Zug ohne große Verspätung von da ab, und schon um 12.30 Uhr sind wir in Goslar. Mit diesem Resultat schon recht zufrieden, stand noch eine Weiterbeförderung in Richtung Haarhausen in Aussicht, doch daraus wurde nichts mehr. Waren es zunächst nur Gerüchte, so bewahrheitete es sich bald zur Tatsache: Die Amerikaner sind im Anmarsch!

Schon fallen die Schüsse am Stadtrand. Blitzschnell leeren sich die Straßen, und die letzten Militärautos verlassen die Stadt an der entgegengesetzten Seite. Auch wir eilen vom Bahnhof weg aus dem Weichbild der Stadt. Auf einem Hügel, in einer Mulde legen wir das Gepäck zur Erde und lagern.

Bald werden wir aus der Nazihölle sein, jetzt kommen die Amerikaner. Panzer auf Panzer rollt in die Stadt, in endloser Reihe. Doch was bedeutet das Schießen über uns? Freund oder Feind? Und jetzt erwidern die Amerikaner das Feuer. Sie müssen auch uns entdeckt haben und Feinde vermuten. Rasend hämmern Maschinengewehr und Handfeuerwaffen, jaulend schlagen Panzergeschosse neben uns ein und bedecken uns mit Schmutz und Erde. Schon schwärmen die khakifarbenen Yankees, langsam und vorsichtig und immer schießend.

Und dass wir diese gefahrvolle Situation gut überstanden, liegt eine besonders Gnade zugrunde, und dass wir Gesellen eine so schöne und romantische Fahrt durch den Frühling machen durften, um wohlbehalten in die Heimat zu gelangen, lässt uns alle, voran aber mich, alle überstandenen Strapazen vergessen. Nun ist zur Tatsache geworden, was ich am Anfang dieser Episode voraussah: Die neue Zeit für uns.

(*Diese Ereignisse in anderer Perspektive dargestellt: vgl. Heinsens Erinnerungen, Anhang A*)

June 24

My mother's birthday has dominated the last few days. Since she is held in great esteem by everyone, their best wishes were directed toward her on this special day. May the sun that was little seen at midday, light up the evening of her life.

Behind me lie some restful weeks interrupted only by several trips to Frankfurt. Once again we have an apartment in Frankfurt, and I have the prospect of a position with the railroad as of July 1.

June 26

I am sitting at my desk in Frankfurt, writing, thinking, and remembering.

Thus, the times have changed. And you, dear Robert, died for this, and you, also, Alfons, and all you others. And you, father, and you, my sister, you are all sacrifices of a time that stormed over the West like a punishment from God.

Who and what will survive, what will pass, and what is yet to come? What is the way and the will of God?

What particularly comes to mind is the Pentacost sermon of the pastor at Reichenbach [*Pastor Waldeck*] and his closing words: "God builds his temple out of ruins."

If on my journey, I was allowed to experience spring amidst the chaos; now a rich fall harvest is coming, and, with God's help, the basis for a better future.

I've employed all my strength this past week, harvesting hay primarily at the Molls, but also at the households of Steinmetz, Maurer, Kurz, and Mina Scherf, where Heinz and Miss Jürgens officiated. With the favorable weather, a great hay harvest was brought in, the likes of which we have not had for a long time.

Before that, I helped in various ways, setting out turnip seedlings in the fields. Strung out across the field in a long line, the helpers work with hearty conversation, and in the end, the once brown land appears transformed. The transplanted seedlings stand in formation, poised to flourish or wither away, custodians of the farmers' hopes and fears. But this year the weather seems to be favorable, thank God!

1945

24. Juni

Im Vordergrund der letzten Tage steht der Geburtstag meiner Mutter. Allerseits hochgeehrt, begegneten ihr an diesem Ehrentag die besonderen Wünsche aller. Möge ihren Lebensabend die Sonne bescheinen, die im Zenit so wenig zu sehen war.

Hinter mir liegen nunmehr einige geruhsame Wochen, unterbrochen von einigen Frankfurtfahrten. In Frankfurt haben wir wieder eine Wohnung und für den l. Juli steht mir eine Anstellung bei der Reichsbahn in Frankfurt in Aussicht.

26. Juni

Ich sitze in Frankfurt an meinem Schreibtisch und schreibe, denke und gedenke.

So haben sich die Zeiten geändert. Und du, lieber Robert, starbst dafür, auch du, Alfons, und all ihr andern. Und du, Vater, und du, meine Schwester, alle seid ihr Opfer einer Zeit, die als eine Strafe Gottes über das Abendland braust.

Wer und was wird bestehen bleiben, was vergehen und was wird kommen? Was ist der Weg und der Wille Gottes?

Mir gedenkt ganz besonders die Pfingstpredigt des Reichenbacher Pfarrers (*Pfarrer Waldeck*) und dessen Schlußwort: Gott baut seinen Tempel aus Ruinen.

Durfte ich auf meiner Reise den Frühling im Chaos erleben, so steht nunmehr ein ernteeicher Herbst bevor und somit durch Gottes Hilfe ein wichtiger Baustein zu einer besseren Zukunft.

In der vergangenen Woche war ich mit besten Kräften bei der Heuernte beschäftigt, voran bei Molls, aber auch bei Steinmetz, Maurer, Kurz und der Mina Scherf, bei welcher Heinz und Fräulein Jürgen amtierten. Bei günstigem Wetter wurde eine Heuernte geborgen, wie sie schon lange nicht mehr so reichlich ausgefallen war.

Vor dieser Zeit habe ich verschiedentlich geholfen, die Pflanzen der Dickwürzrüben auf die Äcker zu setzen. In langer Reihe arbeiten die Helfer bei lustigen Gesprächen und am Ende steht das vorher braune Land wie verzaubert. In Reih und Glied stehen die verpflanzten Pflänzlinge, bereit zu werden oder zu verderben, allzeit umsorgt vom Hoffen und Bangen der Landleute. Doch dieses Jahr scheint das Wetter günstig zu sein, so geb's Gott!

The corn and the wheat also look splendid. The farmers are still feeding their cattle with the first crop of clover, whereas in previous years, for lack of it they were forced to feed the cattle green meadows, which contributed to a significant shortage of hay.

I spent a day with Karl Moll and his fiancée, Emma Scherf, in Bad Homburg, seeing the local doctor at the Department of Health to obtain a "Declaration of No Impediment to Marriage." Although he put no obstacles in their way, this man nonetheless gave them a certificate on the basis of a law that had been issued in 1942. With this, Karl and Emma would have been able to marry in 1942, if….yes, if so many things had been different.

First, things had to fall apart, to put a stop to these unspeakable affairs and to give back the most basic rights of life to so many people; first, huge sacrifices had to be made by all to overthrow this Moloch, this Baal, this Antichrist and, also in the end, to help some of the oppressed and to demonstrate to all that the ostensibly perfect plans of man are lacking and no good if they do not correspond to God's will.

Why should this time be any better than any other, and is it not a foolish hope to believe the world will now be better as long as people remain the same? Truly, we should preach from every pulpit: First better yourselves, so that the world will also be better.

This Sunday, Karl and Emma will step up to the altar, accompanied by my best wishes, because, by marrying, they leave behind an episode that can never be made good, but can be brought to a conclusion..

Yesterday, I was at Georg's mother's house to ask how he was doing. The poor fellow is now in Gelnhausen in the Friedrichsheim (*an infirmary*) ill, very much weakened, yet still hoping for recovery.

It was like in old times again last Sunday, an early morning walk through the woods. I saw two roebucks and watched the sun rise. On the way home through the glorious birdsong-filled forest atmosphere of a Sunday morning, I came upon Mr. Zipp making a glorious bouquet of wildflowers. Following his good example, I likewise put together a bouquet, with red poppies making a charming contrast to white daisies, blue cornflowers and yellow buttercups. My mother was delighted with it.

Auch das Korn und der Weizen stehen prächtig und vom ersten Futterklee füttern die Bauern noch, während sie in früheren Jahren durch Mangel daran die Wiesen grün abfütterten und dabei teilweise beträchtlichen Heuverlust herbeiführten.

An einem Tage war ich mit Karl Moll und seiner Verlobten Emma Scherf in Bad Homburg auf dem Gesundheitsamt beim Kreisarzt wegen der Eheunbedenklichkeits erklärung. Zwar legte dieser Herr keine Hindernisse in den Weg, doch erteilte er dieses Zeugnis auf Grund eines Paragraphen, der 1942 erschienen ist. Somit hätten Karl und Emma schon 1942 heiraten können, wenn ... ja wenn so vieles anders gewesen wäre.

Erst musste dieser Zusammenbruch kommen, um diesen hohnsprechenden Verhältnissen Abbruch zu tun, um so vielen Menschen ihre primitivsten Lebensrechte wieder zu geben, und erst mussten von allen riesige Opfer gebracht werden, um diesen Moloch, Baalsgötzen und Antichristen zu stürzen, aber auch und nicht zuletzt einigen Verfolgten zu helfen und allen den Beweis zu geben, dass es allem menschlichen und scheinbar vollkommenen Planen des Gelingens gebricht, wenn es nicht dem Willen Gottes entspricht, also nicht gut ist.

Warum sollte jene Zeit auch besser sein denn ihre Zeitgenossen; und ist es nicht eine törichte Hoffnung zu glauben, dass es nun besser werde in der Welt, solange die Menschen die gleichen bleiben? Wahrlich von allen Kanzeln müsste man es predigen: Bessert euch zuerst, damit auch die Welt gebessert sei.

Am kommenden Sonntag treten nun Karl und Emma vor den Traualtar, begleitet von meinen besten Wünschen, denn sie treten durch diesen Ehebund aus einer Episode, die zwar nie gutgemacht werden kann, jedoch damit zum Abschluß gebracht wird.

Gestern war ich mal bei Georgs Mutter, um nach seinem Wohlergehen zu fragen; der arme Kerl liegt nun in Gelnhausen im verlegten Friedrichsheim, sehr geplagt, sehr geschwächt, jedoch noch guter Hoffnung auf Genesung.

Am vergangenen Sonntag war ich wieder mal wie in alten Zeiten. Ein Frühspaziergang durch den Wald. Zwei Rehböcke konnte ich beobachten und die Sonne aufgehen sehen. Auf dem Heimweg durch herrliche, vogeldurchklungene Sonntagmorgenwaldstimmung fand ich Herrn Zipp in Zubereitung eines herrlichen Feldblumenstraußes. Durch sein gutes Vorbild angeleitet, suchte ich ebenfalls einen Strauß zusammen, in dem roter Mohn in reizvollem Gegenüber zu weißen Margariten, blauen Kornblumen und Gelben Butterblumen vertreten war. Und meine Mutter hat sich darüber gefreut.

June 27

I have received my assignment from the employment office. With this, nothing stands in the way of starting work with the German Railroad. Things are looking up! Show what you're worth and your place in the world will be determined accordingly. Better to be than to appear. Woe to him who arrogantly disregards his limits; the current of life will wash him up on the shore, toss him onto the banks, and he will be mercilessly forgotten. Therefore, no one should believe that today's certain privileges mean that the place in the sun belongs to him alone. Rather, the only one who will not be disappointed is he who doesn't deceive himself, and who is aware that he will benefit only from what he has earned, not what he has endured.

And because the lessons of these hard times have escaped so many people, they will not benefit from what they have endured.

I met Erich Ehlers again today; we were both very happy to see each other.

I will always have fond memories of Miss Mühle at the employment office. It is she alone I have to thank for the placement with the German Railroad, since what Mr. Rothschild approved as political advisor could only come to fruition through the personal efforts of this woman.

July 4

I've been working for two days now and am quite pleased there. The office is located on the third floor of the industrial office. The director is Mr. Rind. We are mapping the territories of the individual railway bureaus by coloring in black printouts, which requires no more skill to make than some attention to detail.

July 15

What prompts this journal entry is the still fresh events of Anton Reinhard's wedding. We parted just an hour ago, when the nightly American curfew was lifted for the workday. When my hat fell out of my hand, Coach Keller thought I was drunk, but there was nothing to it. It was nice in the church and equally so in the evening at Anton's place. Along with coffee, wine, cake and a good dinner, the companionship was really most pleasant and memorable.

There is little news of significance to report from the office. I'm trying to learn about the subject of railroads by studying the available books. Mr. Kreussler and Mr. Fasterding gave me useful help through explanations and illustrations.

27. Juni

Nun habe ich die Zuweisungskarte vom Arbeitsamt bekommen, und somit steht meinem Dienstantritt bei der Reichsbahn nichts im Wege. Glückauf! Zeige, was du wert bist, und danach ist dein Platz in der Welt bemessen. Mehr sein als scheinen. Wehe dem, der im Dünkel seine Grenzen mißachtet, denn vom reißenden Strom des Lebens wird er an den Rand gespült, über die Ufer geworfen und erbarmungslos vergessen. Glaube da keiner, dem heute gewisse Vorrechte zugebilligt werden, der Platz an der Sonne gebühre ihm allein. Vielmehr nur der wird unenttäuscht bleiben, der sich keiner Selbsttäuschung hingibt und sich bewusst ist, dass allein Erworbenes, aber nicht Erduldetes ihm zum Vorteil gereicht.

Und weil vielen Menschen die Lehre dieser harten Zeit fruchtlos entfallen ist, gereicht ihnen auch nicht zum Vorteil, was sie erduldet haben.

Den Erich Ehlers habe ich heute wieder einmal getroffen; beide haben wir uns sehr gefreut.

Dem Fräulein Mühle vom Arbeitsamt werde ich stets ein freundliches Angedenken bewahren. Ihr allein danke ich die Vermittlung zur Reichsbahn, denn was Herr Rothschild als politischer Berater gutheißt, kann erst durch die individuelle Arbeit dieser Dame zur Tat geraten.

4. Juli

Nun bin ich schon zwei Tage im Amt und kann sagen, dass es mir dort ganz gut gefällt. Das Büro liegt im zweiten Obergeschoß des Industriehauses. Vorstand ist Herr Rind. Wir zeichnen eben in Schwarzdrucke mit Farben die Bereiche der einzelnen Reichsbahnämter ein, was neben etwas Sorgfalt keine weiteren Fähigkeiten zur Bedingung macht.

15. Juli

Anlaß zu dieser Eintragung ist das kaum verklungene Ereignis der Hochzeit Anton Reinhards. Erst vor einer Stunde, mit Beginn der amerikanischen Ausgehzeit, fand die Verabschiedung statt. Trainer Keller erklärte mich für voll, als mein Hut aus der Hand kullerte, jedoch davon keine Spur. Schön war es in der Kirche und ebenso am Abend beim Anton. Neben Kaffee, Wein, Kuchen und gutem Nachtessen war das gesellschaftliche Zusammensein wirklich sehr angenehm und erinnerungswert.

Im Geschäft gibt es nichts wesentlich Neues zu berichten. Ich bemühe mich, mich durch Studien in vorhandenen Büchern etwas in die Materie des Eisenbahnwesens einzuarbeiten. Wertvolle Hilfen durch Erklärungen und Erläuterungen geben mir die Herrn Kreussler und Fasterding.

July 26

After a long layoff, I once again participated in soccer training in Offenbach. The result: sore muscles.

Nonetheless, I contributed to the 5-1 victory over Isenburg on Sunday, as the center half. Erich Nowotny, Heini Alt, Anton Piccard, and I remain of the original Munich contestants. This suggests that by and by the others will also return. I ate at the home of Coach Keller.

July 30

On Monday, the whole Mayer gang came from Wüstems, mother, Heinz, and Gretel with all kinds of food, but no potatoes. For that reason I will go to Wüstems on Tuesday after work and return the next day with my knapsack full of potatoes.

August 2

I completed a work assignment in Hamburg at 1:30. After that I went on to Wüstems and arrived there about five. On the way, I picked and ate very many raspberries.

August 4

I returned to Frankfurt with potatoes Friday morning. On Saturday, I took the 1:49 p.m. train from Höchst to Königstein and then on to Wüstems, my forest home.

26. Juli

Ich habe nach langer Zeit wieder einmal am Fußballtraining in Offenbach teilgenommen. Ergebnis: Muskelkater.

Trotzdem konnte ich am Sonntag beim 5:1-Sieg über Isenburg beitragen, und zwar als Mittelläufer. Von den Münchenkämpfern sind noch Erich Nowotny, Heini Alt, Anton Piccard und ich übrig geblieben. Das heißt nach und nach werden die andern Kameraden schon wiederkommen. Beim Trainer Keller habe ich gegessen.

30. Juli

Am Montag kam die ganze Mayerkompanie aus Wüstems. Mutter, Heinz und Gretel mit allerlei Esswaren, jedoch ohne Kartoffeln. Deshalb bin ich am Dienstag nach Geschäftsschluß nach Wüstems und anderntags mit einem Rucksack voll Kartoffeln zurück.

2. August

Dienstlicher Auftrag in Hamburg bereits um 13.30 Uhr erledigt. Danach bin ich nach Wüstems gewandert und war etwa um 17.00 Uhr dort. Unterwegs habe ich sehr viele Himbeeren gepflückt und gegessen.

4. August

Am Freitagmorgen mit Kartoffeln zurück nach Frankfurt. Am Samstag mit dem 13.49-Uhr-Zug ab Höchst nach Königstein und wieder nach Wüstems, der Waldheimat.

August 5

Big move out of Usinger's room because this shameless company, after doing without rent, now with the American occupation demands rent again. Part of the things were stored in the Moll's residence and barn, and part upstairs with us.

I still had to replace spokes in my bike and so was busy till late afternoon, while Mademoiselle Gretel lay in bed "feeling sickly," yet despite that, in the afternoon flirted with the Americans, all made up and full of beans. Yes, yes, that's typical Gretel.

I drank coffee and ate crumb cake at the Molls' place. In the evening both the "Texas" Americans went hunting with us in the forest, though without any success. While I tagged along on a walk through the woods, Heinz, Walter, and the two Americans amused themselves shooting at "apple targets."

August 6

Had a spill in Oberems. Butter and cottage cheese all over the road and on my coat, and, in addition, three spokes and a backpack broken. Very annoying.

August 11

I was in Offenbach at Keller's house, and learned that a big game was going to be played against F.S.V. (*Fussballsportverein Frankfurt*) on Sunday. I went with Keller to Mr. Dünker's, a former soccer player and today the owner of a sporting goods shop. Coach Keller bought four pairs of soccer boots and ten sports pants. Toward evening, I went to Fechenheim and visited the Boffs and the three Thielemanns.

Everything is as in the old days at Kurt's. Everything is pell mell. I joined him for potato and cucumber salad, followed by a piece of good bread with his homemade jam.

5. August

Großer Umzug aus Usingers Saal, weil diese unverschämte Gesellschaft, nachdem sie beim amerikanischen Einmarsch auf jedes Mietentgelt verzichtete und nunmehr solches wieder begehrt hat. Teils wurden die Sachen bei Molls in die Wohnung und die Scheuer, teils zu uns im 1. Stock untergebracht.

Hiernach musste ich noch Speichen in meinem Fahrrade einziehen, war also bis in den späten Nachmittag hinein tätig, während Mamsell Gretel wegen „Übelkeit" im Bett lag, das ungeachtet am Nachmittag quietschvergnügt und geschminkt mit dem amerikanischen Besuch poussierte. Ja, ja, das ist typisch, Gretel.

Bei Molls habe ich Kaffee getrunken und Streuselkuchen gegessen. Abends waren die beiden „Texas" Amys mit uns im Wald jagen, doch ohne jeden Erfolg. Während ich einen Spaziergang durch den Wald anschloß, vergnügten sich Heinz, Walter und die beiden Amerikaner mit „Apfelschießen".

6. August

Start und Sturz bei Oberems. Butter, Siebkäse auf der Straße und auf meinem Rock, dazu drei Speichen und der Rucksack kaputt. Sehr ärgerlich.

11. August

Ich war in Offenbach beim Keller und erfuhr, dass am Sonntag ein großes Spiel gegen F.S.V. (*Fußballsportverein Frankfurt*) steigen soll. Mit ihm ging ich mit zu Herrn Dünker, ehemaliger Spieler und heute Inhaber eines Sportgeschäfts. Trainer Keller erhielt vier Paar Kickschuhe und zehn Sporthosen. Gegen Abend fuhr ich nach Fechenheim, besuchte Boffs und die drei Thielemänner.

Beim Kurt (Thielemann) ist's noch wie in alten Zeiten. All Pallmall. Kartoffeln und Gurkensalat habe ich mit ihm gegessen, hernach ein Stück gutes Brot mit seiner selbstgekochten Marmelade.

August 12

Big tournament day in Offenbach. Started the day by sleeping in, to save on breakfast. Drove to Offenbach for lunch. That's no way to start a hard day's work in peacetime. We won 1-0 with Weigel in goal, Mayer, Keck, Spiller, Gärtner, Kreiling, Göhlich, Seider, Piccard, Nowotny and Becker. Dutinee played in the first half, and he was the one who scored the goal of the day. The F.S.V. goalie was the nationally ranked goalkeeper, Kress. After the game, we had a friendly get-together over apple wine.

August 13

Today, Heinz came from Wüstems with cake. Just a taste, but good.

August 14

I met Miss Jürgens on Kaiserstrasse, near the main railroad station. In the course of our conversation, she brought up the idea of going to the circus.

The offerings of the Holzmüller Circus from Luxemburg didn't come close to the peacetime performance of an internationally renowned circus, or are my feelings still suffering from the aftermath of the recently ended world tragedy? Other than that, it was quite nice and a pleasant change. While Gretel and Heinz went straight home after the performance, I accompanied Miss Jürgens to Sachsenhausen and then had to hurry home. But I had already broken the nighttime curfew.

August 15

Heinz started a new job in Frankfurt today.

August 19

I experienced another disappointment today, and, as happens so often, it was in sports. I'm going to have to build up some reserves, or I'll lose all self-confidence in my playing ability. Shortly before the game, Keller came up to me and says that I have to sit out the game today. After all the anticipation, a great setback, of course. I smoked a cigar in anger.

August 23

Training in Fechenheim. Perhaps I will play again with the "03" team in the future.

12. August

Großkampftag in Offenbach. Angefangen mit Langschläferei, um das Frühstück zu sparen. Dann nach Offenbach gefahren zum Mittagessen, ist das natürlich kein Auftakt zu friedensmäßiger Leistung. Danach haben wir 1:0 gesiegt. Mit Weigel im Tor, Mayer, Keck; Spiller, Gärtner, Kreiling; Göhlich, Seider, Piccard, Nowotny und Becker. In der 1. Halbzeit spielte Dutinee, welcher auch das Tor des Tages schoß. Im Tor des F.S.V. spielte Nationaltorhüter (Willibald) Kreß. Nach dem Spiel gemütliches Beisammensein beim Apfelwein.

13. August

Heut kam Heinz mit Kuchen aus Wüstems, eine Kostprobe, aber gut.

14. August

Auf der Kaiserstraße nahe dem Hauptbahnhof traf ich Fräulein Jürgens. Im Laufe des Gesprächs kam sie zu dem Vorschlag eines Zirkusbesuches.

Die gebotenen Leistungen im Zirkus Holzmüller aus Luxemburg grenzten zwar bei weitem nicht an die Friedensleistungen eines Weltzirkusses, oder leidet das Empfinden noch unter den Nachwehen dieser nunmehr beendeten Welttragödie? Ansonsten war es ganz schön und eine angenehme Abwechslung. Während Gretel und Heinz nach der Vorstellung sofort nach Hause gingen, begleitete ich Fräulein Jürgens nach Sachsenhausen und musste mich hernach eilen, nach Hause zu kommen. Doch die Polizeistunde war schon überschritten.

15. August

Heute begann Heinz auf einer neuen Arbeitstelle in Frankfurt.

19. August

Heute habe ich wieder eine Enttäuschung erlebt und wie so oft in punkto Sport. Ich werde mir doch einige Reserve auflegen müssen, sonst verliere ich darin alles Selbstvertrauen. Kurz vor dem Spiel kommt Keller und sagt, dass ich heut aussetzen soll. Nach all der Vorfreude natürlich eine Pleite. Aus Zorn habe ich eine Zigarre geraucht.

23. August

Training in Fechenheim. Vielleicht werde ich in Zukunft bei der 03 wieder spielen.

August 26

Won the first game in Fechenheim against Rödelheim, 4-3. Günther Laber is also there again and played with the team. At noon on the same day, I kicked around again with Kickers, but not for long, because I badly twisted my right ankle. For now, that should be my last game in Offenbach too.

September 19

Many things have happened to date that deserve to be recorded in these memoirs.

Seems that Mayer (meaning me) has unintentionally developed into quite the character in the Engineering Office, where liveliness in office demeanor has, until now, been unthinkable for most of the men. For example, when the section supervisor, Mr. Neumann, asked me what I was currently working on, my response made the entire group shake their heads. This was in connection with the journey to Wiesbaden for 80 pounds of potatoes. Neumann and I drove to Wiesbaden. Upon arrival, I looked around for the promised porter, and asked the locals if they were familiar with Frauenlobstrasse. Just then, Neumann came through the crowd, so I asked him if he was also going to Frauenlobstrasse, so that I might join him. But, I pointed out, I don't want to hump around the potatoes yet. This word "hump" was as unintelligible to the good man as was my facial expression, yet caused a great deal of widespread jollity when reported to my co-workers at the office.

Last weekend, I took a foraging trip to Mrs. Sieger's, who had invited me for the purpose. Management gave me the ticket and the vacation time, so I went to the station on Friday evening, since the train to Butzback was scheduled to leave at 4:30. a.m. The night was sleepless, very stressful and seemed without end. Once in the train itself, I sat in the trainmen's car where there was plenty of room and peace. I reached Mrs. Sieger's at 7:30 a.m. and had to wait a while. After that, she gave me coffee, bread with butter and jelly, and, later, lunch. The return train left at about 2:30 p.m. The booty consisted of twenty pounds of white flour, nineteen pounds of rye flour and seven pounds of semolina, as well as a four-pound loaf of bread.

On Sunday, an exhausting and sadly lost game in Bürgel (6-1) and on Monday after work, I went to Königstein for fifty pounds of potatoes, and from Tuesday until today I was in Wüstems where, aside from the obvious benefits, I acquired a dreadful cold and a weariness in all my bones. Therefore, I will close now, and after I've eaten, "hit the hay" to gather new strength for new deeds.

26. August

Erstes Spiel bei Fechenheim gegen Rödelheim 4:3 gewonnen. Günther Laber ist auch wieder da und hat mitgespielt. Am Mittag gleichen Tages habe ich bei den „Kickers" nochmals gekickt, doch nicht lange, weil ich mir den rechten Fuß unglücklich verstaucht habe. Das soll auch vorläufig mein letztes Spiel in Offenbach gewesen sein.

19. September

Bis dato hat sich so mancherlei ereignet, was in den Memoiren festgehalten zu werden verdient.

So scheint sich der Mayer, das bin ich, recht zum Unikum des Büros Technik zu entwickeln, ganz ungewollt, doch ist den meisten Herren Urwüchsigkeit in ihrer Bürofaçon bisher undenkbar gewesen. Als zum Beispiel der Abt. Prokurist Neumann mich gefragt hatte, welche Tätigkeit ich zurzeit ausübe, setzte meine Antwort die ganze Clique in kopfschüttelnde Bewegung. Und in diesem Zusammenhang das Erlebnis der Wiesbadener Reise: 80 Pfd. Kartoffeln. Neumann und ich fuhren nach Wiesbaden. Dort angekommen vermisse ich den versprochenen Gepäckträger und die Leute befragt, ist ihnen die Frauenlobstraße unbekannt. Just kommt mein Neumann durch die Menge, und ich frage ihn, ob er ebenfalls zur Frauenlobstraße gehe, damit ich mich ihm anschließen kann. Nur die Kartoffeln wolle ich mir noch nicht auf den Ast legen. Dieses Wort „Ast" war dem guten Mann aber ebenso unbekannt wie das Mimen, löste jedoch beim Bericht im Büro allgemeine Heiterkeit aus.

Am letzten Wochenende unternahm ich eine Hamsterfahrt zu Frau Sieger, die dazu eingeladen hatte. Die Fahrkarte und den Urlaub gab mir der Vorstand und bereits am Freitagabend ging ich zur Bahn, weil der Zug nach Butzbach bereits um 4.30 Uhr ging. Die Nacht war ohne Schlaf, sehr anstrengend und schier ohne Ende. Im Zug selbst saß ich im Eisenbahnerwagen, und da war viel Platz und Ruhe. Um 7.30 Uhr war ich schon bei Frau Sieger und musste noch etwas warten. Hernach gab sie mir Kaffee und Butterbrot und Gelee und später Mittagessen. Etwa um 14.30 Uhr mittags ging der Zug zurück. Zwanzig Pfd. Weißmehl, 19 Pfd. Schwarzmehl und 7 Pfd. Gries, dazu ein 4 Pfd.-Brot war die Ausbeute.

Am Sonntag ein anstrengendes, leider verlorenes Spiel in Bürgel (6:1) und am Montag nach Feierabend nach Königstein (50 Pfd. Kartoffeln) und am Dienstag auf heute nach Wüstems haben mir neben den sichtbaren Vorteilen einen häßlichen Schnupfen eingebracht und dazu eine Müdigkeit in allen Knochen. Deshalb will ich jetzt schließen und nach vereinnahmter Mahlzeit die „Falle" aufsuchen, um neue Kraft zu neuen Taten zu sammeln.

September 23

I played in the 03 reserve team and earned ten marks.

September 26

On Monday evening I travelled to Königstein and, because Mrs. Scherer wasn't there, went on to Wüstems. I ate dinner at the Molls and repaired two cigarette lighters after that. Tuesday was a day off. I had a wonderful sleep and felt well rested and spent the morning in little Christel's company. Later I put together Mina Scherf's bicycle and around 4:30 p.m., I began the homeward journey, and in passing picked up Kurz's potatoes from the Gasselinks in Königstein. The folks here were beginning to worry about my absence and sought out word from Manager Rind as to whether or not I'd been at work that day. Even Gretel thought I should absolutely have left some kind of word.!?!?!? Management was satisfied with the explanation that I'd been held up in Wüstems because of bicycle trouble.

In the shop, I'm picking up all kinds of interesting and worthwhile bits of technical calculations. On the whole, my work hours are racing by, especially when, as often happens, I'm on the road. In general, the subject of conversation among the older people inevitably revolves around politics. But oh, how they treat the subject! It's as though they were the only victims of the time and all the others were more or less just charlatans and adventurers. Or is there some truth to this depiction? Who are those people who want to play judge today? Are they truly without blame and free and competent to judge and point fingers?

By this I do not mean to defend any Nazi. Absolutely not! Only that these complainers be questioned too. Are they more victimized than a German woman who will never see her sons again or will only see them maimed, and who, beyond that, feels herself defrauded and deceived in her holiest thoughts? Or than the widow of a concentration camp Jew, who, after all the years of hardship, grief and deprivation, can be permitted merely the one satisfaction, that she is free of the Nazi terror, yet who finds herself in virtually the same conditions as before, unable to draw on any visible material benefit?

Oh, there is much that is not as it should be or as it was promised.

23. September

Ich habe in der 03-Reserve gespielt und 10.-- verdient.

26. September

Am Montagabend fuhr ich nach Königstein und, weil Frau Scherer abwesend, dann nach Wüstems. Bei Molls zu Nacht gegessen, habe ich noch zwei Feuerzeuge repariert. Am Dienstag gab's einen „blauen Tag". Vor allen Dingen gut ausgeschlafen, verbrachte ich den Vormittag in Gesellschaft Christelchens. Später montierte ich Mina Scherfs Rad auseinander, und gegen 16.30 Uhr begab ich mich auf die Heimreise und nahm im Vorbeifahren die Kurzschen Kartoffeln bei Gasselink in Königstein mit. Hier hatte man schon Sorgen wegen meines Ausbleibens und bei Vorstand Rind Erkundigungen eingezogen, ob ich im Dienst gewesen sei. Sogar Gretel meinte, eine Nachricht meinerseits hätte unbedingt hinterlassen werden müssen !?!?!?. Der Vorstand war schon mit einer Erklärung zufrieden, dass ich infolge Raddefekts in Wüstems festgehalten worden sei.

Im Geschäft schnappe ich zuweilen sehr interessante und wissenswerte Brocken technischer Berechnungen auf. Überhaupt gehen die Dienststunden sehr behende um, ganz besonders dann, wenn ich, wie öfters, auf der „Achse" bin. Im allgemeinen drehen sich die Gesprächsstoffe bei den Älteren ausnahmslos um Politik. Und wie sie dieses Thema behandeln! Gerade so als seien sie die einzigen Opfer der Zeit und die anderen alle mehr oder weniger Scharlatane und Glücksritter! Oder hätte diese Ansicht etwas Wahres an sich. – Wer sind denn jene, die heute den Richter spielen wollen, sind sie wahrhaft makellos und frei und dazu berufen, zu urteilen und zu richten?

Ich will hiermit keinen „Nazi" in Schutz nehmen. Auf keinen Fall nicht! Nur jenen vorlauten Schreiern etwas auf den Zahn fühlen. Ist er etwa mehr geschädigt als etwa eine deutsche Frau, die ihre Söhne nie mehr oder nur verstümmelt wiedersieht und darüber hinaus sich in ihren heiligsten Gefühlen hintergangen und betrogen sieht; oder etwa einer Witwe eines KZ-Juden, die nach all den Jahren voll Not, Kummer und Entbehrungen lediglich die eine Genugtuung für sich in Anspruch nehmen kann, nun endlich von „Nazi Terror" befreit zu sein, um allerdings unter fast den gleichen Voraussetzungen sich außerstande zu sehen, sichtbaren materiellen Vorteil daraus zu ziehen.

Oh, es ist vieles nicht so, wie es richtig wäre oder wie es versprochen wurde.

October 15

Just finished a letter to the Dietz family in Hünfeld who so kindly hosted us on our homeward journey.

November 3

Twenty-second birthday. Please God that all the good wishes that were directed to me today might come to pass. My dear, good mother remembered me so kindly, also Heinz, Fritz, and Gretel, who baked me a cake. Miss Jürgens gave me a lovely surprise by honoring me with a wonderful bouquet of cyclamen.

At the office, the same sense of fear dominates, and all the more so since Mr. Heck, Mr. Fasterding and Mr. Kühmichel were let go. Just a day after leaving the management team, Kühmichel took the position of stationmaster at Weilburg. So now I find myself sitting next to Mr. Kreussler, who seems to me like a born teacher with his knowledge and uprightness.

November 11

I've just returned from a lecture by Director Fischer at the Northeastern YMCA on the number one subject. Alongside various biblical quotations is a quotation by the antichristian philosopher Nietzsche, along the following lines: Which children have no reason to cry about their parents? A YMCA member must be upright in body and soul, for his children will outgrow him only if the building blocks are a healthy and righteous marriage.

15. Oktober

Soeben beendete ich einen Brief an die Familie Dietz in Hünfeld, welche uns auf unserm Heimweg so freundlich bewirtet haben.

3. November

22. Geburtstag. Gebe Gott, dass all die guten Wünsche in Erfüllung gehen, die mir heute zugedacht wurden. Meine liebe, gute Mutter hat mich so lieb bedacht, dazu Heinz, Fritz und Gretel, die mir einen Kuchen gebacken hat. Freudig überrascht hat mich auch Fräulein Jürgens, indem sie mir einen wunderschönen Strauß Alpenveilchen verehrte.

Im Geschäft hält die Angstpsychose nach wie vor an, umsomehr als inzwischen Herren Heck, Fasterding und Kühmichel entlassen wurden. Kühmichel gerade, nachdem er einen Tag von der Direktion weg war, um die Bahnmeisterei Weilburg zu übernehmen. Nunmehr sitze ich neben Herrn Kreussler, der mir mit seinem Wissen und seiner Aufrichtigkeit der gegebene Lehrmeister scheint.

11. November

Soeben komme ich von einem Vortrag von Dir. Fischer im CVJM Nordost über das Thema 1. Neben verschiedenen Zitaten aus der Bibel ist ein Wort des antichristlichen Philosophen Nietzsche, das so ähnlich lautet: Welche Kinder hätten keinen Grund über ihre Eltern zu weinen. Der CVJMler müsse rechtwinklig an Leib und Seele sein, denn seine Kinder sollen über ihn hinaus wachsen und können dies nur, wenn die Bausteine dazu aus einer gesunden und gottgefälligen Ehe verbürgt sind.

November 16

John 14; 27: "Peace I leave you, my peace I give you. Not as the world gives do I give to you. Do not let your hearts be troubled, nor let them be afraid."

Jesus Christ keeps us in his peace through all the confusion of this age, and through all the troubles that befall us. This is not a peace such as the world gives, in shelter from and in defiance and fear of future wars, but rather, peace of the heart from faith in God, the Almighty Father.

Brother Häseler, a deacon who spent six and a half years in a concentration camp, spoke today at the Northeastern Bible study hour, describing and arguing and castigating the faults of the present age, which are due largely to our unwillingness to consciously renounce evil and only do good.

He said, "There is nothing evil in the world, only the absence of good!"

That is the pure truth. For is not the human love of comfort, the failure to do good, due less to evil than to the absence of goodness? Let him who wants miracles strengthen his own faith!

November 25

All Souls Day. Yesterday I covered Marianne's grave with fir fronds. In the afternoon I visited my colleague Eifert, in Rödelheim. When I got home, Glen, the American friend, had arrived. He gave each of us, Heinz and me, four packs of cigarettes. For mother, he had brought a can of ham, a can of milk, one of coffee, one of butter, and candy for everyone.

This evening I was at the Northeastern YMCA for a commemoration for those who had lost their lives in the war. Mr. Wagner was the speaker. The Bible verse from 2 Peter; 3, verses 3-13. Verse 13: "Nevertheless, we, according to his promise, look for new heavens and a new earth, wherein dwelleth righteousness."

16. November

Johannes 14, Vers 27: „Den Frieden lasse ich euch, meinen Frieden gebe ich euch. Nicht gebe ich euch, wie die Welt gibt. Euer Herz erschrecke nicht und fürchte sich nicht."

In allen Wirrnissen dieser Zeit und über alle Not hinweg erhält Jesus Christus uns seinen Frieden. Nicht ist dies ein Frieden, wie ihn die Welt schließt, in Schutz und Trutz und in Angst vor neuen Kriegen, sondern den Frieden im Herzen, im Glauben an Gott, den allmächtigen Vater.

Heute sprach Bruder Häseler, Diakon und 6 ½ Jahre im KZ, in der Nordost-Bibelstunde und erzählte und überzeugte und geißelte die Misstände der heutigen Zeit, die auch zum größten Teil darin begründet liegen, weil wir nicht gewillt sind, bewusst in Abkehr vom Bösen nur Gutes zu tun.

Er sagte: „Es gibt nichts Böses in der Welt, dies ist nur das Fehlen des Guten!"

Das ist die reine Wahrheit, denn liegt nicht in der menschlichen Bequemlichkeit, in mangelndem Gutestun weniger das Böse als eben das Fehlen des Guten? – Wer Wunder will, der stärke seinen Glauben!

25. November

Totensonntag. Gestern habe ich Mariannes Grab mit Tannenreisern abgedeckt. Am Nachmittag besuchte ich den Kollegen Eifert in Rödelheim. Als ich von dort nach Hause kam, war Glen, der Ami-Freund, eingetroffen. Er hat jedem, Heinz und mir, vier Päcks Zigaretten geschenkt. Für Mutter hat er eine Büchse Speck, eine Dose mit Milch, eine mit Kaffee und eine Dose mit Butter und für die Allgemeinheit einige Süßigkeiten mitgebracht.

Heute abend war ich in Nordost CVJM in einer Gedenkstunde für die Opfer des Krieges. Es sprach Herr Wagner. Das Bibelwort aus 2. Petrus 3, Vers 3-13. Vers 13: „Wir aber warten eines neuen Himmels und einer neuen Erde nach seiner Verheißung, in welchen Gerechtigkeit wohnt."

November 30

Today I was treated to a bottle of wine by my managing director, Mr. Rind, a recognition, an honor, and a motivation for me to stay on the right path. Incidentally, I sent an application to the Central Office of the Reichsbahn yesterday in which I applied for training to become a technical assistant with the RB.

If with God's help my plan works out, I could be finished with my apprenticeship in 1947 and have gained half a year. My main concern is to attain a kind of position and earnings that will enable me to relieve my mother of the double burden of being both breadwinner and housekeeper. Whether I will be successful, only God knows, but I do believe that he will allow the sun to shine again on my mother.

I had a lengthy discussion today with Fritz Cron about the problems that have arisen with regard to his difficult position in our family, since Gretel pretty much deceived him and has now become quite hostile toward him. I advised him not to take everything so seriously, since with the perspective of several years, all these problems will be small and insignificant compared to the other demands life will make of him.

I hope he won't feel any scruples or inhibitions about turning a deaf ear to all the snide remarks and jibes. I regret that we pay so little heed in our house to a guest's right to hospitality, and hope that particularly Gretel and Heinz will never experience outside of our family such a lack of grace and generosity as they today, perhaps unwittingly, show to Fritz Cron.

30. November

Heute war ich bei meinem Bürovorstand, Herrn Rind, zu einer Flasche Wein eingeladen, was für mich Anerkennung, Ehre und Ansporn sein soll, weiter auf rechtem Wege zu bleiben. Übrigens habe ich vorgestern eine Bewerbung an die Reichsbahndirektion gerichtet, in welcher ich mich um die Ausbildung zum technischen RB-Assistenten bewerbe.

Wenn mit Gottes Hilfe das Vorhaben klappt, dann kann ich schon 1947 mit der Ausbildung fertig sein und hätte ein halbes Jahr gewonnen. Hauptsächlich geht es mir darum, eine solche Existenz und solchen Verdienst zu erreichen, dass für meine Mutter endlich einmal diese ewig drückende doppelte Sorge als Ernährer und im Haushalt dazu genommen wird. Ob mir das gelingt, weiß Gott allein, und ich glaube auch, dass er meiner Mutter noch einmal die Sonne scheinen lässt.

Mit Fritz Cron hatte ich heute eine längere Aussprache über die Probleme, die sich in seiner keineswegs heiklen Lage innerhalb unsrer Familie ergeben haben, nachdem Gretel ihn geradezu getäuscht hat und heute ihm direkt feindlich gegenübersteht. Ich habe ihm zugeredet, das alles nicht so tragisch zu nehmen, denn im Abstand einiger Jahre sind ja alle diese Probleme nichtig und gering im Gegensatz zu all den Anforderungen, die das Leben an ihn stellen wird.

Ich hoffe, dass er keine Skrupel noch Hemmungen empfindet, wenn er den spitzen Bemerkungen und Glossen mit tauben Ohren begegnet. Ich bedaure, dass in unsrem Hause so wenig das Gastrecht geachtet wird und hoffentlich lernen, hauptsächlich Gretel und Heinz besonders, die nicht außerhalb der Familie ein solches Vegetieren aus Gnad und Barmherzigkeit kennen, das sie, unbewusst vielleicht heute dem Fritz Cron zuteil werden lassen.

December 10

Christmas is fast approaching. Aunt Jeanne's first letter gave us great joy today. According to the letter, she and the children are well, but she's very worried about their father and her spouse, from whom she has had no word since last March.

Dr. Spieker spoke yesterday at the Northeastern Y on the subject of "America." For some young Germans, his talk could be construed as a word of caution if, blinded by a shining and rich America, they want to recklessly throw overboard all of their ideals without recognizing how crass and repulsive the superficiality of the Americans is for us Germans, and the danger that we might also degenerate!

Yes, Christmas is coming. Will it truly happen … and peace on earth? This peace will not be created at peace conferences until the world is ready for peace.

Oh, don't quarrel with God, for He has been patient with you but you refused to recognize it and remain in misery through envy and strife. How true the Bible verse: "Seek first the Kingdom of God, and all other things will be given to you."

Helga was here for a few days with little Christel, because he had to undergo surgery. Today the little lad was admitted into the hospital at Höchst and tomorrow Helga will return to Wüstems. The Molls are expected to slaughter a pig this week. I really should be there for that, right?

10. Dezember

Mit Riesenschritten geht's nun auf Weihnachten zu. Eine rechte und große Freude bereitete uns heute der erste Brief von Tante Jeanne. Demnach ist sie, wie auch die Kinder, gesund, jedoch sehr in Sorge um ihren Vater und Gatten, von dem sie seit März keine Nachricht mehr erhalten haben.

Gestern Abend sprach im N.O. Herr Dr. Spieker über das Thema „Amerika". Für manchen jungen Deutschen würden seine Ausführungen ein warnendes Halt bedeuten, wenn sie, geblendet vom gleißenden und reichen Amerika, bedenkenlos alle Ideale über Bord werfen möchten, ohne erkannt zu haben, wie krass und abschreckend für uns Deutsche des Amerikaners Oberflächlichkeit entgegensteht und die Gefahr für uns, ebenfalls darin zu verflachen!

Ja, Weihnachten will es werden. Wird es jetzt wahr ... und Frieden auf Erden? Dieser Friede wird nicht auf Friedenskonferenzen erschaffen werden können, solange die Welt nicht friedfertig ist.

Oh, hadert nicht mit Gott, denn er hat Geduld mit euch gehabt, doch ihr habt's nicht erkennen wollen und verbleibt in Unfrieden durch Neid und Streit. Wie wahr das Bibelwort: „Trachtet zuerst nach dem Reiche Gottes, so wird euch alles andere zuteil werden."

Helga war nun einige Tage mit Christelchen hier, weil Klein-Christel sich einer Operation unterziehen muß. Heute kam der Junge nach Höchst ins Krankenhaus und Helga fährt morgen wieder nach Wüstems. Molls sollen diese Woche schlachten. Da müsste ich eigentlich dabei sein?!

December 11

One receives strange and diverse tasks now in the Building Department. Today I had to fetch firewood for the department head, Mr. Neumann, the director, Mr. Endress, and the senior counsel, Mr. Metzig. I carried out the job with two co-workers from Repair Station No. 5. At the distribution center, I saw images and signs of need everywhere, careworn and stooped men, deserving and hateful people, all suffer equally from the merciless cold.

I was supposed to have gotten extra ration cards a few days ago for "Sonny Boy" Dressel, the architect! It's ridiculous, as if he couldn't get his own. His presumptuous demand that his pencils be sharpened for him every morning is yet another reason for our conviction that the guy has a screw loose.

I met Dr. Fisher from the Northeastern Y on the street this morning.

This afternoon, Mr. Rind told me to go home because I was chilled to the bone. He also shared with me that Mr. Link had approved my application, and that I am to begin my training as an assistant after January 1, albeit with the proviso that I continue to be employed as a technical employee, because no civil service applications are being accepted at present.

December 20

Heinz had his twenty-first birthday on the 17th. Tomorrow would have been my father's fifty-seventh birthday if….

Once again, Christmas is approaching and with it an expectant joy, an anticipatory joy evoked by memories of more peaceful times and by the longing for peace and love. Not the peace and love that the world gives, but rather the holy peace of the faithful and the love of the early Christians.

I send Christmas wishes to Mrs. Laber and Master Thielemann. But my thoughts are also with my friends who are imprisoned and those who are no longer among us.

At the office, I'm preoccupied with statistical calculations, for example, calculations regarding a retaining wall. I'm also competing with Franz Eifert in regards to other technical calculations.

11. Dezember

Sonderbare und mannigfaltige Aufgaben erhält man eben im bautechnischen Büro. Heute mußte ich für den Abt. Pr. Neumann, Dir. Endress und Oberrat Metzig Brennholz holen. Mit zwei Arbeitern der BM 5 habe ich den Auftrag ausgeführt. Bilder und Zeugnisse der Not sah ich allenthalben dort an der Verteilungsstelle; verhärmte und gebeugte Menschen, ergebenes und gehässiges Volk leiden gleichviel unter der erbarmungslosen Kälte.

Für den „Sonny-Boy" Baurat Dressel sollte ich schon seit einigen Tagen Freimarken besorgen! Lächerlich, als ob er sich die nicht selbst besorgen könnte. Oder sein anmaßendes Verlangen, dass jeden Morgen seine Bleistifte gespitzt werden sollen, lassen gleichermaßen die Vermutung auftauchen, dass der Kerl etwas am „Sträußchen" hat.

Herrn Dir. Fischer vom Nord-Ost traf ich heute auf der Straße.

Am Nachmittag hat mich Herr Rind nach Hause gehen geheißen, weil ich gar so durchgefroren war. Auch hat er mir offenbart, dass Herr Link meinem Gesuch stattgegeben, und ich ab 1. Januar in Ausbildung zum Assistenten komme, allerdings mit der Einschränkung, dass ich als technischer Angestellter weitergeführt werde, weil offiziell zurzeit keine Beamtenanwärter zugelassen werden.

20. Dezember

Am 17. 12. hatte Heinz Geburtstag und wurde 21 Jahre alt; morgen hätte mein Vater Geburtstag und würde 57 Jahre alt werden, wenn …

Wieder sind die Weihnachtstage näher gekommen und mit diesen Tagen eine erwartungsvolle Freude, eine Vorfreude, die durch die Erinnerung friedvollerer Jahre hervorgerufen und in der Sehnsucht nach Frieden und Liebe. Nicht Frieden und Liebe, wie die Welt gibt, sondern den heiligen Frieden der Gläubigen und die Liebe der alten Christen.

Weihnachtsgrüße sende ich soeben an Frau Laber und Meister Thielemann. Aber auch bei meinen Freunden in der Gefangenschaft weilen die Gedanken und bei denen, die nicht mehr unter uns weilen.

Im Geschäft mühe ich mich zurzeit mit statischen Berechnungen herum, zum Beispiel der Berechnung einer Stützmauer. Oder aber auch mit Franz Eifert im Wettbewerb in anderen technischen Berechnungen.

The world has known the gospel of love through Jesus Christ for almost 2000 years. And yet one could say that in that time the world has only become worse. Why is that?

Today, I was once again at Mrs. Laber's in Fechenheim, and it was a true pleasure to converse with this splendid woman. We don't talk about cabbage and turnips or even about our daily cares, but rather about God and His glory, about the way to Him and about many other things which burden the soul.

I also visited Mrs. Jörger. The poor woman has had to suffer and bear much, and yet does so courageously. For after her son-in-law was killed in the war, and her daughter, Klärchen, a classmate of Marianne's, died, Mrs. Jörger was left to care for a two-year-old girl; then, to add to all her misfortunes, her husband was drafted to go to war and has still not returned. God tests His own, and yet afflictions are also a blessing from above if we can only rightly understand.

It depends on man himself,

And on his will,

Whether he is one way or another, good or bad.

Seit nahezu 2000 Jahren kennt die Welt das Evangelium der Liebe durch Jesus Christus. Jedoch könnte man sagen, dass seit jener Zeit die Welt nur noch ärger wurde. Woran liegt das?

Heute war ich wieder einmal bei Frau Laber in Fechenheim, und es war mir eine rechte Freude, mich mit dieser trefflichen Frau auszusprechen. Dabei reden wir zwar nicht von Kraut und Rüben oder etwas häufiger schon von den täglichen Sorgen, sondern von Gott und seiner Herrlichkeit, vom Weg zu ihm und noch von allerlei, was auf der Seele lastet.

Auch bei Frau Jörger stattete ich einen Besuch ab. Die Ärmste hat auch viel erleiden und erdulden müssen und trägt's dennoch tapfer. Denn nachdem der Schwiegersohn im Krieg gefallen und die Tochter, das Klärchen, eine Klasssengefährtin Mariannens, gestorben war und der Frau Jörger ein zwei Jahre altes Mädchen überließen, musste zu allem Unglück auch noch ihr Mann in den Krieg ziehen und ist bis heute noch nicht zurück. Gott prüft die Seinen, doch ist auch die Heimsuchung eine Gnade von oben, wenn wir es nur recht zu beschauen wissen!!

An den Menschen selbst

Liegt es und an seinem Willen,

ob er so oder so ist, gut oder böse.

Christmas 1945

The following poem was written in 1942:

Rise up and let the bells resound!
Let the music of Christmas
Proclaim in every land
God has sent his Son!

God has shown such love
To this confused world.
And so may you, Lord, in your heavenly tent
Be forever praised.

Oh friend, your eyes are dark with sorrow
Pain and care oppress your heart.
Why do you fear for the morrow?
Just for now look up to heaven!

Why do you give up so quickly
When your heart encounters need?
Leave your crying, moaning, wailing
Look with trust upon your God.

May righteousness guide all your days,
May you live free of stress and strife!
For all the love we give to others
Will one day reap its own reward.

And when one day true love shall find you
And with bliss shall bless your soul,
You will know to bless the hour
In which you yourself gave love.

1945

Weihnacht, 1945

Das nachfolgende Gedicht stammt bereits aus dem Jahre 1942:

Auf, jetzt zieht der Glocken Stränge!
Kündet laut in jedem Land,
weihnachtliche Liederklänge
Gott hat seinen Sohn gesandt!

Solche Liebe hat erwiesen
Gott der ach so wirren Welt;
drum sei alle Zeit gepriesen,
Herr, in Deinem Himmelszelt.

Mensch, dein Aug' trübt schweres Sorgen,
Schmerz und Kummer drückt dein Herz.
Warum bangt es dir vor Morgen?
Schau doch einmal himmelwärts!

Warum willst du gleich verzagen,
wenn dein Herz einmal in Not?
Lass das Weinen, Jammern, Klagen,
schau vertrauend auf zu Gott!

Sei gerecht dein ganzes Leben,
hüte dich vor Streit und Zank!
Alle Liebe, die wir geben,
findet einmal ihren Dank.

Wird dir wahre Lieb begegnen,
dran du deine Seele labst,
dann wirst du die Stunde segnen
wo du selber Liebe gabst!

Romans 7: 24-25: "Oh wretched man that I am! Who shall deliver me from the body of this death? I thank God through Jesus Christ, our Lord."

January 13

It is only now on the thirteenth day of the New Year that I once again feel called to write.

I've just come from a lecture by Deacon Hüseler on the subject of Shakespeare's religious wisdom, which, incidentally, was very skillfully composed. Now, I too am a member of the YMCA and hope to find in this community and brotherhood the spirit and wisdom that will shape me into a true servant of God and an upstanding person.

On New Year's Day, I went to Pastor Waldeck's church service and then took communion. My brother, Heinz, was there, and our presence greatly gladdened Pastor Waldeck. I found his sermon persuasive and have the confidence in him that I did eight years ago when he gave us confirmation instructions. He preached on the verse for the New Year, "I am the Way, the Truth, and the Life. No one comes to the Father except through me."

In the New Year I will pursue my occupational training with all my energy, towards the goal of being a technical assistant for the German Railroad. It is for this reason that I joined the YMCA, because I hope and believe that this way is also "the way" that Jesus Christ ordains in order to attain truth and life. I have great confidence and trust in the Lord.

As part of my job training, I am currently at Repair Station 4 in Bockenheim. I have to go by tram to reach the office because it's much too far to walk. The office manager is Mr. Schilling, who Mr. Rind says was a "stinking Nazi". However, I agree with Mr. Kraussler that Mr. Schilling is a good man, and hope I have not erred in this judgment. Above all, he's very competent and makes an effort to answer my questions thoroughly and clearly.

Römer 7, V. 24-25: „Ich elender Mensch! Wer wird mich erlösen von dem Leibe dieses Todes? Ich danke Gott durch Jesum Christum, unseren Herrn."

13. Januar

Nunmehr erst am 13. Tage des neuen Jahres fühle ich mich wieder zum Schreiben berufen.

Ich komme soeben von einem Vortrag des Diakons Häseler über das Thema „Shakespeares religiöse Lebensweisheit", der übrigens sehr geschickt zusammengestellt war. Nunmehr bin ich auch Mitglied des CVJM und hoffe, in dieser Gemeinschaft und Bruderschaft den Geist und die Lebensweisheit zu finden, die aus mir einen treuen Knecht Gottes und einen aufrechten Menschen formt.

Am Neujahrstage war ich bei Pfarrer Waldeck im Gottesdienst und anschließend zum Abendmahl. Bruder Heinz war dabei, und unsere Anwesenheit hat Pfarrer Waldeck sehr erfreut. Ich fand seine Predigt überzeugend und bringe ihm das gleiche Vertrauen entgegen, das ich ihm schon als sein Konfirmand vor acht Jahren geschenkt habe. Er predigte über die Jahreslosung: Ich bin der Weg, die Wahrheit und das Leben, niemand kommt zum Vater denn durch mich.

Im neuen Jahr gilt es nun auch für mich in der beruflichen Ausbildung zum technischen Reichsbahnassistenten mit aller Kraft zum Ziele zu streben. Aus diesem Grunde bin ich auch dem CVJM beigetreten, weil ich hoffe und glaube, dass auch dieser Weg in meinem Leben „der Weg" sein muss, den Jesus Christus vorschreibt, um zur Wahrheit und zum Leben zu gelangen. Ich bin voller Zuversicht und hoffe auf den Herrn.

Gemäß dem Ausbildungsplan bin ich zurzeit auf der Bahnmeisterei 4 in Bockenheim. Zur Dienststelle muss ich die Straßenbahn benutzen, denn der Weg ist für einen Fußgänger denn doch zu weit. Dienstvorsteher ist Herr Schilling, von dem Herr Rind sagt, daß er ein „stinkiger Nazi" gewesen sei; dagegen stimme ich mit Herrn Kraussler überein, dass Herr Schilling ein guter Mensche ist, und hoffe auch, darin nicht zu irren. Vor allen Dingen ist er sehr tüchtig und gibt sich auch Mühe, meine Fragen gründlich und aufklärend zu beantworten.

After work yesterday, I was at Franz Eifert's in Rödelheim and experienced something strange. Now, I'm accustomed to fulfill promises and to keep appointments. Because the weather that morning was very changeable and seemed unsuited to a trip to the Taunus, I called and arranged to meet Franz at noon. As soon as I arrived, Franz had to fetch wood, which he must have known about earlier that morning, but had apparently forgotten.

But the actual purpose of my visit was to play billiards with Franz. Of course, I helped him fetch and chop the wood. Hardly had we completed this work, though, when Mrs. Eifert showed up with another job, to get more wood from the dealer and once again chop it. All I had to do was to go there; Franz had already gone ahead with the wagon. Okay, I once again helped out and didn't ask why or wherefore, but simply strove to complete the task quickly and so finally to be able to play the anticipated game.

But once the work was done and the wood was stacked in the basement, Franz thought nothing of his promise, blithely filed his finger nails, prattled on about dumb things, and showed such superficiality that I became so frustrated and resigned that I could not focus and therefore lost both the games we later played. I witnessed as well such a contrast in this family's life that I was forced to reconsider, rather shocked, whether the same thing could happen at our house. But then I was ashamed and thought I'd better remain silent rather than say careless words that would disturb the soul.

January 15

Today, Aunt Jeanne wrote and told us she'd had a brief sign of life from Uncle Hans. She's very worried, particularly about her children. Without any income now for eleven months, she's dreadfully afraid of inflation. I wrote back to her straightaway asking if and how we might help and, on behalf of mother, encouraged her to come and stay with us.

January 20

So what now? A public talk on the problems of today by Dr. Scharpf. The lecture by this instructor from our local seminary made a strong impression. He gave answers with symbolically chosen words: seeing, recognizing, and acting. Here, brilliant public speaking combined with extensive knowledge, pedagogical talent with the rich experience of a well-traveled man. A full room and the open support of the gathering promised a good reception for the YMCA's publicity efforts.

Gestern war ich nach Feierabend in Rödelheim bei Franz Eifert und habe Seltsames erlebt. Nun bin ich einmal gewöhnt, gegebenen Versprechen nachzukommen und Verabredungen einzuhalten. Da nun das Wetter morgens sehr unbeständig war und für eine Taunusfahrt ungeeignet erschien, rief ich Büro T an und vereinbarte mit Franz zum Mittag bei ihm zu sein. Dort angekommen, musste Franz nun Holz holen, was er bestimmt am Morgen hätte wissen müssen, jedoch anscheinend vergessen hatte.

Der eigentliche Zweck meines Besuches war aber, mit Franz Billard zu spielen. Natürlich half ich beim Holzholen und beim Schneidenlassen. Kaum war nun diese Arbeit erledigt, kommt Frau Eifert mit einem weiteren Auftrag, noch einmal beim Händler Holz zu holen und dann nochmals schneiden zu lassen. Ich brauche nur hinzugehen, Franz sei mit dem Wagen bereits vorausgefahren. Gut, auch dieses Mal half ich und fragte nicht weshalb und für was, jedoch bestrebt, die Arbeit rasch zu beenden, um dann das erhoffte Spiel noch ausführen zu können.

Als nun auch dies Werk getan und das Holz im Keller verstaut war, dachte Franz gar nicht an sein Versprechen, feilte seelenvergnügt seine Fingernägel, plauderte dummes Zeug und zeigte sich von einer so oberflächlichen Seite, dass ich so enttäuscht und resigniert wurde, dass ich bei dem viel später stattfindenden Spielen nicht bei der Sache war und deshalb beide Male verlor. Außerdem zeigte sich in diesen Familienleben ein Kontrast ab, dass ich erschrocken überdachte, ob es bei uns zu Hause auch so zugehen könnte; dann wollte ich mich schämen und besser schweigen, als dass so manch unnütz Wort gesprochen wird, vor dem die Seele erschrecken muss.

15. Januar

Heute schrieb Tante Jeanne und teilte mit, dass sie ein kurzes Lebenszeichen von Onkel Hans erhalten habe. Sie ist sehr in Sorgen, besonders wegen der Kinder. Seit elf Monaten ohne Einnahmen, bangt es ihr vor einer Inflation. Ob und wie wir helfen können, ich habe sogleich geantwortet und ihr im Auftrage Mutters nahegelegt, zu uns zu kommen.

20. Januar

Und was nun? Ein offenes Wort zu den Problemen der Gegenwart von Dr. phil. Scharpf. Stark beeindruckt hat mich die Rede von diesem Dozenten des hiesigen Predigerseminars. Antwort gab er mit den sinnbildlich gefassten Worten: sehen, erkennen und handeln. Glänzende Rednergabe verband sich hier mit umfangreichem Wissen, pädagogisches Talent mit der reichen Erfahrung eines weitergereisten Mannes. Ein gefüllter Raum und das offene Zeugnis der Veranstaltung verheißt eine gute Aufnahme der Bemühungen des CVJM in der Öffentlichkeit.

On January 27, 28 and 29, Gustav Adolf Gedat, well-known as the author of "A Christian Experiences the Problems of the World," will be speaking to the youth of Frankfurt in the University auditorium. Last Wednesday, I was with Fritz Fischer at the seventh membership meeting of the YMCA. At the Bible study on Friday, January 18, Mr. Wagner spoke on current topics. I didn't find his words as rousing as some more experienced speakers, but I don't doubt that he is sincere.

Early yesterday, my work took me to Höchst, but because of an unsuccessful mission, I continued on to Königstein after I had spoken to the train supervisors. I fixed both kitchen window shutters there in my capacity as a locksmith, but didn't quite finish the job on the second shutter and will have to finish up next time. Everything is all right at the Molls, little Christel and Helga too, though the latter still has many bitter hours before she gains insight into who she is and how little she's capable of changing her situation as long as she doesn't improve herself. If she would just once recognize what Aunt Jeanne has had to go through and what she has already achieved in her life, then how much would she think she deserves?

January 21, 6 a.m.

Today I was up by 4:30 to get a small pack of briquettes from Tommi. Now that I'm back and have some leisure time, I'm preoccupied with yesterday's lecture on Acts 9: 6. Paul's question, "Lord, what is it that you would have me do?" must have arisen in circumstances similar to those depressing people today, especially young men.

"What is it, Lord, that you would have me do?" Are not these words that could have been said yesterday or that might be said today or tomorrow? And yet, faith should also be strengthened in us in the same measure and out of the same sense of need as Saul experienced it and in the same way as faith transformed him into Paul. Surely faith should likewise give courage and confidence to all those in need and sorrow, all those with cares and worries. The Son of Man came to seek and save those who were lost. What a shining standard our Lord and Savior has set before those who believe in Him! He seeks us, the lost, and bestows on us the grace of His word. Who can stand aside in the face of this? Whom does this not concern?

Am 27., 28. und 29. Januar spricht Gustav Adolf Gedat, bekannt als Autor: „Ein Christ erlebt die Probleme der Welt", in der Universitätsaula zu der jungen Welt Frankfurts. Am vergangenen Mittwoch war ich mit Fritz Fischer in der 7. Mitglieder-Vesammlung des CVJM. Am Freitag (18.1.) in der Bibelstunde. Herr Wagner sprach zu aktuellem Thema, nur finde ich, dass er seine Worte nicht so zündend hinauswerfen kann, wie so mancher routinierte Redner, doch zweifle ich nicht, dass er's etwa weniger ehrlich meinte.

Gestern früh war ich dienstlich in Höchst und bin infolge erfolgloser Mission daselbst, nachdem ich mit der Bahnmeisterei 4 gesprochen hatte, nach Königstein weitergefahren. Dort habe ich die beiden Küchenläden angeschlagen nach Schlossermanier, bin jedoch mit dem zweiten Laden nicht mehr ganz fertig geworden und muss es beim nächsten Mal nachholen. Bei Molls ist soweit alles in Ordnung; auch bei Christelchen und Helga, und muss letztere noch viele bittere Stunden auskosten, bis sie zur Erkenntnis gelangt und weiß wer sie ist, wie wenig sie zur Änderung ihrer Lage fähig ist, solange sie sich nicht bessert. Sie sollte sich doch einmal vor Augen halten, was Tante Jeanne zurzeit durchmachen muss und in Anbetracht dessen, was Tante Jeanne schon in ihrem Leben geleistet hat, was wäre denn dann das Maß, welches ihr gerecht wäre?

21. Januar, 6.00 Uhr morgens

Heute war ich bereits um halb fünf aufgestanden, um bei Tommi ein Päckchen Briketts zu holen. Nun da ich wieder zurück bin und Muße habe, beschäftigt mich der gestrige Vortrag in solchem Maße (Apostelg. 9, V. 6). Des Paulus Wort: „Herr, was willst du, dass ich tun soll?" wird wohl in einer ähnlichen Not entstanden sein, wie sie heute den Menschen bedrückt, hauptsächlich den jungen Mann.

„Was willst du, Herr, dass ich tun soll?" Könnte das nicht auch gestern, heute oder morgen gesprochen worden sein oder werden? Doch auch in gleichem Maße und aus gleicher Not, wie sie Saulus empfand, müsste in uns der Glaube sich verstärken, wie der Glaube aus jenem den Paulus gemacht hat; müsste Mut und Zuversicht geben allen denen, die in Not und Leid, in Sorge und Kummer sind. Des Menschen Sohn ist gekommen, zu suchen und selig zu machen, was verloren ist. Welch leuchtendes Panier hat doch unser Herr und Heiland dem vorgesetzt, der an ihn glaubt! Uns, die Verlorenen sucht er und schenkt uns die Gnade seines Wortes. Wer darf da abseits stehen? Wen geht das nichts an?

February 4

These are unforgettable days! These days with Gedat. For three days, the university auditorium was filled with people thirsting after the words of salvation. Did Gedat give them that?

To the young members of the YMCA in any case, he gave a great lift and offered many young, struggling, people a light on their path.

On Sunday, Gedat spoke on the subject, "Coming to Terms with the Past", on Monday, on "Is God Silent?", and on Tuesday, "Is There No Way Out?". On Tuesday evening he spoke again, and only to the youth of Frankfurt.

A second highlight of the week was a lecture by Pastor Busch from Witten, a brother of the pastor in Essen who had performed the marriage of Aunt Jeanne. A warrior type in contrast to Gedat, not so spiritual and artful in his delivery, yet by the same token more solid, earthy, and perhaps more convincing.

I have now officially been received as a member of the YMCA and hope to God that I will be blessed as a result.

Since February 1st, I've progressed another step in my training to become a technical assistant on the railroad, and will be working at the railroad shop for four months. Wilhelm Puth from Fechenheim began his training as railroad inspector the same day as I, but had to stop the next day. He was let go because he had belonged to the Nazi Party! The same thing happened to Mr. Schilling at Repair Station #4. Poor old man! Is that justice?

Today, I received a letter from Rico. Like me, he's glad that the contact worked out.

4. Februar

Es sind unvergeßliche Tage! Jene Tage mit Gedat. Drei Tage die Aula der Universität gefüllt mit Menschen, die nach erlösendem Worte dürsteten. Gab Gedat ihnen das?

Der jungen Mannschaft des CVJM gab er jedenfalls mächtigen Auftrieb und manchem jungen, ringenden Menschen ein Licht auf den Weg.

Gedat sprach am Sonntag über das Thema: „Abrechnung mit der Vergangenheit", am Montag: „Schweigt Gott?", und am Dienstag: „Gibt es noch einen Ausweg?" Am Abend des Dienstags sprach er noch einmal und nur zu der jungen Mannschaft Frankfurts.

Einen zweiten Höhepunkt der Woche bildete der Vortrag von Pastor Busch aus Witten, ein Bruder des Essener Pastors, der Tante Jeanne getraut hat. Ein Kämpfertyp im Gegensatz zu Gedat, nicht so geist- und kunstvoll in der Rede, doch umsomehr wuchtiger, elementarer und vielleicht überzeugender.

Nunmehr bin ich auch offiziell in den CVJM aufgenomen und hoffe zu Gott, dass daraus ein Segen über mich komme.

Seit 1. Februar bin ich in der Ausbildung zum technischen Reichsbahnassistenten eine Station weitergerutscht und nunmehr für vier Monate im Betriebswerk. Wilhelm Puth aus Fechenheim trat am gleichen Tag in die Ausbildung zum technischen Reichsbahn-Inspektor beim Bahnamt ein, musste aber anderntags wieder aufhören. Entlassen wegen Parteizugehörigkeit! Auch dem Herrn Schilling in der Bahnmeisterei 4 ging es so. Armer, alter Mann! Ist das Gerechtigkeit?

Heute erhielt ich einen Brief von Rico; er wie ich freuen uns, dass die Verbindungsaufnahme geklappt hat.

February 22

Once again, small and large matters move me to write. I eagerly await Rico's response to the five-page letter I wrote, or rather, typed. Once again, I don't know the answer to the question of whether I should return to school. Can I ask it of my mother, will I ever have the opportunity of thanking her for it? First of all, I want to complete my training as an assistant on the Reichsbahn, then get some time off from the railroad to study, and then, perhaps, return to railroad work. And yet, those are only daydreams; no doubt the future will turn out differently than we plan it.

Brother Heinz continues to work with the Americans and is well fed there. In general, I don't lust after such delicacies, but it's a strange paradox that the individual American, despite his abundance, has no pity for the need of a shattered people, in the sense that he would be moved more deeply and reveal the aura of his riches not just in cigarettes and chocolates. On the other hand, it seems to me that it is obviously a sign of spiritual poverty that in the face of this deprivation, not even the smallest spiritual solution to these problems can be found.

The vacancy left in the engineering department of the railroad management office by the firing of Mr. Günther has been temporarily filled by Adolf Kneisel. I'm no longer clear about the purpose and results of these terminations.

If a Nazi party member is held accountable for any misdeed, then it is equally obvious that a non-party member should be punished for the same offense. By contrast, if certain judges see party membership as an offense according to general legal, moral, and human perspectives, then I fear we're going to get carried away just as far in the other direction, as was common under the previous regime.

22. Februar

Wieder einmal drängen kleine wie große Dinge zum Schreiben. Sehnlichst erwarte ich Ricos Antwort auf den fünfseitigen Brief aus meiner Feder, oder besser Schreibmaschine. Wieder einmal weiß ich keine Antwort auf die Frage, ob ich doch noch einmal zur Schule gehen soll. Kann ich meiner Mutter solches zumuten, oder werde ich einmal Gelegenheit haben, ihr solches zu danken? Dann möchte ich zunächst meinen Assistenten bei der Reichsbahn fertig machen, dann eventuell von der Bahn beurlauben lassen, um zu studieren und dann gegebenenfalls zurück zur Bahn. Doch das sind ja Hirngespinste, und die Zukunft wird sich wohl anders gestalten, wie man etwa plant.

Bruder Heinz arbeitet weiterhin bei den Amis und wird dort gut in Kost gehalten. Mich gelüstet zwar nicht nach solchen Leckerbissen im allgemeinen, doch ist es seltsam paradox, dass der Amerikaner im Einzelnen trotz seines Überflusses kein Erbarmen mit der Not eines zerschlagenen Volkes kennt, in der Art, dass es ihn etwa tiefer ergriffe und nicht nur mit Zigaretten oder Schokoladenwaren den Nimbus seines Reichtums offenbare. Mir dagegen scheint das eine offensichtliche Geistesarmut zu sein, dass neben diesen Mängeln auch nicht die geringste geistige Lösung all dieser Probleme herbeigeführt werden kann.

Im bautechnischen Büro der Reichsbahndirektion ist durch die Entlassung des Herrn Günther eine neue Lücke entstanden, in die aushilfsweise Adolf Kneisel eingesprungen ist. Mir ist nun bald nicht mehr klar, was mit diesen Entlassungen erreicht und bezweckt werden soll.

Wenn ein Parteigenosse für irgendeine Gemeinheit zur Rechenschaft gezogen wird, dann ist das ebenso selbstverständlich, wie auch ein Nichtparteigenosse für solches zu bestrafen ist. Wenn hingegen gewisse Richter nach allgemein rechtlichen, moralischen und menschlichen Gesichtspunkten in der Mitgliedschaft in der Partei eine Straftat erblicken, dann befürchte ich, dass man nach der Gegenseite ebenso über die Stränge haut, wie es im vergangenen Staat gang und gäbe war.

Easter Sunday, 1946

Once again I feel the urge to write down a few thoughts here.

Spring has arrived once again. It shows itself in the woods and farmlands, the fields, meadows, and gardens; also by the lovely warm days and the first tanned faces of the little boys. But how many people don't even notice, how many mothers, downcast and without hope, mourn for their fallen and missing sons, how many young brides and wives longingly await their loved ones' return from captivity?

And once again, the housewife concerns herself with the daily menu, and so as always joy and sadness go hand in hand. Pity the person who is so overcome by care that he can no longer experience joy, but woe to the person who, swept up by some cursory pleasure, thoughtlessly overlooks the suffering of his neighbor. And woe to our people if the spirit of selfishness drives out their sense of community. Many today pass by heedlessly. I sense it will be a long and hard road back.

Today, I encountered a former schoolmate, Karl Weigand. It was a true joy to see this upright friend again. At the moment, he's studying education at the college in Weilburg with the intention of becoming a teacher. Actually, whenever I walk through Fechenheim, I always encounter many familiar faces.

I have many favorite spots that I like to visit. Foremost is Master Becker's huge smithy. The hammer sounds out a regular beat until late into the evening and announces the untiring industry of a man whose son, Robert, had been my friend.

Opposite the smithy lies the Thielemann house. There's much that links me to the house and its occupants, as the master locksmith and my teacher, Heinrich Thielemann, lives on the ground floor. Though he's a good craftsman, he's an eternally dissatisfied person. Above him lives the widow of the electrician Thielemann with her son Heinz F. and his splendid wife, Hannelore. That's where I most like to visit. Kurt Thielemann, the strangest resident, lives on the third floor. I lived with him for a long time and got to know him as a peculiar fellow. Also eternally dissatisfied, this bachelor lives in constant strife with the other residents and with himself.

Ostersamstag 1946

Wieder einmal drängt es mich, hier einige Gedanken niederzuschreiben.

Wieder einmal ist Frühling im Land; solches offenbart sich in Wald und Flur, Feldern, Wiesen und Gärten, dazu an den schönen warmen Tagen und den ersten braungebrannten Bubengesichtern. Aber wie vieler Menschen Auge sieht das nicht; wie niedergedrückt und hoffnungslos trauern viele Mütter um ihre gefallenen und vermissten Söhne, wie sehnsüchtig erwarten Braut und Frau den Liebsten aus Gefangenschaft.

Und wiederum zergrübelt sich die Hausfrau den Kopf um den täglichen Speisezettel, und so gehen auch jetzt wie allemal Freud und Leid nebeneinander. Es ist schade um den, der ob seines Kummers keine Freude mehr kennt, wehe aber dem, der da im Taumel einer kurzen Freude achtlos an den Leiden seines Nachbarn vorübergeht. Und wehe unserem Volk, wenn der Geist der Selbstsucht den Gemeinschaftssinn vertreibt. Heute gehen viele achtlos dran vorbei. Ich ahne, es ist ein langer und harter Weg zurück.

Heute hatte ich eine Begegnung mit dem früheren Schulkameraden Karl Weigand. Mir war es eine rechte Freude, diesen aufrechten Freund wiederzusehen. Er studiert zurzeit am Lehrerseminar in Weilburg und beabsichtigt, Lehrer zu werden. Überhaupt, wenn ich durch Fechenheim gehe, treffe ich immer viele bekannte Gesichter.

Auch habe ich dort manchen lieben Platz, zu dem ich allemal gern hingehe. Voran in die riesige Schmiede des Meisters Becker. Bis spät in den Abend hinein schlagen die Hammerschläge einen gleichmäßigen Takt und künden von dem unermüdlichen Fleiß des Mannes, dessen Sohn Robert mein Freund gewesen war.

Gegenüber liegt das Haus der Thielemänner. Wohl verbindet mich mit dem Haus und seinen Insassen allerlei, denn im Parterre wohnt der Schlossermeister Heinrich Thielemann, mein Lehrmeister, der zwar ein guter Handwerker, aber ein ewig unzufriedener Mensch ist. Darüber wohnt die Elektromeisterwitwe Thielemann mit ihrem Sohn, Heinz F., und seiner trefflichen Frau, Hannelore. Da gehe ich noch am liebsten hin. Im zweiten Stock wohnt der seltsamste Hausgast, Kurt Thielemann. Bei jenem habe ich lange gewohnt und ihn als sonderlichen Menschen kennengelernt. Auch ewig unzufrieden, lebt dieser Junggeselle in ständigem Hader mit allen Hausbewohnern und mit sich selbst.

A couple streets further on lives Mrs. Böff. I owe much to this singularly faithful and God-fearing woman. Even in the worst of times, she always had a kindly word for me, and oftentimes also a bowl of hot soup. Although she oversees her household honestly and with great strength and good will, those she lives with are not satisfied with her. It's a distressing situation, and Mr. Böff and Willi will only begin to appreciate what their good angel does for them when she no longer is able to care for them.

I've not come to visit Mrs. Laber much recently, but I am nonetheless with her all the more often in my thoughts.

I now have a garden in Bockenheim, which requires a lot of time and energy. However, I hope to reap a good harvest, which would greatly improve our overall situation.

Unfortunately, I've lost the close feeling I had for the YMCA, and for weeks now haven't attended a lecture.

Heinz gave me an English edition of the New Testament, which I am endeavoring to read.

August 9

A shamefully long time has elapsed since I set down my last thoughts, and truly, many a priceless experience has fallen victim to forgetfulness because of it.

I correspond pretty regularly with Rico Engel. We argue and philosophize with each other. He lives with his parents in Marl, near Recklinghausen, attends engineering school there and intends to study chemistry when he's through. Truly an ambitious person! Now he wants to renew his Brazilian citizenship (he was born in Brazil), in case he might contemplate emigrating. The motivation for this last plan isn't clear to me, particularly since I know he was an enthusiastic soldier and fighter for Germany. Will he undermine his idealism for the sake of his personal welfare?

The emigration problem has also recently been the topic of heated discussions in our own family. With all his impatience, Heinz wants to emigrate at any cost, without having any other goal in mind other than simply getting out of suffering Germany. Truly, I would also love to get out into the world sometime, but I tell myself that no individual desire should outweigh one's personal capacity, because otherwise all personal freedom would threaten to disappear only to be replaced by slavery.

Ein paar Straßen weiter wohnt Frau Böff. Dieser einfältig treuen, gottergebenen Frau schulde ich vielen Dank. Selbst in bitterster Zeit hatte sie stets ein warmes Wort und auch meist einen Teller warme Suppe. Obgleich sie rechtschaffen und mit aller Kraft und gutem Willen ihrem Hausstand vorsteht, sind ihre Hausgenossen nicht mit ihr zufrieden. Es ist eine rechte Not damit, und Herr Böff und Willi werden dies auch erst dann zu schätzen wissen, wenn dieser ihr guter Geist nicht mehr um sie sorgt.

Zu Frau Laber komme ich in letzter Zeit recht selten, doch umso öfter bin ich mit meinen Gedanken dort.

In Bockenheim habe ich jetzt einen Garten, der zwar außer einiger Zeit viel Kraft beansprucht, doch erhoffe ich durch die Ernte belohnt zu werden, und die allgemeine Lebenslage wäre entsprechend günstiger gestaltet.

Leider habe ich mit dem CVJM die rechte innere Verbindung verloren und war auch seit einigen Wochen bei keinem Vortrag mehr.

Heinz hat mir eine englische Ausgabe des Neuen Testaments geschenkt, worin ich mich zu lesen bemühe.

9. August

Beschämend lange ist die Zeitspanne, seit die letzten Gedanken festgehalten wurden und wahrlich manches köstliche Erlebnis ist nun leider der Vergessenheit anheim gefallen.

Mit Rico Engel korrespondiere ich einigermaßen regelmäßig, disputiere und philosophiere mit ihm. Er lebt bei seinen Eltern in Marl bei Recklinghausen, besucht zurzeit die Ingenieurschule daselbst und beabsichtigt, anschließend Chemie zu studieren. Wahrhaft ein strebsamer Mensch! Nunmehr will er sich auch die brasilianische Staatsbürgerschaft erneuern lassen (er ist in Brasilien geboren), um gegebenenfalls an eine Auswanderung zu denken. Ungeklärt bei diesem letzten seiner Vorhaben ist mir der seelische Beweggrund, weiß ich doch, dass er begeisterter Soldat und Kämpfer für Deutschland war. Will er um des eigenen Wohlergehens willen seinen Idealismus untergraben?

Auch in unserer Familie ist das Auswanderungsproblem zuweilen heftig disputiert worden. Heinz, in all seiner Ungeduld, will schier mit aller Gewalt auswandern, ohne ein weiteres Ziel vor Augen zu haben als eben fort von dem unseligen Deutschland. Zwar ginge ich auch gerne einmal in die Welt hinaus, doch sage ich mir, dass kein eigener Wunsch stärker denn das eigene Vermögen sein darf, weil sonst alle persönliche Freiheit zu schwinden droht, um einer Sklaverei Platz zu machen.

At work, I'm once again employed in the engineering construction office, where there is lots of work, but I think I've also learned quite a few things in the meantime. As with my apprenticeship as a locksmith, what started as simply looking on, imitating, and trying out something myself, has developed into successful independent work. I've taken on the work of Mr. Kräussler, Mr. Mauroschat, and Mr. Büttgen, and have been able to carry it out satisfactorily.

An abundance of vegetables is growing in my garden, and I feel lucky not to have shied away from the effort of garden work. It's harvest time now, and that's reward enough for all the effort. I've been able to harvest about 60 to 70 pounds of beans, supply peas and carrots for many meals and likewise make available countless heads of white and savoy cabbages to the kitchen...

Future plentiful harvests of peas, beans, white cabbage, savoy cabbage, red cabbage, cauliflower, brussels sprouts, celery, red and sugar beets and carrots, plus lettuce, leeks and onions can be expected and confirm the saying, "No pain, no gain!".

In addition, I'm currently employed as a bricklayer, carpenter, and house painter. We're eager to get the front parlor in shape as quickly as possible now, so that Helga can join us before winter.

Im Geschäft bin ich zurzeit wieder im bautechnischen Büro, gibt es viel Arbeit, doch glaube ich auch inzwischen mancherlei hinzugelernt zu haben. Ähnlich meiner Schlosserlehre beginnt nun nach anfänglichem Sehen, Nachmachen und Probieren als Erfolg das selbständige Arbeiten. Vertretungsweise habe ich schon die Arbeiten der Herren Kräussler, Mauroschat und Büttgen übernommen und zur Zufriedenheit ausführen können.

In meinem Garten wächst ein Reichtum an Gemüse, und ich schätze mich glücklich, die Mühe der Gartenarbeit nicht gescheut zu haben. Jetzt ist Erntezeit und Lohn genug für alle Mühe. Schon etwa 60-70 Pfund Bohnen konnte ich ernten, viele Mahlzeiten mit Erbsen und Gelberüben beliefern und ebenso ungezählte Weißkraut- und Wirsingköpfe der Küche zur Verfügung stellen.

Weitere reiche Ernte an Erbsen, Bohnen, Weißkraut, Wirsing, Rotkraut, Blumen- und Rosenkohl, Sellerie, Rote- und Zucker- und Gelberüben, dazu Salat, Lauch und Zwiebeln steht in Aussicht und bestätigt das Sprichwort: „Ohne Fleiß kein Preis!"

Außerdem bin ich zurzeit als Maurer, Schreiner und Weißbinder tätig. Wir wollen schnellstens nunmehr die vordere Stube instandsetzen, damit Helga bis zum Winter runterkommen kann.

August 29

This day is among the most memorable of my life to date, because today I was favored with a true friendship for the first time in my life. Rico Engel was here, and we discussed "our" problems with one another.

It is true that his ideology is opposed to mine, but it is precisely for that reason that the stimulus is so valuable. He's full of goal-oriented independence and definitely called to achieve excellence. He's striving with all his might to convince me that my demands on life are sunk too deep, and for myself, I'm not yet clear as to how correct his opinion is.

He knows no constraints with respect to family responsibilities; he feels free of any spiritual burden, and in the way he lives life truly does seem to be making a beeline for his desired goal. I, on the other hand, ignorant of my own qualities, seem still to be too depressed because of the recent years, and I think it will be some time yet before I achieve clarity in this regard.

One of my big deficiencies is that my education has gaps too big to be ignored or to be overcome through good will alone. This fellow has really thrown me into confusion and I am persuaded by his constant presence and the example of his energy, to reach where he is and springboard into a livelier world.

He had no sympathy for my perspective on my motivations and said jokingly that, in the final analysis, a motorcycle's engine wouldn't fit into a scooter.

Deeply impressed by our encounter, I wrote to Adolf Kneisel, who recently advised me that I should prepare thoroughly so as to get into the third semester of the State Engineering School. To this end, Adolf Kneisel wanted to introduce me to a student friend of his who would pass on his textbooks to me.

29. August

Dieser Tag gehört zu den denkwürdigsten meines bisherigen Lebens, denn an ihm ward mir zum ersten Male im Leben eine wahrhafte Freundschaft zuteil. Rico Engel war da, und wir besprachen einander „unsere" Probleme.

Seine Ideologie ist der meinen zwar entgegensetzt, doch gerade deshalb sind die Anregungen besonders wertvoll. Er ist voller zielbewusster Selbständigkeit und bestimmt dazu berufen, Vorzügliches zu leisten. Mit aller Gewalt will er mir klarmachen, dass meine Ansprüche an das Leben zu tief veranschlagt seien, und ich selbst bin mir noch nicht klar, wie weit seine Ansicht richtig ist.

Er kennt keine Hemmung in bezug auf Familienrücksichten, er weiß sich frei von jeglicher seelischer Belastung und scheint tatsächlich schnurstracks seinem erstrebten Ziele zuzuleben. Ich hingegen in Unkenntnis meiner eigenen Qualität bin wohl noch zu deprimiert von den rückliegenden Jahren, und es bedarf noch einiger Zeit, bis ich hierüber Klarheit gewinne.

Ein großer Mangel meinerseits ist gewisslich, dass meine Bildung zu große Lücken aufweist, um kurzerhand übergangen zu werden oder allein durch guten Willen ersetzbar zu sein. Der Junge hat mich tatsächlich durcheinander gebracht, und ich bin überzeugt, es durch seine ständige Anwesenheit und dem Beispiel seiner Energie auch dahin zu bringen und auf das Sprungbrett einer lebendigeren Welt zu gelangen.

Ansichten vorgetragenen Beweggründe hatte er kein Verständnis und sagte spaßigerweise, dass in einen Hanomag letzten Endes kein Maybach Motor passe.

Durch unsere Begegnung stark beeindruckt, schrieb ich dann an Adolf Kneisel, der mir kürzlich anriet, durch gründliche Vorbereitung zum Studium in das 3. Semester an der Staatsbauschule einzusteigen. Adolf Kneisel wollte mir die Bekanntschaft eines Studienfreundes vermitteln, der mir seine Kolleghefte zu diesem Zeck überlassen würde.

September 12

Today is Georg Hörnis' birthday. He is in my thoughts and I send him best wishes for his recovery.

This past weekend, I played on the Red-White first team in a competition in Ulm-Laupheim. Although we won in Ulm on Saturday evening, we had to accept defeat in Laupheim. Saturday night I spent as a guest of the Kiesle family in Laupheim (Württemberg), who kindly gave me food and shelter. They even gave me a bag of apples and a sack of white flour for the trip home. Below is the letter I wrote to them today to thank them again for their hospitality.

"Dear Friends! These days a journey is in itself no longer really a pleasure. But the saying "if you take a trip, you'll have something to talk about" always proves true. For me, the trip to Ulm and Laupheim was an occasion I will enjoy thinking back on. I want to express my gratitude above all for your hospitality.

While the problems of these times often lead us only into selfish thought and behavior, your attitude gives me proof, that with only modest means and without life sacrifices, of how much more life would be worth living , if only everyone were willing to the same extent. I personally understand 'life' to be composed less of pleasures or of unique events than of experiencing and understanding the daily ebb and flow and of fulfilling my tasks for the use and blessing of all those who live with me and those who will follow me.

What drives me to soccer and the somewhat coarse circles of its devotees is neither my talent at the sport nor my love for it, but rather the natural, youthful need to let off steam. I much prefer quiet hours spent with books, conversations with understanding friends, and the silence of the forest and flowers.

12. September

Heute hat Georg Hörnes Geburtstag und ich gedenke seiner mit besten Wünschen zu seiner Genesung.

Am vergangenen Wochenende war ich als Spieler der 1. Rot Weiß Mannschaft auf einer Tournee nach Ulm-Laupheim beteiligt. Während wir am Sonnabend in Ulm gewannen, musste in Laupheim eine Niederlage eingesteckt werden. Die Nacht von Samstag auf Sonntag war ich Gast der Familie Kiesle in Laupheim (Württemberg), die in liebenswürdiger Weise mir Obdach und Labsal gewährten. Auf der Heimreise bekam ich noch eine Tüte mit Äpfeln und eine Tüte mit weißem Mehl geschenkt. Nachstehenden Brief schrieb ich heute nach dort, um mich nochmals für die Gastfreundschaft zu bedanken.

„Liebe Familie Kiesle! Heutzutage ist eine Reise anfürsich kein Vergnügen mehr. Aber das Sprichwort: ‚Wenn einer eine Reise tut, dann kann er was erzählen!' bewahrheitet sich immer wieder. Für mich war die Reise nach Ulm und Laupheim ein Ereignis, an das ich gern zurückdenken werde. Vor allem andern Erlebten verpflichtet mich Ihre Gastfreundschaft zum Dank.

Zumal die Not der Zeit uns Menschen nur zu oft in egoistisches Denken und Handeln verleitet, so soll Ihre Haltung mir den Beweis dafür gegeben haben, mit welch geringen Mitteln und ohne Opfer das Leben lebenswerter zu gestalten wäre, wenn nur alle in gleichem Maße dazu willens sind. Ich persönlich stelle mir das ‚Leben' weniger in Vergnügungen oder Ereignissen einmaliger Art vor, sondern im Erleben und Verstehen des alltäglichen Wandels und in Erfüllung der gestellten Aufgaben zum Nutzen und Segen aller, die mit mir leben und mir nachfolgen werden.

Was mich zum Fußball treibt und zu den teilweise rauhen Kreisen seiner Verehrer, ist weder meine sportliche Begabung noch meine Liebe zu diesem Sport, sondern lediglich das natürliche, jugendbedingte Bedürfnis des Austobens. Ich liebe weitaus mehr die stillen Stunden mit Büchern, die Gespräche mit verständigen Freunden, das Schweigen im Walde und Blumen.

Yes, sometimes I hate the overwrought fussing of the sport managers and deeply regret how much this is alienating me from the sport and will probably one day lead me to turn my back on it completely; because I know that sports can be an ideal for the young, but cannot constitute the meaning of life for a mature man. I strive to become a useful person and thus am glad to forego being described as a useful player in a sport report.

My antipathy toward alcohol and nicotine is also not derived solely from reasons of good health, but from my desire not to erect barriers in my future life that could become hindrances to me personally or in my life with my fellow man. I have no wish to be dependent on moods, feelings and desires when it comes to material goods, because then I can always be generous with needy friends without having to keep anything back for myself.

Please accept this sample of my outlook as proof of my grateful thoughts. Warm greetings to all of you. Wishing you all the best in the future, I remain, your 'Guest from Frankfurt,' P. M."

Ja, ich hasse zuweilen das übertriebene Getue der Sportmanager und bedauere zutiefst, wie sehr mich dies dem Sport entfremdet und zuletzt wohl gar den Rücken kehren lässt, weil ich weiß, dass der Sport zwar Ideal der Jugend sein soll, für den reifen Menschen aber keinen Lebensinhalt mehr darstellen darf. Ich strebe danach, ein brauchbarer Mensch zu werden, wobei ich herzlich gern darauf verzichte, in einem Sportbericht als brauchbarer Spieler bezeichnet zu werden.

Meine Antipathie gegen Alkohol und Nikotin stammt auch nicht aus rein gesundheitsvernünftigen Gründen, sondern aus dem Bestreben, in meinem ferneren Leben dort keine Schranken aufzurichten, wo sie mir persönlich und im Zusammenleben mit meinen Mitmenschen hinderlich werden können. Ich will nicht abhängig sein von Launen, Stimmungen und Wünschen, wenn es sich um sächliche Dinge handelt, und dann kann ich eine offene Hand für bedürftige Freunde haben, ohne mir etwas vorenthalten zu müssen.

Nehmen Sie diesen Ausschnitt meiner Gedankenwelt als Beweis dankbaren Gedenkens und seien Sie alle herzlichst gegrüßt. Für die Zukunft alles Gute wünschend, verbleibe ich, Ihr „Frankfurter Gast", P.M.

September 15

Henceforth, I will also write here what I think, what I feel, what is confusing my heart and oppressing my soul. It will be a confession, after which I will be lighter in spirit. Even if no other person ever knows about it, God the Father in Heaven is always in and around the world, he knows my weaknesses, my guilt, my longings and my cares. He alone also knows my prayers for my soul, which is striving for clarity, for purpose and direction and the ability to do good work.

So, have I finally become a man? No, and again, no! An immature youth full of imagination and deficient logic! Who longs for love and yet pays no heed to it, who longs to give but stands there with empty hands. In vain, I dream for days and sometimes nights of a way out. If heaven were to give me a wife, I'd take it as a blessing; but I am not yet mature enough nor am I worthy to be married.

Oh, test me each day, God, and lead me to a place where truth and love abide. You are truth and love; let me know You and praise You. If the world is truly free of problems, why is our heart always ensnared by trivia and never really becomes wise and remains far from the heavenly example of the Lord Jesus Christ?

I wait for Your call and obey Your command. Arm my heart against the lust of the world and prepare my soul with wisdom from Your light that it might shine from afar and bear witness to Your love and the greatness of Your divine wisdom. Protect my family from all evil, send my friends Your wise counsel, help all the oppressed toward Your light. Let me make amends for all that I have failed to do, intercede for me with all those I have hurt or wounded, heal me also of all pride and purify my body and my soul, so that neither vice nor lust find room therein. Jesus, pray for me! Amen

I read the following in a letter:

It's a mystery that a human is composed of three tiers. The animal functions are entrusted to the lower tier; the spiritual work to the heart; but it is to the head that the intellectual work is given. So it's in this manner that we're built up: body, soul, mind; earth realm, emotional realm, heavenly realm. Whoever lives too much in the lower swampy places will have his soul and mind pulled down by materialism and forced into slavery. Sins from there will pollute the entire organism.

15. September

Fortan soll hier auch die Rede davon sein, was ich denke, was ich fühle, was mein Herz verwirrt und meine Seele bedrückt. Es soll eine Beichte werden, nach der mir wieder leicht zu Mute ist. Wenn auch keiner je davon Kenntnis erhält, Gottvater im Himmel ist immer um und in der Welt; er kennt meine Schwäche, meine Schuld, meine Sehnsucht und meinen Kummer. Er allein weiß auch aus meinen Gebeten um meine Seele, die um Klarheit ringt, um Ziel und Richtung und um Befähigung zum gerechten Werk.

Nun bin ich recht zum Mann geworden? Nein und abermals nein! Ein unfertiger Jüngling voll Phantasie und mangelhafter Logik! Der sich nach Liebe sehnt und ihrer nicht achtet, der geben möchte und mit leeren Händen dasteht. Ich grüble Tag und in mancher Nacht umsonst nach einem Ausweg. Wenn mir einmal ein Weib geschenkt wird vom Himmel, ich nehm's als eine Gnade, doch bin ich ja noch nicht reif und einer Ehe wert.

Oh prüfe mich alle Tage, Gott, doch führe mich an einen Ort, da Wahrheit und Liebe wohnen. Wahrheit und Liebe bist Du; lass mich Dich erkennen und lobpreisen. Wenn wahrlich die Welt ohne Probleme ist, warum verstrickt sich unser Herz immer wieder in Nichtigkeiten und kommt nimmer recht voran in der Erkenntnis und bleibt weit entfernt von dem himmlischen Vorbild des Herrn Jesus Christus.

Ich warte auf Deinen Ruf und gehorche Deinem Befehle. Wappne mein Herz wider die Lust der Welt und rüste meine Seele aus mit Weisheit von Deinem Licht, dass es weit leuchte und zeuge von Deiner Liebe und der Größe Deines göttlichen Rates. Bewahre meine Angehörigen vor allem Übel, sende meinen Freunden Deinen weisen Rat, hilf allen Bedrängten hinauf zu Deinem Licht. Lass mich gutmachen, was ich je versäumt, bitte für mich bei allen, die ich beleidigt und gekränkt habe, und heile auch mich von aller Hoffart und reinige meinen Körper wie meine Seele, daß weder Laster noch Wollust in ihnen Raum finden. Jesu, bitte für mich! Amen. –

Ich las in einem Brief folgendes:

Es ist ein Geheimnis darum, dass der Menschen Bau sich in drei Stufen staffelt. Den unteren Partien sind die tierischen Funktionen anvertraut; dem Herzen die seelische Arbeit; dem Kopf aber das Geistige. Also Körper, Seele, Geist – Erdgebiet, Seelenregion, Himmelsreich, so staffelt sich das empor. Wer zuviel aus den unteren Rumpfpartien und Sumpfpartien lebt, wird auch Seele und Geist zur Materie herabziehen und zu Sklaventum erniedrigen. Sünden von dort verderben den ganzen Organismus.

And vice versa. The purpose of this well-planned structure is that a person should gradually grow up into the mental realm, just as a plant grows up through the roots and stem into the blossom. Root, stem, blossom! Dante calls these Hell, Purgatory, Paradise. The roots and stem are the pathways to the blossom, important ways, honorable ways; but the goal is the blossom, the fruit, the mind! That is the crown of victory!

Alexander von Humboldt, Rico's great model, sees the fulfillment of humanity in the work on one's own personality. Of course, what he had in mind in terms of educational level, intellect and ideals, was not achievable for everyone, Not only because they were a long way behind in their intellectual development, but in larger measure because a secure financial base and significant independence from everyday things is necessary for the creation, development, and maintenance of such an ideology, that sadly are not available to the working person.

I long for a leader who could make me strong and free. Have I used my time to this point wisely? I am saddened both by the consciousness of my shortcomings and by the low prospects of attaining the 'high land' of my longings. If I had only been aware of these things, had I known more than I know, I would be more thoughtful, better, and capable, as well as skillful at good works. What will become of me?

Und umgekehrt. Es ist die Absicht dieser planmäßigen Gliederung, daß nach und nach der Mensch in das Geistige emporwachse – genauso wie die Pflanze aus Wurzeldünger, Stengelgebilde emporwächst in die Blüte. Wurzel, Stengel, Blüte! Bei Dante: Hölle, Läuterung, Paradies. Wurzel und Stengel sind die Wege zur Blüte, wichtige Wege, ehrenwerte Wege; aber das Ziel ist die Blüte, die Frucht, der Geist! Das ist die Krone des Sieges!

Alexander von Humboldt, Ricos großes Vorbild, sieht die Vollendung des Menschen in der Arbeit an der eigenen Persönlichkeit. Was ihm dabei an Bildungsgrad, Anschauungsvermögen und dem Ideal vorschwebte, war gemeiniglich nicht für die Allgemeinheit erreichbar. Nicht allein dadurch, dass sie dem Geistesniveau fernstand, sondern in größerem Maße, weil zur Schaffung und Bildung und Erhaltung solcher Ideologie eine sichere finanzielle Grundlage und große Unabhängigkeit gegenüber den Dingen des Alltags notwendig ist, die leider dem arbeitenden Menschen nicht zur Verfügung stehen.

Ich sehne mich nach einem Führer, der mich stark und frei machen könnte. Habe ich meine bisherige Zeit recht genutzt? Es betrübt mich das Bewusstsein meiner Mängel ebenso wie die geringe Aussicht auf das „highland" meiner Sehnsucht. Hätte ich solches nur immer bedacht, ich wüßte heute mehr als ich weiß, wäre besonnener, überlegener und brauchbarer, dazu in guten Werken geschickter. Was wird noch aus mir werden?

October 12

Behind me some unpleasant jazz music is coming from the radio. This acquisition has always been frowned upon in our home, and it was only recently that sister Helga brought this monster from Wüstems. This has meant the fulfillment of yet another of Heinz' fondest wishes. But the biggest piece of news is that Uncle Hans has returned from captivity, the result of a letter that mother gave to my aunt.

The main thing is the result. But now new worries arise, predominantly regarding what type of job, but also concerns about nutrition, for the 1.7 meters tall man, now weighs just 99 pounds and first has to get on his feet again. My learned uncle speaks Latin, Greek, French, English and some Russian. No doubt this former police officer will be able to begin a new existence based on such abilities, and thereby build a future for his lovely children, Martin and Hannele.

My poor mother has lost most of her upper incisors in the last few weeks due to malnutrition. For the time being, she's going around with a caved-in face and with gaps in her teeth until the dentist can fashion her some dentures.

Overnight, I got a dangerous inflammation of the face. It was itchy and burning, an unpleasant illness. Luckily, it's healed sufficiently within the last one and a half weeks so that I can once again shave my face. except for a few spots. A small black goatee, for example, covers a spot where the razor can't yet go.

Little Christel is now talking in such an exceptionally understandable way that it's a good idea not to say a careless word to him or to another person in his company, for he can repeat everything that's said without difficulty and with good powers of memory. Otherwise, he's a loveable boy and only to be pitied because he does not have a father and has a rather uncertain future ahead of him. Little Christel is two years and nine months old today, and a ray of sunshine to his grandmother.

I haven't heard a thing from Rico. I wonder if his visit here gave him reason to be so silent now. My thoughts are often with him, for I regard him as my only friend. I have friendly memories also of the people I knew in Fechenheim. Particularly the members of the Laber family, with whom I unfortunately no longer have any contact.

12. Oktober

Hinter mir ertönt aus dem Radio eine unsympathische Jazzmusik. Seit erdenklicher Zeit war diese Errungenschaft in unserem Hause verpönt, und erst jetzt brachte Schwester Helga dieses Monstrum von Wüstems mit. Heinz ist somit immerhin ein weiterer Herzenswunsch in Erfüllung gegangen. Die größte Neuigkeit aber ist, dass nunmehr Onkel Hans aus der Gefangenschaft zurückgekehrt und dies als Folge eines Briefes den Mutter der Tante mitgegeben hatte.

Hauptsache bleibt das Ergebnis. Nunmehr werfen sich aber neue Sorgen auf, vorwiegend beruflicher Art, aber auch ernährungsmäßig, denn der 1,70 m große Mann ist nur noch 99 Pfd. schwer und muss erst wieder auf die Beine kommen. Der gelehrte Onkel spricht lateinisch, griechisch, französisch, englisch und etwas russisch. Auf dieser Basis wird sich der ehemalige Polizeioffizier gewiß eine neue Existenz gründen können und somit eine Zukunft für seine reizenden Kinder, Martin und Hannele.

Meine arme Mutter hat in den letzten Wochen den Großteil ihrer oberen Schneidezähne eingebüßt, aufgrund ihrer Unterernährung. Zurzeit läuft sie mit eingefallenem Gesicht und zahnlückigem Munde umher, bis der Zahndoktor ein künstliches Gebiss für sie hergerichtet hat.

Über Nacht bekam ich eine nicht ungefährliche Gesichtsentzündung. Juckend und brennend war es überdies, eine unangenehme Krankheit. Heute ist sie glücklicherweise innerhalb von 1 ½ Wochen derart verheilt, dass bis auf geringe Reststellen das Gesicht wieder rasierfähig geworden ist. Ein kleiner schwarzer Kinnbart, zum Beispiel, zeigt eine Stelle, an der das Messer noch keinen Zutritt hat.

Klein-Christel plaudert des öfteren in ungemein verständiger Weise, dass es recht verwunderlich und außerdem angebracht ist, kein unbedachtes Wort mit ihm oder in seinem Beisein mit anderen Personen zu sprechen, weil er ohne Schwierigkeit alles wiederholen kann und über ein gutes Erinnerungsvermögen verfügt. Ansonst ist er ein herzlieber Junge und einzig darum zu bedauern, dass er keinen Vater hat und einer recht ungewissen Zukunft entgegensieht. 2 ¾ Jahre ist Klein-Christel heute alt und für seine Omi ein rechter Sonnenschein.

Von Rico höre ich nichts. Sollte er auf seiner Besuchsreise nach hier einen Anlaß zu solcher Schweigsamkeit gefunden haben? In Gedanken bin ich oft bei ihm, denn ich betrachte ihn als meinen einzigen Freund. Eine freundschaftliche Erinnerung bewahre ich auch meinen Bekannten in Fechenheim. Voran den Angehörigen der Familie Laber, mit denen ich leider keine Verbindung mehr habe.

November 4

My illness has lasted almost five weeks without full recovery. I'll return to work next week; otherwise I'll get too far behind in my training. The days at home have been useful in that they gave me an opportunity to perform urgent tasks. So now the cellar situation has been resolved, the potatoes are stored, the cabbage put up, and thus the fear of hunger has been wrested from the winter.

The fact that intellectual development suffers in the face of unrelenting physical work is the reason why I can't reach agreement with my friend, Rico. By the way, I've been waiting a week for a sign of life from Rico, unfortunately in vain. Why is he so silent? Did I give him a reason? I hope not, and wish I could build a bridge between us soon.

In the meantime, I turned 23 and was well attended on my special day.

I gave myself a particular pleasure by scoring two goals against Hanau 93, one goal in each half, so that today's goal nets will go down in history as my Mayer-Memorial goal nets. I also spent two days with the Red-White team doing community service clearing rubble in Frankfurt am Main. We were assigned to Hochstrasse. Erich Trapp, Herbert Hammer, Kurt Henkel, and Horst Vogel were the only other ones there from our first team. Mr. Hennefeld was likewise untiringly busy. Last Sunday, we won 7-1 in Homburg and find ourselves in the top group of our league division.

4. November

Fast fünf Wochen dauert nun schon meine Krankheit, ohne dass sich die völlige Gesundung eingestellt hat. Nächste Woche werde ich wieder arbeiten gehen, sonst wirft mich dies zu lange in der Ausbildung zurück. Nützlich waren die Tage schon insofern, als mir somit die Gelegenheit geboten war, unaufschiebbare Arbeiten auszuführen. So ist nun die Kellerfrage geregelt, Kartoffeln sind gelagert, Weißkraut eingeschnitten und somit dem Winter die Hungersorge entrungen.

Dass jedoch durch die fortgesetzt körperliche Arbeit die geistige Fortbildung Mangel leidet, ist eben jene Begleiterscheinung, um deretwillen ich mit meinem Freund Rico keine Übereinstimmung erzielen konnte. Übrigens warte ich nun schon wochenlang auf ein Lebenszeichen von Rico, leider vergeblich. Warum er wohl schweigt? Hatte ich den Anlaß dazu gegeben? Ich hoffe nicht und wünsche bald eine Brücke zu schaffen.

Inzwischen bin ich 23 Jahre alt geworden und zu diesem Ehrentag bestens bedacht.

Eine besondere Freude konnte ich mir selbst bereiten, indem ich gegen Hanau 93 zwei Tore schießen konnte, und zwar in jeder Halbzeit ein Tor, so dass die an diesem Tag eingeweihten Tornetze als meine Mayer-Gedächtnisnetze in die Geschichte eingehen. Mit der Gemeinschaft von Rot-Weiß war ich auch zwei Tage zum Trümmerbeseitigen im Ehrendienst an der Stadt Frankfurt am Main. Dabei waren wir in der Hochstraße eingesetzt. Von der ersten Mannschaft waren noch Erich Trapp, Herbert Hammer, Kurt Henkel und Horst Vogel anwesend. Herr Hennefeld war ebenfalls unermüdlich tätig. Vergangenen Sonntag gewannen wir in Homburg überlegen mit 7:1 und befinden uns nun in der Spitzengruppe unserer Liga-Abteilung.

December 12

What could have been the reason for my trip to Recklinghausen, Hannover and Dorfmark? Whatever it might have been, the first destination was the most important for me because it made possible a reunion with Rico.

On Saturday evening (December 7), I left Frankfurt by train and reached Bochum at about six a.m. I immediately caught a tram in front of the station that was going to Herne. Because of the limited Sunday schedule, the connecting ride to Recklinghausen would have been an hour and a half later.

Since I had earlier met a locally knowledgeable man who also wanted to go to Recklinghausen, and since we had no desire to wait in the early morning cold, we quickly decided to set off on foot in the direction of Recklinghausen. This little bit of trouble was worth the effort because part way there we connected with a train that took personnel to Recklinghausen. We reached the town at 7:30 a.m. and were able to catch the train to Marl at 8:00; whereas the first train from Herne would not have left for Recklinghausen before 8:25 am.

Shortly before 9:30, I was able to ring the doorbell at 124 Lipperweg and found Rico at home. He was very happy, and I also got to know his mother. His father was still at the factory and could not return until lunch. On the basis of what I experienced, I can't agree with what others say about the bad food situation in the English sector. It's possible that my hosts went to particular trouble, but even this is evidence for the fact that one mustn't generalize about everything.

Rico's parents live in factory housing. Their apartment has three bedrooms, a bathroom and a kitchen. Books and school papers are piled high on Rico's desk, pretty much in total disarray, which means he doesn't let his mother tidy up for him, so that at every opportunity he can simply pull up his chair and with a little concentration once again focus on his studies. A little king in his kingdom! Perhaps quite unconsciously, his parents have subordinated themselves to their gifted offspring, and actually that is quite a natural thing to do, for Rico is an only child and his advancement is worth any sacrifice.

12. Dezember

Was war wohl der Anlaß zu meiner Reise nach Recklinghausen, Hannover und Dorfmark gewesen? Wie dem auch war, den Höhepunkt für mich nahm ich vorweg, indem das erste Reiseziel ein Wiedersehen mit Rico ermöglichte.

Am Samstagabend (7. 12) startete ich von Frankfurt und erreichte Bochum um etwa 6.00 Uhr morgens. Vor dem Bahnhofsgebäude erhielt ich sofort Straßenbahnanschluß nach Herne. Wegen des eingeschränkten Sonntagsverkehrs wäre dort erst nach 1 ½ Stunden die Weiterfahrt nach Recklinghausen möglich gewesen.

Nachdem ich mich bereits vorher einem ortskundigen Mann, der ebenfalls nach Recklinghausen wollte, angeschlossen hatte und uns das Warten in den frühen, kalten Morgenstunden nicht angenehm schien, gingen wir kurzentschlossen in Richtung Recklinghausen davon. Diese Mühe hat sich wahrlich gelohnt, denn unterwegs erreichten wir eine Bahn, die das Personal nach Recklinghausen beförderte. Erfreulicherweise waren wir schon um halb acht Uhr dort und konnten die um 8.00 Uhr startende erste Bahn nach Marl benutzen; während die erste Bahn von Herne nach Recklinghausen um 8.25 Uhr gefahren wäre.

Kurz vor halb zehn konnte ich im Lipperweg 124 klingeln und fand Rico zu Hause. Seine Freude war groß, und mit seiner Mutter wurde ich auch bekannt. Sein Vater war noch im Werk und kehrte erst zum Mittagessen zurück. Was man ansonsten von der schlechten Ernährungslage im englischen Sektor spricht, kann ich von dem Erlebten nicht bestätigen. Möglicherweise, dass meine Gastgeber sich einer besonderen Mühe unterzogen, doch auch dieses ist schon ein Beweis dafür, dass man nicht alles verallgemeinern darf.

Ricos Eltern leben in einem zur Werksiedlung gehörenden Haus. Die Etagenwohnung enthält drei Zimmer, Bad und eine Küche. Auf Ricos Schreibtisch stapeln sich Bücher und Studienunterlagen in kaum entwirrbarer Fülle; das heißt, er will nicht, dass seine Mutter hier ordnend eingreift, damit er bei jeder Gelegenheit nur mit dem Beirücken seines Stuhles und einiger Konzentration den Faden seiner Studien aufnehmen kann. Ein kleiner König in seinem Reich! Seine Eltern haben sich vielleicht unbewusst ihrem begabten Sprößling ganz untergeordnet, und eigentlich ist dies eine ganz natürliche Sache, ist doch Rico das einzige Kind und sein Fortkommen aller Opfer wert.

Rico is so valuable to me as a friend because he is developing qualities that I myself embrace as the ideal. I wonder if I can maintain this friendship over the long haul? With his advancing knowledge, his intellect will need surroundings at the same level. We're planning things together and trying to clear difficulties out of the way that prevent me from pursuing a similar path, but I'm quite skeptical as to whether I'll ever succeed in breaking free of my present intellectually poor environment in order to grow in another atmosphere and, in my lifetime, come close to finding the meaning of life.

I've also been reflecting on whether the most worthwhile people are those who have been purified through need and deprivation, since because of that experience they demonstrate that their soul is grounded in a true ethic. My thoughts keep circling around Rico, my friend, and create an image of him which would no doubt seem distorted if viewed objectively. And yet it's a joy to me to find in him a person who makes a serious effort and is willing to point the human spirit in the direction of science and service.

When we took leave from each other, he didn't respond to the finality of my words of farewell. It was only after a hearty handshake and a heartfelt "Auf Wiedersehen," expressing the hope that we would someday meet again, that his shadow disappeared among the nearby trees. He set off for school and I returned to Recklinghausen.

My journey, with the many impressions it left, took me from Recklinghausen to Wanne-Eickel and then by train east to Hannover. In Herford, the fast train in the same direction arrived in the station at about 3 p.m. I took advantage of this opportunity to change trains, and after an hour, around 4 p.m., arrived non-stop at the main station in Hannover.

After obtaining information about my destination, Dorfmark, and about train times, I set off for the tram, knowing that lines 5 and 6 went to Kantplatz. Nowadays there seems to be a shortage of public transportation in most major cities, for the overcrowded trams made me think of my hometown, Frankfurt, where people hang from the trams like grapes. Yet in contrast to life in Frankfurt, I saw little military presence in the English sector.

Was mir Rico als Freund so wertvoll erscheinen lässt, muss ich darin suchen, dass Rico die Qualitäten entwickelt, die mir selbst als Ideal vorschweben. Ob ich auf längere Zeit mir diese Freundschaft erhalten kann? Es wird so sein, dass mit dem fortschreitenden Wissen seinem Geist eine Umgebung notwendig ist, die diesem Niveau entspricht. Wohl planen wir gemeinsam und versuchen die Schwierigkeiten aus dem Wege zu räumen, die mir einen ähnlichen Weg verbauen, doch bin ich sehr skeptisch, ob es mir je gelingt, aus meiner derzeitigen, geistig armen Umgebung mich loszulösen, um in einer anderen Atmosphäre zu wachsen und dem Sinn des Lebens auch lebendig näher zu kommen.

Ich habe auch schon darüber nachgedacht, ob nicht jene Menschen die wertvollsten sind, die durch Not und Entbehrung geläutert wurden, weil sie ja damit beweisen, dass ihre Seele in wahrer Ethik beheimatet ist. Meine Gedanken kreisen immer wieder um Rico, meinen Freund, und schaffen von ihm ein Bild, das mir bei nüchterner Betrachtung gewiss verzerrt erschiene. Und doch ist es mir eine Freude, in ihm einen Menschen zu finden, der ernsthaft sich bemüht und willens ist, dem Menschengeist eine wissenschaftliche, dienstbare Richtung zuzuweisen.

Bei unserm Abschied ließ er mein „Leb wohl!" nicht gelten, und erst nach herzhaftem Händedruck und herzlichem „Auf Wiedersehen!" entschwand sein Schatten zwischen den nahen Bäumen. Er ging zur Schule, und ich fuhr nach Recklinghausen zurück.

Von Recklinghausen nach Wanne-Eickel und dann nach Umsteigen in einen Zug nach Hannover ging die Reise mit ihren mannigfaltigen Eindrücken ostwärts. In Herford, etwa um 15 Uhr mittags, erreicht der D-Zug in gleicher Richtung die Station. Ich benutze die Gelegenheit zum Umsteigen und war bereits nach einer Stunde, um 4 Uhr, ohne dass der Zug nochmals gehalten hätte, im Hannoveraner Hauptbahnhof.

Nachdem ich Erkundigungen nach Reiseziel Dorfmark und Fahrgelegenheiten erfragt hatte, begab ich mich zur Straßenbahn, von der ich wußte, dass die Linien 5 und 6 zum Kantplatz führen. Es scheint heute in allen Großstädten an Fahrgelegenheiten zu mangeln, denn die überfüllten Straßenbahnen haben mich unwillkürlich an meine Vaterstadt Frankfurt denken lassen, wo die Menschen wie Trauben an den Trittbrettern hängen. Jedoch im Gegensatz zu hier (Frankfurt) habe ich im gesamten englischen Gebiet wenig Militär gesehen.

Herbert Knigge lives in the ground floor apartment of 73 Berckhuysen Strasse, on the right-hand side. He got to know my sister, Gretel, on a trip to the Alps, after which he visited our home several times. On his last visit, he agreed to get a bottle of schnaps for my brother, Heinz, which I would be able to bring with me to Frankfurt. In addition, I got to know him and his parents as dear people. Herbert had learned the trade of carpenter, and to this day, he's active in this field. He's planning to emigrate at the next possible opportunity, for during his wartime imprisonment in the USA, he got a taste for seeing the world and ever since has had a longing to see more.

The next day, it was December 10th. I left their hospitable home very early in order to go to Dorfmark in the Lüneburg Heath. Before I left, Herbert's mother gave me ample provisions, among other things bestowing on me a honey cake along with four beautiful apples. On the trip there I could see little of the Heath; everything was still asleep and the morning mists were still shrouding the splendid panoramas of the heather. But on my way back that afternoon I got just what I wanted and am most thankful for this travel experience.

The train arrived in Dorfmark about 9:30. This village is located one stop after the town of Fallingbostel. My Aunt Jeanne, Uncle Hans, Martin and Hannele live in a handsome house belonging to a brother of Uncle Hans, who also lives there and is a teacher in the village. In addition to these five people, two of the teacher's aunts and his three children also reside in the house. So things are rather cramped and Aunt Jeanne isn't exactly happy about the situation.

Uncle Hans, who only recently returned from being a P.O.W., looks all right, but I think he suffers from edema. Nowadays, this highly intelligent man is working as a miller's assistant because, as a former police officer, he was dismissed with restrictions and now, following orders from a denazification court, is not allowed any but the most mundane jobs.

Little Hannele is the dearest child. Stars and Christmas apples would be more fitting descriptions for her eyes and her rosy little cheeks. Martin, the seven-year-old son, is a bright boy, hungry for knowledge. When I arrived, he was working on his math exercises, writing down the answers with an awkward hand. The apples from Hannover were a great introduction. Proof: enthusiastic acceptance and a hearty appetite.

In der Berckhuysen-Strasse 73 wohnt in der rechten Parterrewohnung Herbert Knigge. Dieser wurde meiner Schwester Gretel auf einer Alpenfahrt bekannt und besuchte uns anschließend mehrere Male. Bei seinem letzten Besuch vereinbarte er mit Bruder Heinz, ihm eine Flasche Schnaps zu besorgen, die ich nun bei dieser Gelegenheit mit nach Frankfurt nehmen konnte. Außerdem lernte ich in ihm und in seinen Eltern liebe Menschen kennen. Herbert hat Zimmermann gelernt und arbeitet noch heute in seinem Fach. Er plant, bei der nächstmöglichen Gelegenheit auszuwandern, denn während seiner Kriegsgefangenschaft in USA hat er den Blick für die Welt und eine Sehnsucht nach ihrer Weite bekommen.

Am folgenden Tage, es war der 10. Dezember, verließ ich schon frühmorgens das gastliche Haus, um nach Dorfmark in der Lüneburger Heide zu fahren. Zuvor hat mich Herberts Mutter noch bestens versorgt und mir u.a. noch einen Honigkuchen nebst vier schönen Äpfeln geschenkt. Auf der Hinfahrt konnte ich von der Heide wenig sehen, alles lag noch im Schlaf und der Morgennebel verhüllte den Augen dann die herrlichen Panoramen der Heide. Umso mehr kam ich am Nachmittag bei der Rückfahrt auf meine Rechnung und bin für dieses Reiseerlebnis sehr dankbar.

Etwa um 9.30 Uhr lief der Zug in Dorfmark ein. Dieser Ort liegt eine Station nach der Kreisstadt Fallingbostel. Meine Tante Jeanne, Onkel Hans, dazu Martin und Hannele wohnen in einem stattlichen Wohnhaus bei einem Bruder von Onkel Hans. Dieser ist dort Lehrer. Außer den vorgenannten Personen leben noch zwei Tanten des Lehrers und drei eigene Kinder in der Wohnung. Somit ist auch alles sehr beengt, und Tante Jeanne ist ob der Umstände auch nicht gerade glücklich.

Onkel Hans, der erst kürzlich aus Kriegsgefangenschaft zurückkam, sieht wohl gut aus, doch schätze und vermute ich etwas Wasser in den Geweben. Der hoch intelligente Mann arbeitet heute als Müllerknecht, weil er als ehemaliger Polizeioffizier geächtet, entlassen und noch vor einem Spruchkammerbescheid stehend, keine anderen als gewöhnliche Arbeiten verrichten darf.

Allerliebst ist das kleine Hannele. Sterne und Weihnachtsäpfel wären bezeichnendere Ausdrücke für ihre Augen und die roten Pausbäckchen. Martin, das siebenjährige Söhnchen, ist ein kluger und wissbegieriger Junge. Bei meiner Ankunft saß er gerade über seinen Rechenaufgaben, deren Resultate er mit ungelenker Hand niederschrieb. Hier waren auch die Hannoveraner Äpfel die beste Einführung. Beweis: begeisterte Annahme und herzhafter Appetit.

117

The gifts I brought along with me almost made Aunt Jeanne lose her composure, and at first she didn't want to accept everything. A good thing that I had left some items in Frankfurt. Martin was quite curious, but, of course, I couldn't give away the secrets of the Christ Child, who brings the gifts. After only three hours, I had to head back to the train, but still had enough time to talk with Uncle Hans. I hope very much that peace, order, and confidence will once again be the order of the day for this family.

I spent from 4 to 8 p.m. waiting in the railroad station at Hannover. There I made an effort to reflect on recent events and to gather my thoughts together in a letter to Rico. My observations at this time confirmed the sad fact that both the standard of living and the feeling of togetherness and love of neighbor have been lost or greatly decreased.

I also got to know a young German from the Sudetenland who, now homeless and without a career, is facing a difficult life situation; he has had no news of his parents and can't make a living from what he learned from his college prep courses in high school. For now, he's traveling around the country trying to sell arts and crafts, trying to earn his living in this way. We shared my food and when we said good-bye he promised to write to me sometime.

The fast train to Frankfurt left at 10 p.m. on the dot. After an uncomfortable night, during which I mostly had to stand, the train arrived in Frankfurt at about 8:30 a.m.

In the course of the morning, I asked for another vacation day from work, and although I was tired, I didn't miss practice that evening. After that, I sought out Mr. Mensch in Sachsenhausen in order to get the address of a colleague who teaches at the engineering school in Idstein.

The next day, the 12th of December, at 6:45 a.m. a train took me to Idstein. I was able to talk with Mr. Zelenka during a break between classes. The recommendation from Mr. Mensch no doubt also influenced him to write down my resume and to promise me to bring my concern to the attention of the school's director. He said he would inform Mr. Mensch of the decision before Christmas and I'd be able to find out from him if I could soon begin my studies at Idstein.

On my return, I wrote to Rico again, reported on my bold venture, and expressed my skepticism with regard to a potential outcome. I wonder what will become of it?

Mein Mitbringsel brachte Tante Jeanne fast außer Fassung, und sie wollte es gar nicht alles annehmen. Nur gut, dass ich noch einiges in Frankfurt gelassen hatte. Martin war recht neugierig, doch konnte ich ihm die Geheimnisse des Christkinds doch nicht verraten. Bereits nach drei Stunden musste ich zurück an die Bahn, konnte jedoch noch mit Onkel Hans reden. Es wäre doch sehr zu hoffen, dass auch für diese Familie wieder Ruhe, Ordnung und Zuversicht zum Tagesprogramm gehören.

Die Wartezeit von 16 Uhr bis 20 Uhr verbrachte ich im Bahnhofsbunker von Hannover. Dort gab ich mir zunächst Mühe, die rückliegenden Ereignisse zu ordnen und meine Gedanken in einem Brief an Rico zusammenzufassen. Meine Studien bei dieser Gelegenheit bestätigten die traurige Tatsache, dass einmal das Lebensniveau und dazu das Zusammengehörigkeitsgefühl und die Nächstenliebe verlorengegangen bzw. sehr gesunken sind.

Auch lernte ich einen jungen Sudetendeutschen kennen, der nunmehr heimatlos und ohne Beruf einer schweren Lebenssituation gegenübersteht, weil er von seinen Eltern nichts weiß und von seiner Gymnasiastenzeit keinen Broterwerb herleiten kann. Heute reist er als Vertreter von kunstgewerblichen Artikeln durch das Land, bemüht, diese Artikel abzusetzen und dadurch seinen Lebensunterhalt zu verdienen. Mit meinem Reiseproviant hielten wir gemeinsame Mahlzeit, und beim Abschied versprach er, mir einmal zu schreiben.

Pünktlich um 22.00 Uhr fuhr der D-Zug nach Frankfurt am Main ab. Nach einer beschwerlichen Nachtfahrt, meist musste ich stehen, lief der Zug etwa um 8.30 Uhr in Frankfurt ein.

Im Laufe des Vormittags erbat ich mir im Büro einen weiteren Urlaubstag und versäumte am Abend trotz der Müdigkeit das Training nicht. Anschließend suchte ich Herrn Mesch in Sachsenhausen auf, um von ihm die Adresse des Kollegen zu erfahren, der an der Idsteiner Bauschule als Lehrkraft beschäftigt ist.

Anderntags, am 12. 12., morgens um 6.45 Uhr brachte mich ein Zug nach Idstein. In einer Unterrichtspause konnte ich Herrn Zelenka sprechen. Die Empfehlung von Herrn Mensch bestimmte ihn wohl auch, meine Daten aufzuschreiben und das Versprechen zu geben, dem Anstaltsleiter das Anliegen vorzutragen. Den Entscheid wird er vor Weihnachten dem Herrn Mensch mitteilen, und von diesem werde ich dann erfahren können, ob ich demnächst in Idstein mit dem Studium beginnen kann.

Nach der Rückkehr schrieb ich abermals an Rico, berichtete von dem Unterfangen und brachte darin meine Bedenken dem positiven Ausgang gegenüber zum Ausdruck. Was dann wohl wird?

January 7

Today, it's already the 7th of January of the year 1947. Thus Christmas and the turn of the year are already behind me. It has been a colorful, eventful time and, thanks to many memorable events, a pleasant time.

Together with mother, Heinz and Mrs. Floding, I went to the Christmas Eve midnight service in the off-limits area.

On Monday, the day before, I accepted an invitation to the Sports Club and was as happily surprised by the celebratory program as I was by the many unexpected gifts.

On Christmas day, I participated in a soccer match in Offenbach (score was 0-2) and the next day, I was a guest in the home of Mr. Kreussler. On December 29, I played with the junior team in Dudenhofen with a score of 6-6.

By and large, however, the holiday season provided an opportunity for reflection, and it gave me great pleasure to demonstrate my gratitude and appreciation to some of my colleagues. My visit to Mr. Kreussler's offered me a particular opportunity, since I'd already had the opportunity some time earlier to get to know the splendid family of this man whom I respect greatly as my supervisor and teacher.

And so, another year came to a close, a year which, besides bringing a lot of work and some struggle, also brought with it so very much that was wonderful, that allowed me to know life beyond life in the shadows, and which, along with hope, also gave me faith in a future for me and for my sorely tested fatherland.

I said my farewells to 1946 without any alcohol, so the last few hours gave me plenty of opportunity for a retrospective, in which I prayed for all my friends, acquaintances, relatives, and strangers, praying that nothing would stand in the way of their wishes being fulfilled in the new year.

A cold bath before midnight refreshed me greatly and gave me the clarity of spirit that I hope to have for the rest of my life. May a pathway be prepared for me into the future, on which my destiny can be accomplished to my satisfaction and to the blessing of all those who are gathered around me and to whom I belong today. In the same way that I believe that God holds his hand over me and makes his will come to pass, in the same way He allows me to recognize that the crown of life is surely there for those who have fought the good fight, if they have taken His will seriously. So forward with God and as God wills it! Here's to the New Year!

7. Januar

Heute schreiben wir bereits den 7. Januar des Jahres 1947. Somit liegen die Weihnachtstage und die Jahreswende bereits hinter mir. Es war eine bunte, ereignisreiche Zeit und eingedenk der vielen erinnerungswerten Ereignisse eine schöne Zeit.

Am Heiligen Abend besuchte ich gemeinsam mit Mutter, Heinz und Mrs. Floding einen Mitternachtsgottesdienst im Sperrgebiet.

Am Montag, tags zuvor, folgte ich einer Einladung des Sportvereins und war von dem dargebotenen Programm der Feier ebenso freudig überrascht wie von den mannigfachen, unerwarteten Geschenken.

Am ersten Feiertag folgte ein Spiel in Offenbach (0:2), und am zweiten Feiertag war ich bei Herrn Kreussler zu Gast. Am 29. 12. spielte ich mit der Juniorenmannschaft in Dudenhofen mit dem Resultat von 6:6.

Im Großen und Ganzen gaben die reichlichen Feiertage jedoch auch genug Gelegenheit zur Besinnung, und mir war es die größte Freude, auch manchen Kameraden gegenüber meine Dankbarkeit und Aufmerksamkeit zu beweisen. Besonderen Anlaß bot mir der Besuch bei Kreusslers, hatte ich doch schon vor einiger Zeit Gelegenheit, die trefflichen Angehörigen des Mannes kennenzulernen, dem ich als einem Vorgesetzten und Lehrer meine besondere Hochachtung zuteil werden lasse.

So ging ein Jahr zu Ende, das mir neben viel Arbeit, manchem Kampf, so unendlich viel Schönes brachte, das mich das Leben anders erkennen ließ, als nur im Schatten, und das mir neben der Hoffnung auch den Glauben an eine Zukunft für mich als auch für mein hartgeprüftes Vaterland bescherte.

Mein Abschied von 1946 vollzog sich unter jeglicher Enthaltung des Alkohols, wobei mir die letzten Stunden willkommenen Anlaß zu einer Rückschau gaben, bei der ich alle Freunde, Bekannte, Verwandte und Unbekannte in das Gebet einschloß, dass im Neuen Jahre allen der Erfüllung aller Wünsche nichts mehr im Wege stehe.

Ein kaltes Bad vor Mitternacht erfrischte mich prächtig und gab mir den klaren Geist, den ich mir für die Folge meines Lebens wünsche. Möge auch mir in Zukunft ein Weg bereitet sein, eine Bahn, in der sich mein Schicksal vollzieht, zu meiner Zufriedenheit und zum Segen derer, die dereinst um mich geschart sind und denen ich schon heute zugeordnet bin. So wie ich glaube, dass Gott seine Hand darüber hält und seinen Willen geltend macht, so lässt er mich erkennen, dass einem kampfreichen Leben letztenendes die Krone des Lebens gewiss ist, wenn es der Kämpfende recht ernst mit seinem Willen nimmt. Also mit Gott und wie Gott will! Auf ein Neues!

Photographs and Documents

Alice and Friedrich's formal portrait at the time of their marriage in Strassburg

Alice and five children: Helga, Paul, Marianne, Heinz, and Gretel

Young Paul Mayer

Gretel, Helga, Heinz, and Paul

Paul With His Parents

Paul's father, Friedrich Mayer,
after returning from Buchenwald and losing business

Friedrich Mayer's Letter
From Auschwitz Birkenau

Original Family Home in Fechenheim - Second Floor

The building survived the war. Friedrich's store was around the corner.

Feeling unsafe in the Fechenheim apartment, the family moved to a "more secure" location at 5 Eiserne Hand in Frankfurt. Helga and her infant son, Chris, were in the basement and narrowly escaped.

"Stolperstein" commemorative stone and plaque placed in front of modern day building at 5 Eiserne Hand in Frankfurt, Germany.

This project was initiated by German artist, Gunter Demnig, in 1992. As of October 2018, 70,000 stones have been placed throughout Europe at the last place of residency or work prior to falling victim to the Nazi terror.

Feli Gürsching of the Bibliothek Der Alten assisted in the research resulting in the placement of this stone in memory of Paul's father, Friedrich Mayer.

The Moll Home in Wüstems
After the bombing of the Mayer home in Frankfurt,
the Moll family offered rooms in their farmhouse in Wüstems.

Opa and Oma Moll
Helga (second from the left) and
Heinz (on right) with friends

Heinz with his guitar

Paul in Wüstems

Paul and Heinz in Wüstems

Paul's completed project for Journeyman Locksmith

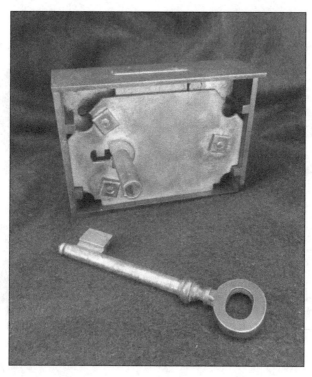

*1939 Hilter Youth
"Kreissieger"
Industrial Award Badge*

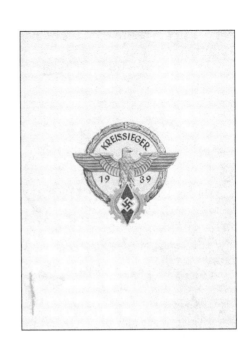

*Paul with
Herr Thielemann,
his locksmith master*

Marianne.

A poem by Paul for Marianne
The English translation appears on page 188.

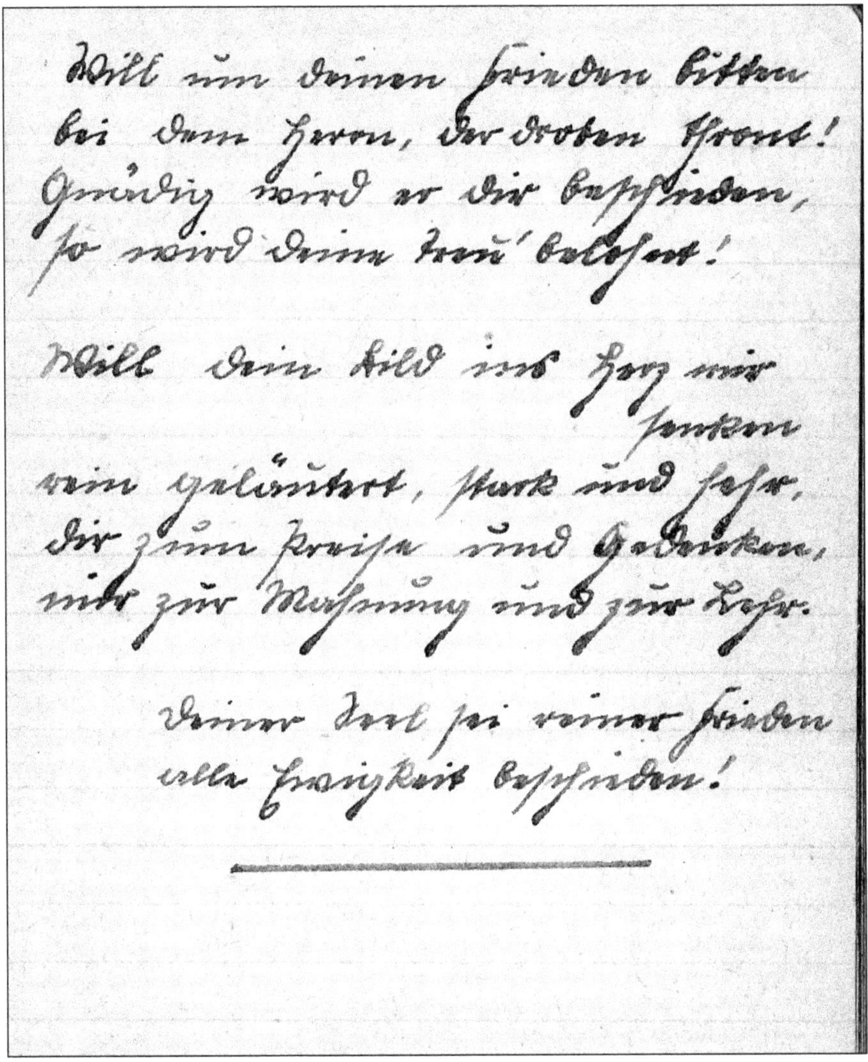

Willst um deinen Frieden bitten
bei dem Herrn, der droben thront!
Gnädig wird er dir bescheiden,
so wird deine treu' belohnt!

Willst dein Bild ins Herz mir
                                      senken
ein geläutert, stark und sehr,
dir zum Preise und Gedenken,
mir zur Mahnung und zur Lehre.

      Deiner Seel sei einer Frieden
      alle Fröhlichkeit beschieden!

_____

135

ach kurzer, schwerer Krankheit
nsere herzensgute, innigstgeliebte

Marianne

kurz vor ihrem 27. Geburtstag von
uns gegangen.

In tiefer Trauer: Familie Fritz Mayer
Georg Fischer.

Frankfurt a. M.. Eiserne Hand 5, III.
den 3. September 1942.

Feuerbestattung findet am 7. Sept.,
16 Uhr, auf dem Hauptfriedhof statt.

———

Die Betriebsführung und Gefolg-
schaft der Fa. Louis Filsinger wird
der verstorbenen Arbeitskameradin
ein ehrendes Andenken bewahren.

Death Notice of Paul's Sister, Mariane

```
Frau
Alice Mayer
Frankfurt a,Main
Eiserne Hand 5 III

Ihr Ehemann,Fritz Israel Mayer geb. 21.12.88 in
Freiburg(Baden) ist am25.8.43 um 9 Uhr 30 Min.im
Lager Auschwitz  an Myocardinsuffienz verstorben.


Mitgeteilt am:                    Reichsvereinigung der Juden
  3.9.43                              in Deutschland
```

Letter from Auschwitz about the Death of Friedrich Mayer

Memorial at Jewish Cemetery in Frankfurt

Kickers Offenbach in Munich 1943
Paul in center

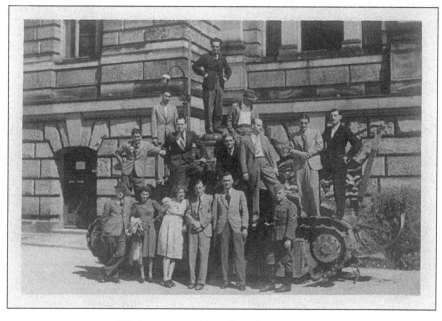

Kickers and Friends, Munich 1943

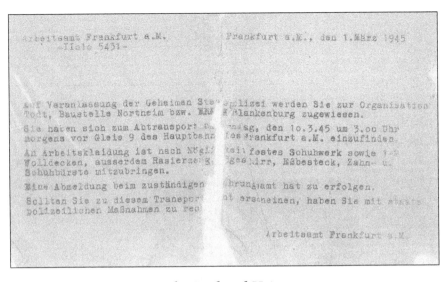

Summons for Paul and Heinz to report
to the Organisation Todt "Labor Camp" in Derenburg

Pre-war photograph of Hotel Weisser Adler, Derenburg
where Paul and brother, Heinz, slept on cots
throughout Labor camp internment

The technical book in Paul's pocket showing impact of bullet when he was shot while crossing line of fire after escaping the labor camp

After the labor camp, Paul both played and coached soccer.

Kickers Offenbach Team, 1945
Paul - third from the right

Paul as Coach of Young Kickers Team, 1946

Photographs of Paul Mayer's Journals
and a book of poetry (bottom row, left)

United States of America

05710 ✳

CERTIFICATE OF IDENTITY IN LIEU OF PASSPORT

U. S. Consulate General, ___Frankfurt/Main, Germany___

Date ___January 23, 1947___

1. This is to certify that ___Paul Gustav Wilhelm Mayer___, born at
    (name in full)

___Germany___, ___Frankfurt/Main___, ___ , on ___25___
    (country)   (town)   (district)   (day)

of ___November___, ___1923___, ___male___, ___single___
    (month)   (year)   (sex)   (marital status)

_____, intends to immigrate to
    (given & maiden name of wife)

the United States of America.

2. He (she) will be accompanied by ___unaccompanied___

(Here list all family members by name,
birthplace & date, together with citizenship of each)

_____

_____

_____

3. His (her) occupation is ___locksmith___

4. DESCRIPTION

PHOTOGRAPH

Height ___5___ ft. ___9.9___ in.

Hair ___brown___ Eyes ___brown___

Distinguishing marks or features:

___xxxxx___

___scar on left eye___

5. He (she) solemnly declares that he has never committed nor has he been convicted of any crime except as follows ___no exceptions___

6. He is unable to produce birth certificate, marriage license, divorce papers and/or police record for the following reason(s) ___he can produce___

I hereby certify that the above are true facts, proper photograph and description of

Paul Gustav W. Mayer
(Signature of applicant)

Sworn to and Subscribed before me this 21st day of May, 1947.

James P. Osbourn
(Signature of consul)

James P. Osbourn
Vice Consul
(Date)

Service No. ___7637___ _no fee acct_

MAY 27 1947

Initial U.S. Certificate issued in lieu of a passport

Paul Mayer's Ship Ticket

144

1947

Heute schreiben wir bereits den 16. Februar
1947. Wissen kann jeder die große Lücke seit
Schreibbeginnen brauchen, wie ich es
auch höchstpersönlich selbst tue. Ich will
hierfür weder eine Entschuldigung
anführen noch gelten lassen, denn
es ist meines Erachtens keiner
Entschuldigung noch einer Anklage
wert. Gewisslich ist, könnte man
in späteren Tagen die Versäumnisse
der Jugend wiedersehen, so würde
man mit einiger Genugtuung noch
jeder Erkenntnis wachsen und
dem Ideal ähnlich und ähnlicher
werden.

Sample page from initial journal written in Germany

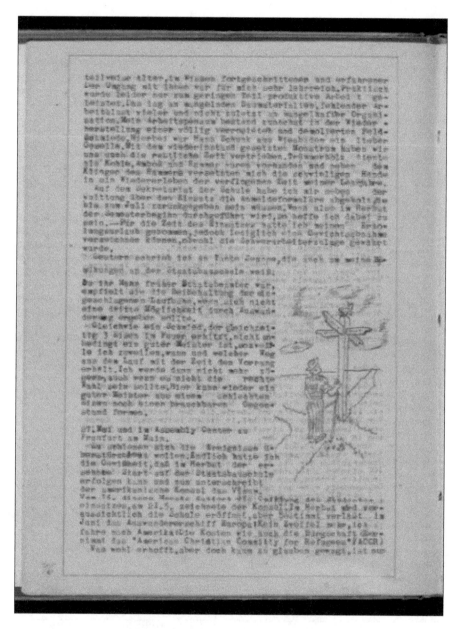

Sample page from Von Main zum Ohio, the typed version Paul created and illustrated, using original journal entries, as a gift for his mother after immigration to the US.

1-31-48   Tonight I have read two very interesting reports in the paper.

Queen Wilhelmina of Holland, who has reigned for 50 years will relinquish her crown to her daughter Juliane this month. The report praises mainly her great affection to her home country. During World War II she went to London and directed and strengthened the resistance of her people against the German conquerers. Now she is tired, physically as well as spiritually. Juliane as the successor has with her youth the energy and the better qualifications to lead the Dutchmen out of their post war calamities (as they hope!)

The second story has stimulated a greater interest. When one might think the resignation of queen W. is one of the subsequent incidents of our up to day history so is the report about Mr. Charles Eustic Bohlen a pointing career. Driven by his own desire to

Sample page from later journal written in Cincinnati, Ohio

After immigrating to Cincinnati, circa 1947

*Paul standing in front of
Clifton Methodist Church
Cincinnati, Ohio*

*Heinz and Paul
in their new neighborhood*

Paul at work project in Cincinnati

Paul at University of Cincinnati
International Weekend

*Photograph of the original Vom Main Zum Ohio,
the typed version Paul made as a gift for his mother*

Part Two

February 1947-April 1948

Vom Main zum Ohio

From the Main to the Ohio

Original in German with English Translation

Memory

Who loves them not, the quiet hours
In which life's many bygone splendors
Reappear in twilight dreaming
As sunshine yields to close of day

When water babbles in the streamlet
Birds sing their music to the night,
When my head bows down in silent
Contemplation of the light?

No longer can I see the sun set
on ridges of the far-off hills.
Yet now I see in shapes before me
Loved ones from those bygone days.

Accept my greetings, all you dear ones
Who come unbidden to my heart,
To join in that great celebration
In which we never more will part.

And may that which, in happy times
As brothers joined us close in life,
Keep us together as we venture
Toward that far-off sunny land.

I love them, all the quiet hours
When daily cares have slipped from view.
For then I live, in dreams remembered
Of the past I spent with you.

Erinnerung

Wer liebt sie nicht, die stillen Stunden,
Wenn sich vergangene Lebenspracht,
In Träumen wieder eingefunden,
Im Sonnenscheiden vor der Nacht!

Wenn von dem nahen Bach das Rauschen,
Der Vögel letztes Lied erklingt.
Wenn mir der Kopf in stillem Lauschen
Gedankenvoll vornüber sinkt.

Nicht mehr am Grat der Bergeshalden,
Seh' ich die Sonne untergehn.
Dann seh ich vor mir die Gestalten
Vergangner Tage auferstehn.

Seid mir gegrüßt, ihr lieben Freunde!
Die ungerufen alle da
Zur großen Feiertagsgemeinde
Vollzählig meinem Herzen nah'.

Und was uns einst in frohen Zeiten
Im Leben brüderlich verband,
Das lässt uns heut gemeinsam schreiten
Nach dem verfloss'nen Sonnenland.

Ich liebe sie, die stillen Stunden,
Die von des Tages Last befreit,
Dann leb' ich gegenwartsentschwunden,
Träumend in der Vergan

February 16

Today, as I write, it's already the 16th of February, 1947. By now everyone will be able to understand the long gap in my narration, as I myself personally can too. But in my estimation it's not worth bemoaning, and I will neither offer an excuse nor accept one. What is certain is that if one could undo the omissions of one's youth later on in life, one would quite deliberately learn from each new insight and become more and more like the ideal.

And what would be more worth pursuing than that? So the question is, what is needed to attain this end? Is one's place in life, one's career, or one's wealth the determining factor? Does luck or a favorable fate help pave the way? In the case of the latter the response is clear and a resounding No! For then it would be the task of persons either to seek happiness in a conventional sense and trust the stars, or to apathetically embrace an illusion.

And thus it seems to me that my task is through work to attain a career, a place in life, and financial security. My education as a technical assistant with the railroad is now completed. The written examination (February 2nd) is behind me and this whole episode will be finished up with the oral examination on February 18th. If the combined result is favorable, then I especially have to thank my superiors, who taught me many things and gave me much advice. Because I recognize and fully acknowledge this, I don't think I'm being ungrateful or presumptuous if I see this not as an ultimate objective but rather simply a stage along the way.

For some time now, with the excellent help of my friend, Rico, I have been preoccupied with the thought of studying at a technical school. In so doing I am hardly dreaming of some ivory tower or big salary. Instead, what prompts me to think this way is the reflection that choosing for oneself a difficult path will sooner lead to a goal and prevent missing out on things than a youth full of boredom and laziness. If these words should seem somewhat rash, I nonetheless hope and strive to pursue my future in this manner.

16. Februar

Heute schreiben wir bereits den 16. Februar 1947. Bisjetzt kann jeder die große Lücke beanstanden, wie ich es auch höchstpersönlich selbst tue. Aber es ist meines Ermessens keine Anklage wert und ich will hierfür weder einen Entschuldigungsgrund anführen noch gelten lassen. Gewisslich ist, könnte man in späteren Tagen die Versäumnisse der Jugend widerrufen, so würde man mit einiger Konsequenz nach jeder Erkenntnis wachsen und dem Ideal ähnlich und ähnlicher werden.

Und was wäre erstrebenswerter als solches? Die Frage lautet nun: Was ist vonnöten, um dieses zu erreichen? Ist die Lebensstellung, der Beruf oder das Vermögen maßgebend? Ist das Glück oder das günstige Schicksal wegbereitend? Im letzteren scheint mir die Antwort klar und zwar mit Nein! Denn dann wäre es die Aufgabe der Menschen, entweder das Glück im landläufigen Sinne zu suchen und sich einem günstigen Stern anzuvertrauen oder apathisch einer Illusion zu huldigen.

Also erscheint es mir auch meine Aufgabe, durch Arbeit zum Beruf, zur Lebensstellung und zu Vermögen zu gelangen. Nunmehr ist meine Ausbildung zum technischen Assistenten bei der Bahn beendet. Die schriftliche Prüfung (3. 2. 47) liegt hinter mir, und mit dem mündlichen Examen am 18. Febr. wird diese Episode abgeschlossen sein. Wenn das Gesamtergebnis ein günstiges Resultat zeigen wird, dann verdanke ich dies nicht zuletzt meinen Vorgesetzten, die mich in vielen Dingen unterrichtet und beraten haben. Indem ich dies erkenne und voll würdige, glaube ich doch nicht undankbar oder gar überheblich zu sein wenn mir dies kein Ziel, sondern nur Etappe dünkt.

Seit einiger Zeit, mit vorzüglicher Hilfe meines Freundes Rico, befasse ich mich in Gedanken mit dem Besuch einer technischen Lehranstalt. Dabei schweben mir für die Zukunft bestimmt keine Luftschlösser oder hohe Gehälter vor, sondern es bewegt mich zu dieser Denkart lediglich die Überlegung, dass zur Vorbeugung gegen etwaige Versäumnisse ein selbstgewählter schwieriger Weg eher zum Ziele führt als eine Jugend voller Langeweile und Müßiggang. Mögen diese Worte auch etwas voreilig erscheinen, so hoffe und erstrebe ich doch in dieser Art meinen Werdegang.

Doesn't the red sky in the morning announce the approaching day? Isn't it inevitable that my efforts in Idstein or Frankfurt will lead to the goal? On the 14th of February an unheated train brought my half-frozen bones to Idstein. I had come to make sure that the documents I'd sent along had really arrived and that my application for acceptance into the State School of Civil Engineering had been successful. Mr. Zelenka, a certified engineer and teacher in the land surveying department, lived close to the institution at Idstein, and it was there I was to seek him out, because classes had been interrupted by a "coal-vacation." Although the purpose of my visit did not meet with immediate success, since this spring it is not possible to start a first-semester course of study, nonetheless during a two-hour talk I had a memorable experience. This Mr. Zelenka, a German from Sudetenland and a refugee, had earlier been employed by the rail authority in Breslau and had been recommended to me by my colleague, Max Mensch. On parting, he promised to send me a program for self-study to prepare me and help make up for not attending school. In doing so he used the following words: "I'll keep an eye on you, for, you know, if a man has no one to pull him up out of the masses, then he'll just remain one of the masses."

On my return to Frankfurt, along with the returned application documents (sent by certified mail) I found a letter from the Frankfurt School of Civil Engineering, in which they promised to open up lower level classes this fall, but made acceptance dependent on participation in a 14-day work detail. I went straight to the School's admission office and told them I agreed to the work detail and also that I hoped to be admitted to the second semester of study. This decision seems rather daring now, but I'll just have to work hard this summer and then I'll make it happen.

Kündet nicht das Morgenrot den nahenden Tag? Müssen meine Bestrebungen in Idstein oder Frankfurt nicht zum Ziele führen? Am 14. Februar brachte ein ungeheizter Zug meine halberfrorenen Glieder nach Idstein. Ich wollte dort in Erfahrung bringen, ob meine übersandten Papiere dort eingegangen und ob meine Bewerbung um Aufnahme an der Staatsbauschule von Erfolg begleitet war. Herr Zelenka, Diplomingenieur und Lehrer im Vermessungsfach, wohnt unweit der Idsteiner Anstalt, woselbst ich ihn aufsuchen musste, weil der Unterricht durch Kohlenferien unterbrochen wurde. War auch dem Zweck meines Besuches kein direkter Erfolg beschieden, da in diesem Frühjahr kein 1. Semester gestartet werden kann, so wurde mir doch während eines zweistündigen Spazierganges ein denkwürdiges Erlebnis zuteil. Jener Herr Zelenka, ein Sudetendeutscher und Flüchtling, war früher bei der RBD Breslau beschäftigt gewesen und wurde mir von dem Berufskollegen Max Mensch empfohlen. Beim Abschied versprach er, mir als Ersatz für den Schulbesuch ein Programm zum vorbereitenden Selbststudium zu übersenden, und gebrauchte die Worte: „Ich werde Sie im Auge behalten, denn wissen Sie, wenn man gar niemanden hat, der einen aus der Masse herauszieht, so bleibt man eben Masse."

Nach Frankfurt zurückgekehrt, fand ich neben den per Einschreiben zurückgesandten Bewerbungsunterlagen ein Schreiben der Staatsbauschule Ffm, in dem sie die Eröffnung der unteren Klassen für den Herbst dieses Jahres in Aussicht stehen, die Aufnahme jedoch von einem 14tägigen Arbeitseinsatz abhängig machen. Sofort begab ich mich zum Sekretariat der Schule und gab außer meiner Bereitwilligkeit meine Bewerbung ins 2. Semester kund. Nunmehr erscheint mir diese Erklärung etwas gewagt, dann muss ich eben im Sommer fleißig arbeiten, und dann wird der Anschluss sehen klappen.

February 20

Two days after the successful examination. What I had hoped and wished for has actually happened. I can also say today that all the work, effort, and desire for knowledge was worth it. Compared to the other candidates I had a distinct superiority, as was subsequently noted in the grade of "good". The examination that I had anticipated with some anxiety turned out to be relatively harmless; what contributed significantly to that was Mr. Häuser being such an understanding examiner. The ceremony concluded with a short speech by the president, the announcement of results, and the congratulations. It was only when I knew my favorable results that I told my mother about the exam and its result. Her joy was just as great as her surprise had been in 1941 when I used the same tactics with my journeyman exam.

In contrast to what I've believed, now I'm not supposed to stay in the civil engineering department of the RBD railroad. I regret this and still hope for notification to the contrary. The decision does make me wonder, for, since this place keeps employing so many loafers, I feel this sort of personnel policy is quite contradictory. If I'm forced to leave and am transferred to a job in a field office, I'll disappear from the stage and run the risk of being forgotten. For this reason it seems all the more urgent to prepare to study at a college, so as not to fall victim to the arbitrariness of the authorities.

20. Februar

Zwei Tage nach der bestandenen Prüfung. Es ist tatsächlich so gekommen, wie ich es gewünscht und erhofft habe. Heute kann ich auch sagen, dass sich alle Wissbegierde, alle Arbeit und Mühe gelohnt hat. Gegenüber den anderen Anwärtern hatte ich ein deutliches Übergewicht, wie es auch im „gut" des Urteils zum Ausdruck kommt. Die mit so mancher Sorge erwartete Prüfung erwies sich als verhältnismäßig harmlos, wozu Herr Häuser als verständnisvoller Prüfer wesentlich beigetragen hat. Die Zeremonie schloss mit einer kurzen Ansprache des Vorsitzenden, der Urteilsverkündung und der Gratulation. Ich hatte von dieser Prüfung und dem Ausgang meiner Mutter erst dann Mitteilung gemacht, nachdem mir das günstige Resultat bekannt war. Ihre Freude war eben so groß wie ihre Überraschung anno 1941, als ich anläßlich meiner Gesellenprüfung mit der gleichen Taktik verfuhr.

Entgegen meiner bisherigen Auffassung soll ich nun doch nicht im Bautechnischen Büro der RBD bleiben. Ich bedaure dies und erhoffe noch einen gegenteiligen Bescheid. Wundern darf mich das doch, denn da man hier so viele Faulenzer festhält, erachte ich diese Personalpolitik als sehr widersprechend. Wenn ich also abtreten muss und einer Außenstelle zugeteilt werde, verschwinde ich gleichermaßen von der Bildfläche und gerate in Gefahr des Vergessens. Mithin erscheint mir umso dringlicher, einen Schulbesuch nunmehr vorzubereiten, um nicht der Willkür beschränkter Machtbefugnisse anheimzufallen.

February 28

Today is the last day of February, but nonetheless the old truism, "Spring is on its way!" seems rather daring, for it's snowing outside like in the depths of winter. I'm sitting in the warm office and I have the walk here behind me, toward the end of which I looked like a wandering snowman. Once again I'm thinking of my friend, Rico, whom I wrote yesterday, though I didn't respond to every issue he raised. In contrast to that of his former superior army officer in captivity, his human sensitivity touched me as proof of his very noble disposition. Though I didn't get to know the ideology of the soldiers on the front directly, it can differ from high human ideals only when it distinguishes between friend and foe. Or is there no such distinction? Despite my at times rather sad youth, I can't hate anyone because of his actions. For where there is hatred, reason is abandoned. Because of this, I think back to some earlier situations with the smile of someone who knows better, but without hatred, and forgive all chicanery because I know it had its origins in foolish bedazzlement or sheer stupidity.

All the more, therefore, I recollect with gratitude all those events which helped preserve my courage to face life and my faith in goodness. In this, my dear Rico, I agree with you wholeheartedly. It's not just a case that we should, but that we must help and try to make good the injustice that has occurred, if we can do nothing to prevent it. In this I only regret my shortcomings and my limited means. Those affected are not only former members of the Nazi Party or the so-called racially, politically, or religiously persecuted, but regular people who have had to suffer through no fault of their own because of the necessities of the times. It is those people to whom a sympathetic person means something special in their joyless existence, and it to them that a little attention affords great joy. In this respect I'm certainly not selfless to the point of self-sacrifice, just an egoist who does it for his pleasure.

Digressing completely from these details: it is the ineluctable human tragedy that no group in power has ever understood or has ever been in a position to treat opposite positions justly and peacefully without making some kind of concession to their own kind by oppressing the underdog. That's how I see the situation in overall terms.

28. Februar

Heute ist der letzte Februartag, und trotzdem scheint mir die alte Binsenwahrheit: Es muss doch Frühling werden!, etwas gewagt, denn draußen schneit es wie im dicksten Winter. Ich sitze bereits im warmen Büroraum, habe also den Marsch nach hier hinter mir, auf dem ich zuletzt einem wandelnden Schneemann glich. Wieder denke ich an Freund Rico, dem ich vorgestern schrieb, jedoch nicht in allen Dingen geantwortet habe. So hat mich sein menschliches Empfinden gegenüber seinem eingesperrten früheren Vorgesetzten bei der Wehrmacht als ein Beweis seiner überaus edlen Gesinnung angesprochen. Ich habe zwar die Ideologie des Frontsoldaten nicht unmittelbar kennengelernt, doch kann diese von den hohen menschlichen Idealen nur in den Dingen abweichen, wo sie eine Grenze zwischen Freund und Feind kennt. Oder besteht diese Grenze nicht? Ich kann trotz meiner zuweilen recht traurigen Jugend keinem um seiner Handlungen willen einen Hass entgegenbringen. Denn wo Hass ist, geht alle Vernunft verloren. So gedenke ich mancher zurückliegenden Situation zwar mit dem Lächeln des Überlegenen, aber ohne Hass und verzeihe alle Schikanen, weil ich weiß, daß sie in törichter Verblendung oder gar Dummheit ihren Ursprung hatten.

Umso mehr gedenke ich voller Dankbarkeit aller Begebenheiten, die mir den Lebensmut und den Glauben an das Gute erhalten haben. Und hierin, mein lieber Rico, stimme ich Dir mit ganzem Herzen zu. Wir sollen nicht nur, nein, wir müssen dort helfen und versuchen, geschehenes Unrecht wieder gutzumachen, wenn es sich vorher nicht mehr verhüten lässt. Ich bedaure hierbei nur die Mängel und die Beschränkung der Mittel, über die ich verfügen kann. Auch sind die Betroffenen nicht ehemalige PGs (*Parteigenossen*) oder die sogenannten rassisch, politisch und religiös Verfolgten, sondern es sind die Menschen des Alltags, die unter der Not der Zeit ohne eigene Schuld zu leiden haben. Denen in ihrem freudearmen Dasein ein mitfühlender Mensch etwas Besonderes dünkt und denen eine kleine Aufmerksamkeit große Freude bereitet. Ich bin hierin gewiss nicht bis zur Selbstaufopferung selbstlos, sondern eben doch Egoist, der solches zu seinem Pläsier treibt.

Ganz abschweifend von diesen Einzelheiten, ist es die unabänderliche menschliche Tragödie, dass keine Machtgruppe je verstanden hat oder in der Lage wäre, die Gegensätze gerecht und friedlich auszugleichen, ohne durch Unterdrückung der Unterlegenen den Gleichwertigen irgendwelche Konzessionen zu machen. So sehe ich die Lage im Großen!

There's a great deal of talk about wars, causes, and consequences. The consequences are particularly illuminating because we have suffered from the results of the war. The war and its consequences day to day are worth thinking about. I consider the military defeat less humiliating than the decline of human morals in our fatherland. What's particularly revealed here is how destructive and regressive the consequences of a lost war are on culture and on the spiritual state of a people.

March 1

As agreed with Mrs. Sieger, I went to Griedel this morning. In my backpack was the coat for Helmut, the young miller.

The train conductor was quite rude, but my equally decisive demeanor had the effect of my being allowed to ride in the service car. The rest of the train was filled beyond capacity. In Griedel, Mrs. Sieger prepared me the treat of a big breakfast, serving up plentiful ham along with good bread. I took advantage of the opportunity and my fears of stomach pains were quelled with the herbal tea she offered me. I was her guest again at lunch.

There were two rare sausages floating around in the big soup pot. Because I got a large helping I had plenty of opportunity to get a good taste of them. Baby Ursula has also arrived in the Rainmühle. Her mother, Lily, is doing fine and Helmut, although he's a rather young father, is also a very happy one. He gave me two little sacks of white flour and one of semolina for 15 Reichsmarks. The train ride didn't cost me a thing, and so both the hassles of the trip and the expenses are bearable. It would just be nice if I could visit more often.

Es wird sehr, sehr viel geredet über Kriege, Ursachen und Folgen. Die Folgen sind deshalb besonders einleuchtend, weil wir die Leidtragenden des letzten Krieges sind. Der Krieg und seine Folgen im Alltäglichen sind einer besonderen Betrachtung wert. Ich halte die militärische Niederlage für weniger schimpflich, als der Niedergang der menschlichen Moral in unserm Vaterland. Hierin wird besonders offenbart, wie verderblich und zurückwerfend für die Kultur und das geistige Niveau die Folgen eines verlorenen Krieges sind.

1. März

Wie mit Frau Sieger vereinbart, fuhr ich heute morgen nach Griedel. Es befand sich in meinem Rucksack der Mantel für Helmut, den jungen Müller.

Der Zugschaffner war zwar reichlich grob, doch bewirkte mein ebenso entschiedenes Auftreten, dass ich im Eisenbahnerabteil fahren durfte. Der Zug ansonsten war überfüllt. In Griedel bereitete mir Frau Sieger den Genuss eines bäuerlichen Frühstücks, indem sie mir zu gutem Brot reichlich Schinken auftischte. Ich nahm die Gelegenheit gründlich wahr und meine Befürchtung wegen Leibschmerzen wurde mit einem dargebotenen Magentee entkräftet. Zum Mittagsmahl war ich nochmals Gast. Im großen Suppengericht schwammen zwei seltene Exemplare von Würsten umher, deren Geschmack ich durch einen reichlichen Anteil ebenfalls zu kosten bekam. In der Rainmühle ist auch eine kleine Ursula angekommen. Die Mutter, Frau Lilly, ist wohlauf und Helmut, wenn auch ein sehr junger, so doch ein recht glücklicher Papa. Für 15.-- RM gab er mir zwei Säckchen Weißmehl und ein solches mit Grieß. Die Bahnfahrt kostete mich nichts und so sind neben den Wegstrapazen auch die Unkosten erträglich. Nur wäre wünschenswert, dass mein Besuch öfters willkommen sei.

March 2

It's been the topic of conversation all week! Is the weather going to hold? So that the match in Marburg can take place? Well, since yesterday's snowfall wasn't such that a cancellation would have been necessary, it was arranged that the rendezvous be at the Bockenheim police post at 8:30.

I was up early, mistrustful that mother's watch was on time. However, the Radio Frankfurt chronometer on Eschersheimer Landstrasse showed me that my worries were unfounded. In order not to wander in at the rendezvous too early I decided to go by foot. It took almost an hour and was past nine o'clock before all the other traveling companions arrived and the nice drive commenced in the blue coach. We ate lunch in Marburg at the Felsenkeller restaurant. For the times, the meal was good and plentiful. I enjoyed the pleasant company of Brono Wirth's girlfriend, Helma, until it was time to go.

Then the bus took us to the playing field. The good field conditions allowed us to play in a superior fashion, so that our mood about the match, like that of the numerous spectators, was satisfied with the game, which we won 6:2. Our return journey let us see the many charms of the countryside. The setting sun sank like a red fireball on the horizon and overspread the snowy landscape with a magical light. After it got dark, we all sang songs. Because of this, the journey didn't seem too long and actually could be described as a memorable experience in the history of the Red-White team.

2. März

Schon die ganze Woche sprach man davon! Wird das Wetter unverändert bleiben? Damit das Spiel in Marburg stattfinden kann? Nun ja, die Schneefälle waren gestern nicht der Art, dass eine Spielabsage notwendig geworden wäre. Also Treffpunkt 8.30 an der Bockenheimer Warte.

Bereits vor der Zeit war ich auf den Beinen und misstrauisch, ob Mutters Uhr auch die rechte Zeit anzeigt. Der Chronometer von Radio Frankfurt in der Eschersheimer Landstraße belehrte mich jedoch, dass meine Zweifel unbegründet waren. Um nun nicht zu früh am Treffpunkt einzutrudeln, zog ich vor, den Weg zu laufen. Bis die andern Reisegefährten alle zur Stelle waren, dauerte es bald 1 Stunde und erst nach 9.00 Uhr begann die schöne Fahrt mit dem blauen Autobus. In Marburg wurde im Restaurant „Felsenkeller" zu Mittag gespeist. Die Mahlzeit war zeitentsprechend gut und reichlich. Die Zeitspanne bis zum Aufbruch verbrachte ich in angenehmer Gesellschaft von Bruno Wirth's Freundin, Helma.

Zum Sportplatz brachte uns dann der Bus. Bei guten Platzverhältnissen zeigten wir eine überlegene Spielweise, sodaß unsere Spiellaune, wie auch die zahlreichen Zuschauer von dem Gastspiel befriedigt waren. 6:2 haben wir dort gewonnen. Die Heimfahrt zeigte uns viele landschaftliche Reize. Die untergehende Sonne versank gleich einem roten Feuerball am Horizont und überschüttete das verschneite Land mit zauberhaftem Licht. Nach eingetretener Dunkelheit sangen wir gemeinsam Lieder, sodass uns die Reise keinesfalls langweilig wurde und überdies noch zu einem denkwürdigen Erlebnis in der Vereinschronik von Rot-Weiß zu stempeln wäre.

March 10

I really should have gone to the Molls in Wüstems long ago because a considerable period had elapsed since my last visit. So yesterday it finally happened. The Königstein train took me the stretch of the trip that can be done on wheels, and after that I set off through the snowy woods on foot. You could barely have discerned the trace of a human, let alone encountered one. Toward noon I arrived in that picturesquely situated village in the Taunus Mountains that had been a refuge to us in the last years of the war and had provided other essentials. The joy of seeing our former hosts was mutual. Grampa, Grandma, and Richard Moll were present.

The relative special aspect of this journey has without doubt to do with pleasure. First and foremost are the foods we enjoyed, because of the times (and nature), although the spiritual experience--walking in the lonely woods, and the sincere friendship of the Moll family really ought to be given a higher value. In any case it was very nice and there are even good things to be said retrospectively about getting up early and about a night hike. Both of these were necessary in order to show up in time for work the next day.

10. März

Eigentlich hätte ich schon längst wieder einmal zu Molls nach Wüstems fahren müssen, denn seit dem letzten Besuch war eine geraume Zeit vergangen. Gestern war es nun soweit. Der Königsteiner Zug brachte mich die fahrbare Etappe vorwärts und dann auf Schusters Rappen quer durch den verschneiten Wald. Kaum dass man eine menschliche Spur entdecken konnte, noch viel weniger solchen begegnen. Etwa gegen Mittag kam ich in jenem malerisch gelegenen Taunusort an, der uns während der letzten Kriegsjahre ein Asyl und noch andere lebensnotwendige Dinge gewährt hat. Die Wiedersehensfreude mit den früheren Wirtsleuten war beiderseitig. Opa, Oma und Richard Moll waren anwesend.

Die relative Besonderheit dieser Reise ist ohne Zweifel auf dem Gebiet der Genüsse zu suchen. Dabei stehen die einverleibten Speisen zeit- (oder natur-)gemäß an erster Stelle, obwohl das geistige Erlebnis, das Wandern im einsamen Wald und die aufrichtige Freundschaft der Moll-Leute eigentlich noch höher eingeschätzt werden müsste. Auf jeden Fall war es sehr schön, und selbst dem Frühaufstehen und einer Nachtwanderung kann man einige Reize nachsagen. Dies ist jedesmal notwendig, um anderntags wieder rechtzeitig im Geschäft zu erscheinen.

March 26

I'm always glad to get letters from Rico. As he wrote, the long winter has caused him some inconvenience. Thank God he has now more or less recovered. Now he's living in Essen, the city where his school is, which no doubt benefits his studies.

Today is a splendid spring day and yesterday it was already quite warm. It was especially hot for me because I made a pilgrimage to Bockenheim on my bike towing the side cart loaded with three defective paper sacks. The sacks were filled with lime, which is now in a garden shed, waiting to be used in my garden as fertilizer. This year's garden preparation is made the more difficult because all of my garden tools have disappeared. It's virtually impossible to find replacements these days so I'm glad that I'm able to use the Elter's tools.

26. März

Über Ricos Briefe freue ich mich immer. Wie er schreibt, hat ihm der lange Winter manche Ungelegenheit bereitet. Gottlob ist er nun wieder einigermaßen hergestellt. Auch wohnt er jetzt in Essen, dem Ort seiner Schule, was seinem Studium zuträglicher ist.

Heute ist ein herrlicher Frühlingstag und schon gestern war es recht warm gewesen. Mir speziell war es sogar heiß geworden, als ich mit meinem Fahrrad und dem mit drei defekten Papiersäcken beladenen Leiterwagen als Anhänger nach Bockenheim pilgerte. In diesen Säcken war Muschelkalk, der nun in einer Gartenhütte liegt, um demnächst in meinem Garten als Düngemittel Verwendung zu finden. Die diesjährige Gartenbestellung wird deshalb erschwert, weil meine sämtlichen Gartengeräte abhanden gekommen sind. Die Ersatzbeschaffung ist heutzutage kaum möglich, und darum ist es angenehm, daß mir die Elter's Geräte zur Verfügung stehen.

1947

April 1

Since time immemorial people have played silly tricks on their friends on April 1. I've had a silly joke played on me in that, though the sun is shining outside and is interrupted now and then by the rain showers that are so typical of April weather, I've again come down with those vexing sores and have been banned to the house. This time I've entrusted myself to the care of the specialist, Dr. Wichert, and hope for a complete recovery. I've been on sick leave since March 28, and he's directed me to cover my beard area with salve and bandages. The procedure has to be repeated mornings and evenings. Wrapped up like this I look a bit like the turban-wearing Muslims. And yet I don't feel in the least bit sick. I awake at the usual time in the mornings. My books, pencil, and paper are within reach. Yesterday I was, contrary to orders, at the main rail freight station to take delivery of a hundredweight of coal. Today I disassembled the kitchen oven, which, in combination with the stove, provided additional warmth for us during the winter. I also gave the cellar a good cleaning.

On March 30th we (the Red-White team) had a decisive match against Friedberg which we managed to win 2:1. So we need another seven points from the remaining six matches in order to win the unchallenged championship of our league. On Easter Sunday, Red-White will play the Konkordia Wandsbek guest team from Hamburg at the Bornheimer Hang.

1. April

Bereitet man seit altersher seinen Bekannten scherzhafte Überraschungen. Mir selbst widerfährt insofern ein schlechter Scherz, denn während draußen die Sonne scheint und im Rahmen des Aprilwetters von Regenschauern abgelöst wird, bin ich wieder einmal von den leidigen Geschwüren heimgesucht und ins Haus verbannt. Diesmal habe ich mich dem Spezialisten Dr. Wichert anvertraut und erhoffe vollkommene Heilung. Vom 28. März an wurde ich krankgeschrieben, um nach seiner Weisung die Bartfläche mit Salbe und Verband zu bedecken. Die Prozedur muss morgens und abends wiederholt werden. Dabei habe ich eine gewisse Ähnlichkeit mit den turbantragenden Muselmännern. Jedoch fühle ich mich nicht im geringsten krank. Morgens werde ich zur gewohnten Zeit wach. Greifbar liegen Studierbücher, Bleistift und Papier zum Gebrauch. Gestern war ich sogar verbotenerweise im Hauptgüterbahnhof, um einen Zentner Eierkohlen abzuholen. Heute habe ich in der Küche den Ofen abmontiert, der uns im Winter durch eine Kombination mit dem Herd zusätzliche Wärme spendete. Auch habe ich den Keller wieder ordentlich aufgeräumt.

Am 30.3 hatten wir (Rot-Weiß) ein entscheidendes Spiel gegen Friedberg daselbst mit 2:1 gewinnen könnten. So benötigen wir aus den 6 noch ausstehenden Spielen sieben Punkte, um unangefochten die Meisterschaft unserer Liga zu erringen. Am Ostersonntag spielt Rot-Weiß am Bornheimer Hang gegen einen Hamburger Gast „Konkordia Wandsbek".

April 8

Now even the Easter days are past, as if they flew by. They were restful days, only the aforementioned soccer match upset my equilibrium a bit when, during an unfortunate collision, I suffered a severe laceration above the left eyebrow, which bled heavily. Fresh blood ran down my face almost every time I headed the ball, so that I was forced to sit out the game towards the end. That was on the first day of the holiday. I retired totally for the second. My books were dear companions for the day, among them Eckermann's Gespräche mit Goethe (*Conversations with Goethe*), a valuable treasure trove. Here are a few quotations:

"...but do people do what we old folks say? Every one thinks he knows best, yet in going their own way, some get lost and some stray for a long time. But now there's no more room to err. We old folks have been through what we've been through. And moreover what would all our seeking have been worth if the younger folk just want to make the same mistakes? We'd never advance. It was considered all right when we old folks strayed, because we didn't find the paths already forged for us. But more is demanded of him who has come into the world at a later date. He shouldn't repeat the straying and the seeking, but rather take the advice of the elders and straightaway set off on the right path. It shouldn't suffice that one takes steps which eventually lead toward the goal, rather, each step should be a goal in itself and be regarded as a step."

On the value of the present circumstance, of the present in general, he writes: "...always keep firm hold of the present. Every situation, indeed every moment, is of infinite value, for it is the representation of all eternity." Another time he writes: "Conflict with the world is only interesting if something comes of it." And, "He who is not driven into the wide world by great purposes would be much happier if he were to stay at home."

The following saying might have been formulated yesterday rather than over 100 years ago: "Humility has not been given to this world, not to the powerful so that no abuse of power can take place; and not to the masses, so that they might be satisfied with adequate conditions in expectation of gradual improvements. If humanity could be made perfect, then perfect circumstances would be imaginable. But in reality things will forever have their ups and downs; one part will suffer while the other is comfortable, egoism and envy, those two evil demons, will always play their game, and the battle of the parties will have no end."

8. April

Nun sind auch die Ostertage vorbei, wie verflogen. Es waren geruhsame Tage, lediglich durch das bereits erwähnte Fußballspiel kam ich etwas aus dem Gleichgewicht, denn bei einem unglücklichen Zusammenprall erlitt ich eine starkblutende Platzwunde über der linken Braue. Fast bei jedem Kopfstoß rann neues Blut über mein Gesicht, sodass gegen Ende mein Ausscheiden notwendig wurde. Dies war am 1. Feiertag, den 2. verbrachte ich in vollkommener Zurückgezogenheit. Hierbei waren mir meine Bücher liebe Genossen, zu denen sich in Eckermanns „Gespräche mit Goethe" eine wertvolle Schatzgrube zugesellt hat. Hier einige Zitate:

„aber tut man denn, was wir Alten sagen? Jeder glaubt, er müsse es doch am besten wissen, und dabei geht mancher verloren und manche hat noch lange daran zu irren. Es ist aber jetzt keine Zeit mehr zum Irren, dazu sind wir Alten gewesen, und was hätte uns all unser Suchen geholfen, wenn die jüngeren Leute dieselben Wege laufen wollten. Da kämen wir ja nie weiter! Uns Alten rechnet man den Irrtum zugute, weil wir die Wege nicht gebahnt fanden; wer aber später in die Welt eintritt, von dem verlangt man mehr, der soll nicht abermals irren und suchen, sondern er soll den Rat der Alten nutzen und gleich auf dem rechten Weg fortschreiten. Es soll nicht genügen, dass man Schritte tue, die einst zum Ziele führen, sondern jeder Schritt soll ein Ziel sein und als Schritt gelten."

Über den Wert eines augenblicklichen Zustandes, der Gegenwart im allgemeinen, heißt es: „... halte immer an der Gegenwart fest. Jeder Zustand, ja jeder Augenblick ist von unendlichem Wert, denn er ist der Representant einer ganzen Ewigkeit."Ein andermal: „Der Konflikt mit der Welt hat nur insofern etwas Interessantes, wenn etwas dabei herauskommt." und: „Wen nicht große Zwecke in die Ferne treiben, der bleibt weit glücklicher zu Hause."

Der folgende Ausspruch könnte erst gestern und nicht etwa vor über 100 Jahren getan worden sein: „Es ist dieser Welt nicht gegeben, sich zu bescheiden; den Großen nicht, dass kein Mißbrauch der Gewalt stattfinde, und der Masse nicht, dass sie in Erwartung allmählicher Verbesserungen mit einem mäßigen Zustande sich begnüge. Könnte die Menschheit vollkommen gemacht werden, so wäre auch ein vollkommener Zustand denkbar; so aber wird sie ewig herüber und dann hinüber schwanken, der eine Teil wird leiden, während sich der andere wohl befindet, Egoismus und Neid werden als böse Dämonen immer ihr Spiel treiben, und der Kampf der Parteien wird kein Ende haben

"We are most clever in the morning, but also most worried, for worry is a kind of wisdom, even if a passive kind. But stupidity knows not worry!"

I've absolutely got to write to my friend Rico soon, for what will he think if my reply is always so late in coming! I hope he's recovered his health fully and can devote all his energy to his studies. It's got to be pretty dismal at the moment in his part of the country, the Ruhr district. Driven by worry, hunger and deprivation, the inhabitants are protesting again the general distress by strikes and mass demonstrations. I wonder if they'll be successful against the universal need?

April 18

Although my facial illness does not look like it's healed, I've been back at work for three days now. I've also just become a civil servant. Technical Railroad Assistant, a title without much clout, for, from what I've learned, I'll be earning 152 Reichsmarks gross for the next four years. Herr Thomas says that I can improve my situation only by marrying and having children.

My friend, Rico, has been close to my thoughts today as well. Last night I dreamt that he'd come to visit me. But I was away at a soccer match, so that, to our mutual disappointment, we couldn't get together. Oh, may this never happen in real life!

Günther Gleiter, the goalie in our first team, is a nice fellow. Only thing is that he tends to say and promise things that he later fails to carry out due to forgetfulness and negligence. Nonetheless, I like him, because he also has to find his way through life alone without a father's guidance.

Last Saturday, various "sponsors" of the team arranged an evening of drinking. It started at 8 in the evening and lasted till the following morning. A total of 90 bottles of wine and 4 bottles of liquor were consumed, which

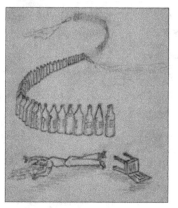

meant, of course, that most of the guys got totally drunk. Günther among them, unfortunately. As a consequence he totally forgot his promise to take me to visit a sports venue the next day.

„Am Morgen sind wir am klügsten, aber auch am sorglichsten, denn auch die Sorge ist eine Klugheit, wiewohl eine passive. Die Dummheit weiß von keiner Sorge!"

An meinen Freund Rico werde ich unbedingt bald schreiben, denn was soll er nur denken, wenn die Antwort immer so lange ausbleibt! Hoffentlich ist er nun wieder ganz gesund und kann sich mit aller Kraft dem Studium widmen. In seiner Heimat, inmitten des Ruhrgebietes, muss es augenblicklich recht traurig zugehen. Von Sorgen, Hunger und Entbehrungen aufgeputscht, protestieren die Bewohner mittels Streik und Massenkundgebungen gegen die allgemeine Not. Mit Erfolg??

18. April

Obwohl meine Gesichtserkrankung keineswegs als geheilt anzusehen ist, stehe ich seit 3 Tagen wieder im Dienst. Nun bin ich auch Beamter geworden. Technischer Reichsbahnassistent, ein Titel ohne Mittel, denn nach meinen Erkundigungen werde ich etwa 4 Jahre den Bruttoverdienst von 152 RM erhalten. Nach der Meinung des Herrn Thomas kann ich mich nur noch verbessern, wenn ich heirate und Kinder bekäme.

Meinem Freund Rico auch heute ein herzliches Gedenken. Heute nacht träumte ich davon, dass er gekommen wäre, um mich zu besuchen. Ich hingegen war abwesend und zu einem Fußballspiel gegangen, sodass wir uns zu beiderseitigem Leidwesen nicht erreichen konnten! Möge solches nie eintreffen.

Der Günther Gleiter, Torwart unserer 1. Mannschaft, ist ein sympathischer Junge. Nur schneidet er etwas auf, das heißt, er spricht und verspricht manches, was er hernach durch Vergesslichkeit und/oder Nachlässigkeit einzuhalten versäumt. Trotzdem mag ich ihn gut leiden, weil er auch ohne einen Vater und dessen Leitung seinen Weg durchs Leben selber suchen muss.

Am vergangenen Samstag hatten verschiedene „Gönner" der Mannschaft einen Saufabend arrangiert. Er begann um 8 Uhr abends und dauerte bis gegen den Morgen des folgenden Tages. Insgesamt wurden 90 Flaschen Wein und 4 Flaschen Schnaps verkonsumiert, was natürlich zur Folge hatte, dass die meisten Kameraden maßlos betrunken waren. Leider auch Günther. Sein Versprechen, mich anderntags zu einem Sportplatzbesuch abzuholen, hat er daraufhin total vergessen.

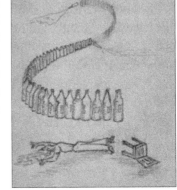

A further strange occurrence is that my colleague, Herr Marrter, claims to have lived in the same building in Fechenheim at the time of my birth. As a result, we were able to name various mutual friends and recall various memories of the place. When I reported this to my mother, she was delighted for she had clear memories of Mrs. Marrter, just as Mrs. Marrter confirmed her recollections to her husband.

April 19

From a letter to my friend Rico:

I hope you've recovered completely now. In that respect, things are going okay with me, even if the frequently recurring pustules on my beard area aren't very comfortable. So I've stayed home the past fourteen days, treating my chin with salve and my innards with pills, though with no success. Today I'm back to work, but I remain under my doctor's supervision.

I was offered numerous congratulations on being named a civil servant, and I'm sure many of my contemporaries would have been ecstatic in the same situation. However, I'm quite clear that this career path is not only limited and surrounded by high fences, but also that it can't be an appropriate career goal for a young man thirsty for knowledge.

Outdoors, spring is unfolding all its splendor. Yesterday the temperature climbed to 28°C, and some people, hungry for the sunshine, today are already sporting tanned faces that could compete with real Negroes. The end of the winter signifies for me the end of a calm period in which I was able to pursue my preparatory studies unencumbered and free. Now the garden demands not only a portion of my energy but also the majority of my leisure time so that even with an increased desire to do so, intellectual activity cannot keep pace with the increase in physical demands. (If there's a will, is there a way?) My concern is whether I can in fact start in the fall, in other words, whether Frankfurt or Idstein will be in a position to implement their intended programs. Strange worries, aren't they?

Because of the food shortages, which are growing worse daily, a healthy diet becomes difficult. I'm not complaining for myself, but it seems obvious that the current crisis will give even freer rein to the contemporary havoc, to the detriment of the common good. So it's less physical privation about which I'm complaining, for with a relatively good will that can be alleviated within a few years. Rather, I'm concerned about the spiritual need which follows, the need that leads to bad qualities and evil passions. It takes much longer and is much more difficult to conquer them and that's a path taken only by people who, recognizing their mistakes, want to regain their lost level of life.

Eine weitere besondere Begebenheit ist die, dass der Bürokollege, Herr Marrter, zu der Zeit meiner Geburt im selben Haus in Fechenheim gewohnt haben will. Hierbei konnten wir gemeinsame Bekannte zitieren und manche Erinnerung an jenen Ort wachrufen. Als ich meiner Mutter davon berichtete, war sie hocherfreut, denn sie konnte sich noch gut an Frau Marrter erinnern, wie auch diese ihrem Mann gegenüber ihre Erinnerung bestätigte.

19. April

Aus einem Brief an Freund Rico:

Hoffentlich bist Du nun wieder ganz gesund geworden. Mir geht es in dieser Hinsicht zufriedenstellend, wenn auch die oftmals wiederkehrenden Bartpusteln bestimmt keine angenehme Sache sind. So war ich letzthin 14 Tage zu Hause geblieben, die Bartflächen mit Salben und mein Inneres mit Pillen traktierend, jedoch ohne Erfolg. Heute bin ich wieder im Dienst, aber weiter in ärztlicher Behandlung.

Bei meiner Ernennung zum Beamten wurden mir zahlreiche Gratulationen zuteil, und gewiss viele Zeitgenossen wären in der gleichen Situation heilfroh; mir dagegen ist recht deutlich klar, dass dieser Weg nicht nur begrenzt und von hohen Zäunen umgeben ist, sondern auch für einen wissensdurstigen jungen Mann kein Ziel bedeuten darf.

Draußen entfaltet der Frühling seine ganze Pracht. Gestern stieg das Thermometer auf 28° C, und mancher Sonnenhungrige läuft schon heute den echten Negern zur Konkurrenz mit einem braungebrannten Gesicht umher. Das Ende des Winters ist für mich gleichbedeutend mit dem Ende einer geruhsamen Zeit, in der ich frei und ungebunden meinen vorbereitenden Studien nachgehen konnte. Nunmehr verlangt der Garten neben dem Anteil an Kraft auch den Großteil meiner Freizeit, sodass dem Wachsen der körperlichen Beanspruchung eine gleichbleibende geistige Tätigkeit selbst bei größerem Wollen nicht mehr folgen kann. (Wo eine Wille, ist auch ein Weg?) Meine Sorge ist, ob wohl im Herbst der Start vonstatten gehen kann, ob also Frankfurt oder Idstein sein vorgehabtes Programm durchzuführen imstande ist. Komische Sorgen, wie?

Besonders in Anbetracht der täglich größer werdenden Ernährungsschwierigkeiten. Ich klage nicht wegen meiner Person, aber es ist doch offensichtlich, dass die gegenwärtige Krise dazu angetan ist, allem Unbill der Zeit noch freiere Bahn zu lassen, der Allgemeinheit sehr zum Schaden. Es ist also weniger die leibliche Not, die ich beanstande, denn jene kann mit einigermaßen gutem Willen in wenigen Jahren behoben sein, sondern die in ihrem Gefolge erscheinende geistige Not, die Förderin der schlechten Tugenden und bösen Leidenschaften, zu deren Überwindung ein viel längerer und viel schwierigerer Weg erforderlich ist, und der auch wieder nur von Menschen beschritten wird, die in Erkenntnis der Fehler das verlorene Lebensniveau wiedergewinnen wollen.

May these reflections lose some of their pastoral tone when I reflect on my own shortcomings, yet may such thoughts be shared at times with the younger generation and may the old saying "Beware of beginnings" (meaning of bad things) become a general rule of life. Of course no-one's belly gets filled through such sayings. Rather, it seems to be one of those sayings that are made public by magazines and the radio as a distraction to deflect public attention from the actual catastrophic circumstances. But these are reflections of a young man who believes he has recognized that, alongside the truly great need of the body which has been deprived of many basic necessities, there is an even greater, more serious need. It is a spiritual need, one which clouds the vision of most people so that they can no longer recognize what might be necessary to their well-being. Now no one has proven which is the one religion that can make one blessed, so it's up to each individual to become blessed in his or her own way.

Mögen diese Gedanken durch die Betonung der mir eignen Mängel etwas von ihrer pastoralen Färbung verlieren, doch sollten besonders der jungen Generation solche Gedanken zuweilen eingegeben und das alte Sprichwort Wehre den Anfängen! (des Schlechten nämlich) eine allgemein anerkannte Lebensregel werden. Davon wird natürlich niemand satt; vielmehr scheint es eine der vielen Phrasen zu sein, die in Zeitschriften und Rundfunk publik gemacht werden, um als Ablenkungsmanöver den Blick des öffentlichen Interesses von den tatsächlich bestehenden katastrophalen Zuständen abzuziehen. Hier aber handelt es sich um die Überlegung eines jungen Menschen, der zu erkennen glaubt, dass es neben der gewiss großen Not des Leibes in seiner Entbehrung mancher lebensnotwendigen Dinge noch eine größere, leidvollere Not gibt. Jene geistige Not die den meisten Menschen den Horizont verdunkelt, sodass sie nicht mehr erkennen können, was zu ihrem Heile vonnöten wäre. Hierbei ist allerdings keinesfalls erwiesen, welche die allein „seligmachende" Religion sei und es bleibt den Individuen überlassen, nach ihrer Façon selig zu werden.

April 28

Last week I met Walter Waruschin, a former classmate from vocational school. Already at the time he was quite an alert guy, and he's since completed his engineering studies. Nowadays, like so many, he indulges in idleness, looks healthy and well dressed and perhaps also believes that this, along with various other affectations, qualifies him as a man of the world.

Should I or shouldn't I? Can I or can't I? Every time I went past an advertising pillar, doubts rose up in me as to whether or not I should respond to the call of the Frankfurt Union for the Education of the People. Even when my will to learn was for it, the weight of my other obligations and my own comfort resisted it. I was pretty upset with my lack of will power. By way of punishment I forced myself to go to the office of that institution and enroll for three classes. Then I said to myself: If you give in now, you're a big wimp, for, besides your work, you have time to do sports and that means there's enough time for you to go to school.

May 20

The last four weeks were filled with work, work which won't let up in the near future. But it was also an experientially rich time which opened up valuable avenues for me. The courses were on Algebra III, Geometry III, as well as Physics and Chemistry, which the Frankfurt Union for the Education of the People offered in this time period. The courses are held on Tuesdays, Thursdays, and Fridays, from 6-7.30 p.m.

According to the stipulations of the Frankfurt State Engineering School I was supposed to participate in the student work detail to rebuild the School by working 100 hours between May 5 and 17th. Since each student was permitted to work up to ten and a half hours a day, I took advantage of the opportunity and completed 91 hours in nine days. Since, thanks to this achievement, a sixteen-hour premium was awarded, the work required of me is now accomplished, with seven additional hours.

Some of my colleagues during this work were older, more advanced in their knowledge and more experienced. Working with them taught me a great deal. Practically speaking, a minimal amount of productive work was actually done. The reason for this was insufficient building materials, a lack of a desire to work on the part of many, and not least, the inept organization. My work assignment was first of all to get a totally rusted and dilapidated field smithy working again.

28. April

Vergangene Woche traf ich einen ehemaligen Kameraden aus der Berufsschule, Walter Waruschin. Schon seinerzeit ein ganz geweckter Junge, hat er inzwischen sein Studium zum Ingenieur beendet. Heute allerdings frönt er wie so viele dem Nichtstun, sieht gesund und gut angezogen aus und glaubt auch vielleicht, dies im Verein mit gewissen Allüren stempele ihn zu einem „Weltmann".

Soll ich oder soll ich nicht? Kann ich oder kann ich nicht? Diese Zweifel lösten jedesmal die Anschläge des Frankfurter „Bund für Volksbildung" in mir aus, wenn der Weg an einer Litfaßsäule vorbeiführte. War mein Wille zum Lernen dafür, so sträubten sich die Summe der anderen Obliegenheiten plus Bequemlichkeit dagegen. Ich war recht böse auf meine Unschlüssigkeit. Zur Strafe zwang ich mich zum Büro dieser Institution, schrieb mich für 4 Kurse ein, und dann habe ich mir gesagt: Wenn du jetzt kneifst, bist du ein großer Feigling. Denn hast du Zeit, um neben deiner Arbeit noch Sport zu treiben, so ist auch genug Zeit, um die Schule zu besuchen.

20. Mai

Die letzten vier Wochen waren angefüllt mit Arbeit, die auch in Zukunft nicht aufhören wird. Daneben war es aber eine ereignisreiche Zeit, die mir wertvolle Aufschlüsse übermittelte. So fallen die Anfänge der Kurse Algebra III, Geometrie III sowie Physik und Chemie, die der Frankfurter Bund für Volksbildung durchführt, in diesen Zeitraum. Die Kurse verteilen sich auf Dienstag, Donnerstag und Freitag jeweils von 18.00 bis 19.30 Uhr.

Vom 5. bis 17. Mai sollte ich laut Aufforderung der Frankfurter Staatsbauschule an dem Studenten-Arbeitseinsatz zum Wiederaufbau der Staatlichen Ingenieurschule teilnehmen und 100 Stunden ableisten. Da man jedoch 10,5 Stunden arbeiten konnte, nahm ich die Gelegenheit wahr und hatte in 9 Tagen 91 Stunden absolviert. Da dank dieser Energieleistung außerdem eine Prämie von 16 Stunden zuerkannt wurde, so liegt die geforderte Leistung, um sieben Stunden überschritten, längst hinter mir.

Die Kollegen dieses Einsatzes waren teilweise älter, im Wissen fortgeschrittener und erfahrener. Der Umgang mit ihnen war für mich sehr lehrreich. Praktisch wurde leider nur zum geringen Teil produktive Arbeit geleistet. Das lag an mangelnden Baumaterialien, fehlender Arbeitslust vieler und nicht zuletzt mangelhafter Organisation. Mein Arbeitspensum bestand zunächst in der Wiederherstellung einer völlig verrosteten und demolierten Feldschmiede.

Hans Schunk from Wiesbaden was a good workmate in this. We spent the rest of the time dealing with the repaired monster. Trash wood served as coal, hammer and anvil were at hand, and I relived memories of my apprenticeship because of the sound of the hammer as well as the blisters on my hands.

At the administrative office of the school I obtained both a receipt for my assignment and the registration forms, which had to be sent in by July. So when the semester begins in the fall, I hope to be part of it. I used my disability time off for the work period, and just lost a little weight, even though I received supplemental food because of the strenuous work.

Yesterday I wrote to Aunt Jeanne, who knows about my hopes for the State Engineering School. Since her husband used to be a civil servant, she recommended that I stay the course I was already on, if a third possibility did not open up through emigration.

Just as a blacksmith who heats three pieces of iron at the same time in the fire is not necessarily a good master, I have doubts at times when and which direction will be given preference over the course of time. When the time comes I'll no longer hesitate, even if it is not the right choice. A good master can devise a useful object from a poor piece of iron.

Hierbei war Hans Schunk aus Wiesbaden ein lieber Geselle. Mit dem wieder instandgesetzten Monstrum haben wir uns auch die restliche Zeit vertrieben. Trümmerholz diente als Kohle, Amboss und Hammer waren vorhanden, und neben dem Klingen des Hammers versetzten mich die schwieligen Hände in ein Wiedererleben der verflogenen Zeit meiner Lehrjahre.

Auf dem Sekretariat der Schule habe ich mir neben der Quittung über den Einsatz die Anmeldeformulare abgeholt, die bis zum Juli zurückgegeben sein müssen. Wenn also im Herbst der Semesterbeginn durchgeführt wird, so hoffe ich dabei zu sein. – Für die Zeit des Einsatzes hatte ich meinen Erholungsurlaub genommen, jedoch lediglich eine Gewichtsabnahme verzeichnen können, obwohl die Schwerarbeiterzulage gewährt wurde.

Gestern schrieb ich an Tante Jeanne, die auch um meine Bemühungen an der Staatsbauschule weiß. Da ihr Mann früher Staatsbeamter war, empfiehlt sie die Beibehaltung der eingeschlagenen Laufbahn, wenn sich nicht eine dritte Möglichkeit durch Auswanderung ergeben sollte.

Gleichwie ein Schmied, der gleichzeitig 3 Eisen im Feuer erhitzt, nicht unbedingt ein guter Meister ist, so zweifle ich zuweilen, wann und welcher Weg aus dem Lauf mit der Zeit den Vorrang erhält. Ich werde dann nicht mehr zögern, auch wenn es nicht die rechte Wahl sein sollte. Hier kann wieder ein guter Meister aus einem schlechten Eisen noch einen brauchbaren Gegenstand formen.

May 27, in the Assembly Center in Frankfurt am Main

Events seemed to want to run over themselves. I finally had the certainty that my longed-for studies at the State Engineering School would commence, when the American consul approved my visa. My receipt for the work done in the student deployment is dated the 16th of this month; the Consul signed on 21st of May. Presumably school will open in the fall, but the ship carrying emigrants will definitely leave Europe in June. I have absolutely no doubts any more; I'm leaving for America. The American Christian Committee for Refugees (ACCR) is taking care of the expenses and also sponsoring me.

What we hoped for but hardly dared believe has now become fact. My brother, Heinz, and I can now emigrate to the States, to a brighter future. Taking leave of mother doesn't constitute an insurmountable obstacle; indeed, I hope to see her again very soon. This morning, our lodger, Mr. Meixner, brought our luggage here, and after we registered we were allowed to move into a room. The camp here isn't a camp, strictly speaking, more like an apartment complex which had to be vacated by civilian residents. You can take walks on clean park paths, and alongside the good food, the Assembly Center certainly offers other comforts if we get to know it better. What will my friend, Rico, say about all this? And Aunt Jeanne? Our efforts have been progressing for a year now, and we've been nearing the goal step by step. So I've kept my silence and have a big surprise in store for everyone.

27. Mai und im Assembly Center zu Frankfurt am Main

Es schienen sich die Ereignisse überstürzen zu wollen. Endlich hatte ich die Gewissheit, dass im Herbst der ersehnte Start auf der Staatsbauschule erfolgen kann und nun unterschreibt der amerikanische Konsul das Visum. Vom 16. dieses Monats datiert die Quittung des Studenteneinsatzes, am 21. 5. zeichnete der Konsul. Im Herbst wird voraussichtlich die Schule eröffnet, aber bestimmt verlässt im Juni das Auswandererschiff Europa! Kein Zweifel mehr, ich fahre nach Amerika! Die Kosten wie auch die Bürgschaft übernimmt das „American Christian Community for Refugees" (ACCR).

Was wohl erhofft, aber doch kaum zu glauben gewagt, ist nun Tatsache geworden. Bruder Heinz und ich können nach den Staaten auswandern, in eine hellere Zukunft. Da bedeutet der Abschied von der Mutter kein unüberwindliches Ereignis; ich hoffe sogar zuversichtlich, sie bald wiederzusehen. Heute morgen brachte Herr Meixner, unser Untermieter, das Gepäck hierher und nach der Registratur konnten wir ein Zimmer beziehen. Das Lager hier ist kein solches im Sinne des Wortes, sondern Wohnblocks, die von der Zivilbevölkerung geräumt werden mussten. Man kann auf sauberen Parkwegen spazierengehen, und neben guter Verpflegung bietet das Assembly Center gewiss noch manches Angenehme, wenn wir es näher kennenlernen. Was wird Freund Rico sagen? Und was Tante Jeanne? Seit einem Jahr laufen unsere Bemühungen, und nur Schritt für Schritt konnten wir dem Ziele näher kommen. Also habe ich auch geschwiegen und habe eine große Überraschung für alle.

May 29

This morning our cargo luggage was weighed and retained. For me this meant my big black trunk with the yellow pig leather straps. My travel necessities are packed in the smaller suitcase as hand luggage. The weight limit of 160 pounds required a careful selection process of the things I wanted to take. My mother was responsible for gathering the necessary linens and clothing, while I picked out a small selection of items I wanted to bring along. My first priorities were my technical textbooks and books of tables; all other literary desires had to take a backseat. My slide-rule, compass case, square, and India ink were permitted on the journey, whereas my drawing board and guide because of their inordinate size had to forego this opportunity to prove their seaworthiness. May they become a valuable tool for some other studious person when they find their new owner when my room gets cleared out. The skis can be useful to my mother because they're a valuable object for bartering. I don't need to say good-bye to any of the other knick-knacks, since I didn't grow close to any of them. It's such a pity that just yesterday my only piece of jewelry, the ring of my deceased sister, Marianne, lost the stone from its setting, and so now has to remain at home.

You can take leave here, and Heinz has already gone away. I still want to finish up my journal writing, shave, and eat lunch here. Then I'll also go home. Outside it's another glorious spring morning. Birds are singing their hearts out in the trees that edge the paths, and I'm dreaming. Yesterday I visited Bruno and his brother, Hans Wirth, again, and later met with my lads from the Red-White team, whom I had trained. Folks in Bockenheim are really sad to see me go, because my departure's left a hole on the team. The first team has to present a cohesive unit, particularly in the difficult qualifying games that are coming up, in order to beat out the competition among those aspiring to the first league. I hope the very best for my team-mates, although I can't quite believe that they'll succeed.

29. Mai

Heute morgen wurde unser Schiffsgepäck gewogen und gleich dort behalten. Als dieses gilt mein großer schwarzer mit gelben Schweinslederriemen umgürteter Koffer. Als mein Handgepäck sind in einem kleineren Koffer die Reiseutensilien eingepackt. Die Beschränkung des Gesamtgewichts auf 160 Pfund machte eine sorgfältige Sichtung der mitzunehmenden Sachen notwendig. Meiner Mutter oblag die Zusammenstellung der erforderlichen Wäsche und Kleidung, während ich eine kleinere Auswahl wünschenswerter Gegenstände ausgesucht habe. An erster Stelle stehen natürlich meine technischen Lehr- und Tabellenbücher, denen zulieb jede andere literarische Besonderheit zurückgestellt wurde. Auch Rechenschieber, Zirkelkasten, Winkel und Tusche dürfen die Reise mitmachen. Reißbrett und Schiene dagegen mußten infolge ihrer ungebührlichen Größe auf einen Beweis der Seetüchtigkeit verzichten. Mögen sie dereinst einem andern Studienbeflissenen ein wertvolles Werkzeug werden, wenn sie dereinst bei der Entrümpelung den neuen Besitzer finden. Die Skier können meiner Mutter insofern dienlich sein, als sie für Tauschzwecke ein wertvolles Objekt darstellen. Allem andern Tand brauche ich nicht Lebewohl zu sagen, denn ich war nie mit ihm verwachsen. Zu schade, dass gerade gestern mein einziges Schmuckstück, meiner verstorbenen Schwester Marianne's Ring, den Stein aus der Fassung verlor und nun zuhause bleiben muss.

Hier kann man Urlaub bekommen und Heinz ist schon weggegangen. Ich will noch mein Tagebuch nachtragen, mich rasieren und noch hier zu Mittag essen; dann werde ich auch nach Hause gehen. Draußen ist wieder ein herrlicher Frühlingsmorgen. Auf den die Wege säumenden Bäumen jubilieren die Vögel und ich träume. Gestern war ich nochmals bei Bruno und dessen Bruder Hans Wirth gewesen, später auch bei meinen Jungs von Rot-Weiß, die ich vorher trainiert habe. In Bockenheim bedauert man meinen Abgang sehr, der eine Lücke in die Mannschaft gerissen hat. Besonders in den schweren kommenden Aufstiegsspielen müsste die 1. Mannschaft ein geschlossenes Ganzes bilden, um aus der Konkurrenz der Oberligaaspiranten als Sieger hervorzugehen. Ich wünsche dies meinen Kameraden von ganzem Herzen, obwohl ich nicht recht an das Gelingen glauben kann.

Marianne

The grim reaper now has snatched you
From the living here on earth.
In grief and pain we long for you
And we miss your loving heart.

All are mourning for your life,
Asking God and himself: why?
Can you not give us an answer?
Alas, you, too, must silent be.

Cheerful courage was your power
Duty was your strength in life.
You did all your work with vigor
Until death snatched you away.

I will pray for your soul's peace
To the Lord enthroned above.
That he may be gracious to you
And reward your faith and love.

I'll hold you always in my heart.
Pure, transmuted, strong, sublime.
In honor of your memory
To guide and lead me through my time.

May your soul be granted peace
Now and in all eternity. Amen

Marianne

Schnitter Tod hat dich entrissen
Aus der Erdenbürger Kreis.
Schmerzlich wird man dich vermissen
Und entbehren deinen Fleiß.

Alle trauern um dein Leben,
Fragen Gott und sich: Warum?
Kannst du uns die Antwort geben?
Aber nein, auch du bleibst stumm.

Froher Mut war deine Stärke
Pflichtbewusstsein deine Kraft.
Nimmermüd gingst du zu Werke,
Bis der Tod dich hingerafft.

Will um deinen Frieden bitten
Bei dem Herrn, der droben thront,
Gnädig wird er dir beschieden,
So wird deine Treu belohnt.

Will dein Bild ins Herz mir senken,
Rein, geläutert, stark und hehr.
Dir zum Preise und Gedenken,
Mir zur Mahnung und zur Lehr.

Deiner Seel sei reiner Frieden
alle Ewigkeit beschieden! Amen!

Leaving my Parents' Home

Detached now from the parent tree
A twig wends its way downstream.
Will it come to grief?
Who can dare to ponder fate?
Or will it reach a welcoming shore
A land where it can set new roots?

              I have likewise yearned to wander.
`   To my home, a fond farewell.
              Let me depart.
              Let nothing sadden this good-bye.
              Farewell to all of you, my loved ones.
              I start my voyage well prepared.

Steadfast and constant in my faith
And the Lord in heaven
Praise always.
These cornerstones will guide my way.
And no earthly thief can rob me
Or my reward take away.

              No matter what I may encounter
              In far-off lands I'll never bring
              Shame on you!
              Yet if the world should bring me blessings
              I will without hesitation
              Give, love, thank.

Abschied vom Elternhaus

Abgelöst vom alten Stamme
Treibt das Reis auf Stromeswellen!
Wird's zerschellen?
Wer kann's Schicksal je ergründen?
Wird es neue Ufer finden?
Findet es Land zu neuem Stamme?

    So es mich zum Marsch gelüstet
    Elternhaus „Aufwiedersehen",
    Lasst mich gehen!
    Nichts soll mir den Sinn noch trüben.
    Lebet wohl! Ihr meine Lieben.
    Und zum Kampf bin ich gerüstet.

Treu und Redlichkeit im Glauben
Und den Herrn im Himmel oben
Immer loben!
Das sind Markstein meines Wandelns
Und die Früchte meines Handelns
Kann kein ird'ger Dieb mir rauben.

    Sollte auch der Grund mal schwanken,
    Nimmer bin ich fern im Lande
    Euch zur Schande!
    Doch gereicht die Welt mir Segen
    Will ich ohne überlegen
    Geben, lieben, danken.

June 6

Today I find myself in Bremen. The second phase on the way to America is called Emigrant Staging Area. During the last days of my stay in Frankfurt the rather dull camp life in the Assembly Center was relieved somewhat by truly wonderful experiences in the Brentanobad, an outdoor swimming pool complex in Rödelheim. There I had a great time with a group of some of the younger sports comrades. We played soccer, romped around, and swam. Marion Wahl was a good buddy. The fact that I ran barefoot and on uneven ground in what was at times a hotly contested play for the soccer ball resulted in several painful blisters on the soles of my feet. However, in view of the lasting memories of all of my comrades there, this is a secondary and temporary situation of no great importance.

When a list of the names of those emigrants who were scheduled to be transported to Bremen was nailed up around noon last Tuesday, the whole company gathered around, only to return with more or less relieved hearts, for not all found their names on the list. Heinz, comrade Dorwood, and I were on the list. A farewell evening at home made it clear that, even there, people were willing to go along with the new circumstances. Following a local move, the Meixner family is now living and sleeping in our bedroom and our front kitchen. Fortunately, my share of garden work is also being shared by them and also by sister, Helga, and friend, Werner. Leaving my job with the railroad has not caused me any concern, since I know it wasn't an ideal situation. Despite the security of the position, which should not be underestimated, it involved too much dependency and lack of freedom. My parting visit to the Kreussler family took place on the Saturday before Pentecost. Fräulein Kreussler was not present. I remember all the other acquaintances, friends, and supervisors collectively with gratitude, because they passed some knowledge on to me and showed me some kindness. In general, I was fairly well-liked, and I'm sure that Paul Mayer will not soon be forgotten at the RBD.

Among the last tasks to be undertaken in the Frankfurt camp were returning bed linens and our food cards, as well as receiving a ticket which was to be attached to your coat. Two trucks appeared punctually at 7.30 p.m. to take everyone to the nearby south train station. There, all 88 emigrants were accommodated in two large passenger cars in an express train.

6. Juni

Heute finde ich mich bereits in Bremen. Emigrant Staging Area heißt die zweite Etappe auf dem Weg nach Amerika. In den letzten Tagen meines Frankfurter Aufenthaltes wurde das etwas stupide Lagerleben im Assembly Center abgelöst von wirklich schönen Erlebnissen im Brentanobad in Rödelheim. Dort habe ich mich im Kreise jüngerer Sportkameraden sehr wohl gefühlt; wir haben Ball gespielt, getollt und gebadet. Auch Marion Wahl war ein lieber Spielgeselle. Dass ich mir bei dem manchmal tollen Spiel mit dem Ball, barfuß und auf unebenem Rasen, mehrere schmerzende Blasen an die Fußsohlen praktizierte, ist eine nebensächliche und vorübergehende Erscheinung, die neben der bleibenden Erinnerung an alle Kameraden einen denkbar untergeordneten Wert besitzt.

Als am vergangenen Dienstag um die Mittagszeit die Liste aller Namen jener Emigranten angeschlagen wurde, welche für den Transport nach Bremen bestimmt waren, sammelte sich das ganze Volk, um dann mit mehr oder weniger erleichtertem Herzen zurückzugehen, denn nicht alle fanden ihren Namen verzeichnet. Heinz, Kamerad Dorwood und ich waren dabei. Ein letzter Abschiedsabend zu Hause zeigte uns auch dort, dass man sich mit den neuen Verhältnissen vertraut zu machen gewillt ist. Nach einem lokalen Umzug wohnen und schlafen Familie Meixner nunmehr in unserm Schlafzimmer und in der vorderen Küche. Mein Arbeitspensum im Garten wird erfreulicherweise auch von ihnen geteilt und außerdem von Schwester Helga und Freund Werner wahrgenommen. Das Scheiden aus dem Bahndienst hat mir bisher keinen Kummer bereitet, weiß ich doch, dass es nichts Ideales war, denn trotz der nicht zu unterschätzenden Sicherheit dieses Verhältnisses barg es zuviel Unfreiheit und Abhängigkeit in sich. Mein Abschiedsbesuch bei Familie Kreussler geschah am Pfingstsamstag; Fräulein Kreussler war nicht anwesend. Aller andern Bekannten, Kameraden und Vorgesetzten gedenke ich noch Summarum in Dankbarkeit, weil sie mir manches Wissen vermittelt und manche Freundlichkeit erwiesen haben. Im Allgemeinen habe ich mich einer gewissen Beliebtheit erfreuen können, und ich bin gewiss, dass man den Paul Mayer in der RBD nicht so schnell vergessen wird.

Zu den letzten Handlungen im Frankfurter Lager zählten die Rückgabe von Bettwäsche und Esskarte sowie der Empfang einer Fahrkarte, die in Form eines Anhängers am Rock zu befestigen war. Pünktlich um 19.30 Uhr erschienen 2 Trucks, die alle Personen zu dem nahen Südbahnhof brachten, woselbst die 88 Emigranten in zwei großen D-Zugwagen untergebracht wurden.

Among others, Dorwood and Hans Schmitt were seated in our compartment, the last one in the train, adjoining the one with the American staff. Hans, a witty if somewhat cheeky youth, was notable for his organizational talent, thanks to which we had enough to eat during the train journey. The parting meal in Frankfurt was a joke, for besides the usual cabbage soup there were two pieces of something like cookies, which we often received later on during the journey. The children who were hanging around were grateful recipients of the baked goods and appeared to have developed a certain routine in seeking and finding such opportunities.

Although we were supposed to depart at 11 p.m., this did not alter the fact that the train didn't leave until midnight. Meanwhile a tumultuous storm broke, and I had to wonder if Werner's younger sister would once again be so terribly afraid. The thunder and lightning could not trouble us much, for our thoughts were preoccupied with more personal matters and with wondering when the American milk train would arrive, onto which we would be coupled until Bremen, on its way to Denmark.

Now if I were to say in advance that we did not arrive at our destination until late in the afternoon (5 p.m.) after such a long journey, then I should add right away that the time certainly did not seem unbearably long to myself nor to the others in our compartment. I want to report on this in more detail.

In unserm Abteil, das letzte im Zuge und neben dem der amerikanischen Zugbegleitung gelegen, saßen unter anderen auch Dorwood und Hans Schmitt. Letzterer, ein witziger, wenn auch etwas vorlauter Junge, glänzte durch sein „Organisationstalent", wodurch wir während der Bahnfahrt keinen Hunger zu leiden hatten. Das Abschiedsessen in Frankfurt war eine Farce, denn neben einer gewöhnlichen Krautsuppe gab es 2 Stück von keksähnlichem Gebäck, das wir später auf der Fahrt in reichem Maße erhielten und des öfteren aus dem Zuge reichen konnten. Dankbare Abnehmer waren hierfür herumlungernde Kinder, die sich eine gewisse Routine im Aufsuchen und Finden solcher Gelegenheiten angeeignet zu haben schienen.

War die Abfahrt auch für 23.00 Uhr festgesetzt, so ändert dies nichts an der Tatsache, dass erst nach 24.00 Uhr der Zugstart vonstatten ging. Inzwischen entlud sich ein heftiges Gewitter, und ich musste daran denken, ob wohl Werners jüngere Schwester wieder so mächtige Angst haben würde. Uns selbst konnte das Donnern und Blitzen wenig anhaben, denn unsere Gedanken bewegten sich um persönlichere Dinge und wann wohl jener amerikanische Milchzug eintreffen würde, dem wir dann auf seiner Fahrt nach Dänemark bis Bremen angehängt wurden.

Wenn ich jetzt schon vorausschickte, dass wir nach überlanger Fahrt erst am Spätnachmittag (17.00 Uhr) das Ziel erreichen konnten, so muss ich gleich hinzufügen, dass mir wie auch den andern Abteilgenossen die Zeit keinesfalls unerträglich lang erschien. Hierüber will ich eingehender berichten.

I was the last one to leave the truck, was one of the last to climb up into the train car, and found only the last compartment still unoccupied; it was perfect for us. It's more than an ordinary coincidence that, in addition, the staff, complete with a store of provisions, were settled in next door along with two big boxes of the aforementioned cookies on the backwards-facing platform. In short, the main reason that alleviated all concerns about having enough to eat was this: in addition to the obligatory packets of cookies, butter, canned fish and small bars of chocolate, we had our "organized" prizes: two tins of Argentinean orange marmalade and, from Dorwood's personal supply, there was still some rye bread, bacon, and cheese available. I believe the availability of all this food was the reason for the harmonious progress of the journey, although I will also mention other factors that made the trip pleasant and memorable for all of us. In this respect what should be mentioned first of all is Miss Naumann, who hails from the Kaiserslautern area. Because of her calm presence she was a pleasant companion and moreover she kept the compartment thoroughly clean by taking care of housekeeping duties. Our two instruments (guitar and mandolin), a harmonica and a portable gramophone provided musical entertainment. Jokes and cheerfulness provided the necessary element of good humor, and a conciliatory spirit all around ensured peace, which was the most important quality of all.

The tracks of the railroad yards around Bremen almost reach the Emigrant Staging Area. Thus, once our cars had been uncoupled from the milk train, which would travel on, we were shunted there and shut down. Our luggage was loaded onto vans and we went on foot to the former navy barracks, which were nearby. Initially, the sight of these military-style buildings evoked little sympathy in us. But I was soon able to change my attitude and come to the realization of how seldom a momentary feeling turns out to be true in the face of subsequent events. This is a general observation. And in particular, the bad experiences I had in Frankfurt after the initial good impressions, and now here a similar experience with the omens reversed.

Als letzter Mann verließ ich den Truck, erkletterte als einer der Letzten den Eisenbahnwagen und fand nur noch das letzte Abteil unbesetzt; es war wie für uns geschaffen. Da außerdem das Begleitpersonal samt Verpflegungsarsenal nebenan und 2 große Kisten mit den bereits erwähnten Keksen auf der rückwärtigen Plattform etabliert waren, ist mehr als ein gewöhnlicher Zufall. Kurzum, hierin liegt der Hauptgrund, durch den wir allen Essensorgen enthoben wurden. Neben den obligatorischen Kekspaketen, Butter, Fischkonserven und kleinen Schokoladentäfelchen standen uns als „organisierte" Errungenschaft zwei Dosen argentinische Orangenmarmelade und aus Dorwoods Privatbesitz noch etwas Schwarzbrot, Speck und Käse zur Verfügung. Ich glaube auch in diesen Gegebenheiten die Ursache für den harmonischen Verlauf der Reise suchen zu dürfen, obwohl es nicht unerwähnt bleiben soll, was ferner uns allen die Fahrt angenehm und erinnerungswert gestaltet hat. Hier gehört an die erste Stelle Frl. Naumann aus der Gegend um Kaiserslautern, die durch ihr ruhiges Wesen ein angenehmer Gesellschafter war und darüber hinaus durch die Wahrnehmung hausfraulicher Pflichten das Abteil gründlich reinhielt. Unsere beiden Instrumente (Guitarre und Mandoline) im Verein mit einer Mundharmonika und einem Koffergrammophon sorgten für die musikalische Unterhaltung, Witze und Frohsinn für den nötigen Humor und der versöhnliche Geist aller für den noch wichtigeren Frieden.

Bis ganz nahe an das „Emigrant Staging Area" reichen die Gleise der Bahnanlagen um Bremen. So konnte auch unser Transport nach der Trennung von dem weiterfahrenden Milchzug dorthin rangiert und dann abgestellt werden. Das Gepäck wurde auf Lastautos geladen und zu Fuß gingen wir zu der nahen ehemaligen Marinekaserne. Der Anblick dieser Gebäude militärischen Charakters erweckte in uns zunächst wenig Sympathie. Doch bald konnte ich meine Ansicht ändern und dafür die Feststellung machen, wie wenig das augenblickliche Empfinden oft vor den Beweisen der nachfolgenden Erlebnisse zu bestehen vermag. Dies im allgemeinen. Und im besonderen die nach den ersten guten Eindrücken gemachten schlechten Erfahrungen in Frankfurt und nun hier ein ähnliches Erlebnis mit umgekehrten Vorzeichen.

Within a few minutes we were free of our luggage, had been searched, disinfected, and provided with a pass, a food card, and bed linens as white as snow. Dorwood, Heinz and I were assigned once again to the same room, which accommodated a total of 10 people. Roomy, clean and plentiful sinks, showers, and lavatories testify to the aesthetics of modern barracks and how such facilities can also serve peaceful purposes. German staff demonstrated their legendary thoroughness in housekeeping and in the good meal preparation, so that a quick comparison with conditions in the Frankfurt barracks showed a distinct advantage in favor of this institution. The meals, made from American ingredients and prepared accordingly, are altogether new to me, but the qualitatively excellent meals seemed nonetheless not quite up to my quantitative expectations. Nonetheless, there certainly isn't any hunger here and I would only wish that the entire German population might experience a comparable level of nutrition in the near future.

Since today is an American holiday, our visit to the ACCR office was in vain, and we hope to knock on that office door again tomorrow with better success. In the afternoon, we three roommates headed into town. Strangely enough, the city center here is intact, but the outskirts have been destroyed by the events of the war. The use and recycling of materials from the ruins in Bremen can't have been nearly as problematic as in Frankfurt, as the houses here are made almost exclusively out of brick.

Heinz and Dorwood sent telegrams to Miss Jürgens and his father, respectively, from a post office in the city center. At the moment, Miss Jürgens from Frankfurt is staying with relatives near Bremen and intends to visit us again. It's possible that the rendezvous set for next Monday won't occur, for if we were to be part of the next transport (departing Bremerhaven June 12), for which ship passes will be distributed on Monday, then the only possible solution would be to send another telegram canceling the meeting.

Now we find ourselves quite at the edge of our fatherland, remote from what's happening in our old homeland. We are looking for a new home! I can judge all expressions of home and fatherland appropriately without overlooking the fact that the human heart needs a home, and finds one in the place where it is understood, where it flourishes and can love, so that it can be loved in return. The only thing I'm afraid of is going to a strange land without knowing if I'll find such a home. For certainly, if I return, my old home will have grown unfamiliar to me.

Denn in wenigen Minuten waren wir des Gepäcks ledig, untersucht, desinfiziert und mit einem Pass, einer Esskarte und mit blütenweißer Bettwäsche versehen. Bei der Zimmerzuweisung kamen Dorwood, Heinz und ich wieder in einen Raum, wo allerdings insgesamt 10 Personen untergebracht waren. Große, saubere und zahlreiche Wasch-, Dusch- und Abortgelegenheiten zeugen von der Ästhetik moderner Kasernenbauten und wie solche Einrichtungen auch friedlichen Zwecken dienen können. Deutsches Personal beweist im Reinemachen wie im Zubereiten der Speisen die sprichwörtliche Gründlichkeit, sodass nach den bisher gemachten Erfahrungen ein kurzer Vergleich mit den Frankfurter Lagerverhältnissen ein deutliches Übergewicht der hiesigen Institution zutage treten lässt. Für mich sind die dargebotenen Speisen aus amerikanischen Beständen und entsprechend zubereitet überhaupt neu, sodass die qualitativ hervorragenden Mahlzeiten den quantitativ unvernünftigen Ansprüchen noch etwas gering erschienen. Es kann jedoch von Hunger keine Rede sein und ich wünsche nur recht bald dem ganzen deutschen Volk ein derartiges Ernährungsniveau.

Da heute ein amerikanischer Feiertag ist, war auch unser Gang zu dem Büro des ACCR vergebens, und wir hoffen morgen mit besserem Erfolg dort anzuklopfen. Am Nachmittag zogen wir drei Zimmergenossen in die Stadt. Hier ist seltsamerweise der Stadtkern intakt, während die Peripherie von den Kriegsgeschehnissen heimgesucht wurde. In Bremen dürfte die Trümmerverwertung und ihre Wiederverwendung kaum so problematisch wie in Frankfurt sein, denn die Häuser waren hier fast ausschließlich Backsteinbauten.

In einem Postamt in der Stadtmitte sandten Heinz und Dorwood Telegramme an Frl. Jürgens beziehungsweise seinen Vater. Fräulein Jürgens aus Frankfurt weilt augenblicklich bei Verwandten in der Nähe von Bremen und beabsichtigt uns nochmals zu besuchen. Möglicherweise wird sich das vereinbarte Rendezvous am kommenden Montag gar nicht durchführen lassen, denn sollten wir dem nächsten Transport angehören (ab Bremerhaven am 12. 6.), zu dem am Montag die Schiffskarten ausgegeben werden, dann ist ein neuerliches Telegramm mit einer Absage die einzig mögliche Lösung.

Nun stehen wir ganz am Rande unseres Vaterlandes, abseits und desinteressiert an den Geschehnissen der alten Heimat. Wir suchen eine neue Heimat! - Ich weiß alle Phrasen von Heimat und Vaterland richtig einzuschätzen ohne zu übersehen, dass das menschliche Herz eine Heimat braucht und sie dort findet, wo es verstanden wird, wo es sich aufschließen und lieben kann, um wieder geliebt zu werden. Allein davor bangt es mir, in die Fremde zu gehen, ohne zu wissen, ob ich diese Heimat finden werde. Denn bei einer Umkehr ist mir die alte Heimat gewiss fremd geworden.

But today there's no turning back; and the experience of the unfamiliar, with its new and multifaceted impressions, will be more useful for any young person than idly wasting away one's youth confined to the old homeland. What is for me a real loss is giving up formal education, and yet life itself is such a many-sided school for learning that to a student hungry for knowledge much that's worth knowing is offered here or there. It will be possible for such a student to pursue his goals in keeping with the level of his own intelligence. It is on this that I want to build, assuming I can recognize the goal and path of my life with God's guidance and help.

June 7

The unaccustomed, carefree passage of time is a new experience each day. I'm enjoying this time and view it as a representation of eternity. The minute I set foot on American soil, this existence will be over and the daily routine will make its own demands.

Here, each day begins with the sound of a bell, which is rung shortly before 7 a.m. As I sleep upstairs in a typical military bunkbed and brother Heinz and below him Dorwood are my neighbors, it doesn't take long till six legs are planted on the ground; equally many hands reach for wash cloths, and cheery chatting in the cold showers reveals that these lads who've enjoyed a good night's rest are no softies. Brushing our teeth and shaving are part of the daily morning routine.

Heute gibt es kein Zurück mehr, und das Erlebnis der Fremde mit seinen neuen und vielseitigen Eindrücken wird jedem jungen Menschen nützlicher sein als das unnütze Verdösen seiner Jugend in der engen Heimat. Als einen wirklichen Verlust empfinde ich das nunmehrige jegliche Entsagen von einem Schulstudium, doch ist das Leben eine derart vielseitige Schule, dass dem gelehrigen Schüler hier wie dort viel Wissenswertes geboten wird. Ganz nach dem Maß der eigenen Intelligenz wird es ihm auch hierdurch möglich sein, einem Ziele näherzukommen. Und darauf will ich bauen, wenn ich mit Gottes Rat und Hilfe Ziel und Weg meines Lebens erkennen kann.

7. Juni

Ein täglich neues Erlebnis ist der ungewohnt sorglose Ablauf der letzten Zeit. Ich genieße diese Gegenwart und betrachte sie als einen Repräsentanten der Ewigkeit. Von der Stunde an, welche mich in den Staaten auf eigne Füße stellt, ist dieses Dasein zu Ende und der Alltag wird seinen Tribut fordern.

Hier beginnt der Tag mit dem Ton einer Glocke, die kurz vor 7 Uhr geläutet wird. Da ich im oberen Bett der üblichen Militärschlafstätten ruhe und Bruder Heinz mit seinem Untermann Dorwood meine Nachbarn sind, dauert es nur wenige Zeit, bis sich sechs Beine auf die Erde stellen, ebensoviele Hände nach den Waschutensilien greifen und das muntere Plätschern unter den kalten Duschen verrät, daß hier keine verweichlichten Burschen gut ausgeschlafen haben. Zähneputzen und Rasieren gehört zu der alltäglichen Morgenbeschäftigung.

Breakfast is between 7.30 and 8.30 in the big dining room called Patton Hall. Arranged on a tray are morning soup, real coffee, white bread, cookies, and schmalz. Well-satisfied, we dedicate the rest of the morning to cleaning shoes and clothing. Often, there's also time for a relaxed conversation or an opportunity to play some music. There's plenty of reading material on hand in a library. In general, the social games that are available are eagerly taken up so that I could observe how, according to a person's temperament or disposition, tennis, chess, checkers, or nine men's morris, among other games, were embraced by some, while others studied books. Another meal is taken in Patton Hall between 12.30 and 1.30. Similar to the breakfast routine, people put on their trays soup, mashed potatoes, a vegetable such as split peas or bean puree with meat sauce or, like today, a pair of wieners with a slice of white bread, coffee or tea. Meals are eaten at the long tables, and we sit on benches, which, because of the way they're made, we have to climb onto.

Everyone is free to leave the camp between the hours of 8 a.m. and 11 p.m., and many emigrants use this opportunity to take care of various errands or walk in the town. But today it's such cold, unfriendly weather, with scattered showers, that I prefer to bring my journal up to date in the recreation room than to go outside and get a red nose and an undesirably large appetite. Though I reported many praiseworthy things about this camp earlier, I now realize I haven't mentioned everything, for the evenings offer opportunities for a whole range of entertainment, like listening to music, dancing, or watching a movie. Dorwood, Miss Naumann and Heinz had such a good time at the dance yesterday that when the public dancing was over they further indulged their desire to dance with the help of the portable record player.

In der Zeit von 7.30 bis 8.30 Uhr wird im großen Speisesaal der „Patton-Hall" das Frühstück vereinnahmt. Auf einem Tablett summieren sich der Reihe nach eine Morgensuppe, Bohnenkaffee, Weißbrot, Kekse und etwas Schmalz. Recht gesättigt wird der übrige Vormittag dem Reinemachen der Schuhe + Kleider gewidmet. Oft ist auch Zeit zu einer zwanglosen Unterhaltung oder Gelegenheit zum Musizieren. In einer Bibliothek steht reichhaltige Lektüre zur Verfügung. Allgemein wird den vorhandenen Gesellschaftsspielen lebhaft zugesprochen, sodass ich beobachten konnte, wie je nach Temperament oder Veranlagung dem Tennisspiel, Schach, Dame, Mühle und anderen Spielen neben dem Studium der Bücher gehuldigt wurde. Von 12.30 bis 13.30 Uhr wird wieder in der Patton-Hall gespeist. Ähnlich dem Vorgang beim morgendlichen Frühstück wird Suppe, Kaffee oder Tee neben dem Kartoffelbrei, etwas Gemüse in Form von Erbsen- oder Bohnenbrei und dazu noch eine Fleischsoße oder wie heute 1 Paar Wiener Würstchen mit einer Schnitte Weißbrot auf das Tablett geladen. An den langen Tischen und auf Bänken, die man infolge ihrer Eigenart erst ersteigen muss, werden die Speisen vereinnahmt.

Es steht jedem frei, das Lager in der Zeit von 8.00 bis 23.00 Uhr zu verlassen, und so nutzen viele Emigranten diese Gelegenheit zu Erledigungen und Spaziergängen in der Stadt. Heute ist aber ein kaltes, unfreundliches und zu Regenfällen neigendes Wetter, sodass ich es lieber vorziehe, im Recreation Room mein Tagebuch zu vervollständigen als mir draußen neben einer roten Nase einen unerwünscht großen Appetit zu erwerben. Wußte ich bisher so viel Lobenswertes über dieses Lager zu berichten, so ist doch noch nicht alles erwähnt, denn in bunter Folge bieten die abendlichen Veranstaltungen Gelegenheit zum Aufsuchen von Unterhaltungsmusik, Tanzmusik oder einer Kinovorstellung. – Bei der gestrigen Tanzmusik amüsierten sich Dorwood, Frl. Naumann und Heinz derart, dass sie nach Beendigung des öffentlichen Tanzvergnügens mit Hilfe des Koffergrammophons weiter ihrer Tanzlust frönten.

About 900 emigrants are waiting longingly for the opportunity to be relocated. The variety of their backgrounds is expressed in the mélange of accents. Bygone fates must be just as varied as the dreams of the new home. But there's one observation I can make about the majority of the emigrants. Almost all of them are outfitted with some kind of objects of value, whether they are rings, watches, cameras, or other optical equipment, coin or stamp collections or other similar things, so that we two brothers actually seem quite poor in comparison. We trust firmly in our ability to work, our health, and good fortune, and hope to be able to advance without entering into speculation. It depresses me somewhat to go over there without any kind of contact (other than the ACCR), but my frequently cited slogan, "Don't cry before you are hit," absolutely holds true in this circumstance as well. So all I can do is wait and see, keep my eyes open, and put a shoulder to the wheel when necessary.

Etwa 900 Emigranten warten sehnsüchtig auf die Möglichkeit des Abtransportes. Die Verschiedenheit ihrer völkischen Abstammung drückt sich im Sprachengewirr aus. Ebenso verschieden mögen die rückwärtigen Schicksale wie auch die Wünsche in der neuen Heimat sein. Eine Beobachtung konnte ich beim Gros der Auswanderer machen. Fast alle sind ausgerüstet mit irgendwelchen Wertobjekten, seien es Ringe, Uhren, Photoapparate, andere optische Geräte, Münzen- oder Briefmarkensammlungen oder ähnliche Gegenstände, sodass wir beiden Brüder eigentlich recht arm aussehen. Wir vertrauen jedoch fest auf unsere Arbeitskraft, unsere Gesundheit, den guten Willen und hoffen, auch ohne Spekulationen ein Vorwärtskommen zu finden. Es betrübt mich etwas, so ganz ohne Anhaltspunkt (außer ACCR) nach drüben zu gehen, doch mein oft zitiertes Sprichwort: Nicht eher heulen als geschlagen, hat auch in diesem Falle unbedingt Gültigkeit. Also abwarten, Augen aufmachen und zugreifen, wo es notwendig ist.

Sunday, June 8.

As befits the literal meaning, the sun is shining, at least on this Sunday. That's the first thing I noticed on waking at seven. Yesterday evening an orchestra gave a concert in the dining room of Eisenhower Hall. Along with the rest of the complex of which Patton Hall is a part, these two horseshoe-shaped buildings currently house all the emigrants.

Unfortunately. the restless audience didn't pay the necessary attention to the music, which was truly good and played with technical virtuosity. The small children of parents with no common-sense disturbed just as much as did the improper behavior of the teenagers. I managed to be able to concentrate for most of the time and had a good impression of the one and a half hour concert. Heinz, Dorwood, and Traude Naumann subsequently sought further pleasure on the dance floor. A wide range of thoughts were going through my head, but I couldn't find diversion or distraction either by studying the English dictionary or by solving math problems. In order to be alone soon, I said my goodnights, took a bath, and went to bed. It took me a long time to fall asleep, but when the others came back I was already sleeping deeply, and only awakened to the sun-drenched Sunday morning I mentioned earlier.

After breakfast, we three musketeers attended a church service in the Bremen cathedral. This monumental house of God built in the gothic style clearly demonstrates how great the religious influence on life must have been during the Middle Ages to cause the coming together of architectural and building skills and know-how in works of this type. It's such a shame that even this work of art suffered significant damage during the war. The roof of one of the naves was almost totally destroyed, and I observed in the rear part of the cathedral that many repairs had been carried out deep in the crypt area, as protection against further damage.

Sonntag, den 8. Juni

Gemäß der wörtlichen Bedeutung scheint wenigstens am heutigen Sonntag die Sonne. Dies war die erste Beobachtung, als ich um 7 Uhr aufgewacht war. Gestern abend veranstaltete ein Unterhaltungsorchester ein Konzert im Speisesaal der Eisenhower-Hall. Mit dem Gebäudekomplex der „Patton-Hall" sind diese beiden hufeisenförmig angelegten Bauten das derzeitige Domizil aller Emigranten.

Leider wurde von dem unruhigen Publikum der wirklich guten und mit virtuoser Technik dargebotenen Musik nicht die notwendige Aufmerksamkeit gewidmet. Die Kleinkinder unvernünftiger Eltern störten ebenso wie das ungebührliche Benehmen der Halbwüchsigen. Ich selbst konnte mich die meiste Zeit genügend konzentrieren und habe von den 1 ½ Stunden einen guten Eindruck gewonnen. Anschließend suchten Heinz, Dorwood und Traude Naumann im Tanzen weiteres Vergnügen. Mir gingen die verschiedensten Gedanken durch den Kopf, dass auch das Studium eines englischen Wörterbuches und das Lösen mathematischer Aufgaben keine Abwechselung und Ablenkung brachten. Um dann bald allein zu sein, verabschiedete ich mich, nahm mein Bad und ging zu Bett. Noch lange fand ich keinen Schlaf, doch als die andern kamen, lag ich schon in tiefen Träumen und erwachte erst wieder im Anblick des vorhin erwähnten, sonnenbeschienenen Sonntagmorgens.

Nach dem Frühstück besuchte unser Kleeblatt den Gottesdienst im Bremer Dom. Dieses monumentale, im gotischen Stil erbaute Gotteshaus lässt wohl mit Bestimmtheit vermuten, wie groß der religiöse Einfluß im Mittelalter gewesen sein muss, dass sich alle Baukunst und Intelligenz an solchen Werken zusammenfand. Zu schade, infolge des Kriegsgeschehens wurden auch diesem Kunstwerk beträchtliche Schäden zugefügt. Allein das Deckengewölbe des einen Schiffes ist fast gänzlich zerstört und im hinteren Teil des Domes konnte ich beobachten, wie bis in die tiefsten Kellergewölbe zum Schutz gegen weitere Zerstörungen umfangreiche Reparaturen durchgeführt werden.

The sermon of the young pastor was rousing and executed with great seriousness, in keeping with the Bible passage and the pastor's fine exegesis. With the help of the church choir, the worship service had the task of conveying a certain atmosphere; in contrast to this, the small congregation managed to fill only a diminutive section of the church interior. I find in this a clear demonstration of the receding of ecclesiastical influence on popular life and an obvious consequence with respect to the decline of people's morals and customs.

The sign to the town hall beer cellar catches the eye opposite the cathedral's exit, and the entire town hall hints at the splendor this Hanseatic city enjoyed in its heyday. Roland, the symbol of the city, still stands with his stony face facing the cathedral, while part of the old apothecary shop and many other buildings at the edge of the market square have fallen victim to the catastrophe.

Bremen doesn't actually have much of a big-city feel to it, but it's fairly spread out so that the punctual and frequent trams are an agreeable feature. Very much in contrast to Frankfurt, the street cars are not overfilled and the friendly conductress always announces the next stop in advance. Consequently every passenger has ample time to get ready to get off, and entering and exiting take place without a hitch. The female police officers are something new to me. Like their male colleagues, they wear clean, blue uniforms decorated with the coat of arms of the city in shiny silver, and fulfill responsible positions both on the streets and in their offices. The shop windows are pleasing for their variety, and if one could imagine away the rationing system, one would often be lured into the shops. Snow-white bread is sold in the bakeries, and lately it's only been the lack of items to put on the bread that's caused the citizens of Bremen and elsewhere many a headache.

Die Predigt des jungen Geistlichen war mitreißend und von großem Ernst getragen, wie es der Bibeltext und seine feine Auslegung durch den Pfarrer erforderte. Der Gottesdienst hatte in der Mitwirkung des Kirchenchores eine besondere Note aufzuweisen, hingegen konnte die wenig zahlreich vertretene Gemeinde nur einen geringen Teil der Räumlichkeiten füllen. Hierin erblicke ich eine klare Demonstration des Rückgangs kirchlicher Einflüsse auf das Volksleben und eine zwangsläufige Folgerung im Hinblick auf den moralischen und sittlichen Niedergang im Volke.

Gegenüber dem Domausgang fällt das Ratskellertransparent ins Auge, und das ganze Rathaus verrät, welche Pracht die Hansestadt in ihrer Blüte zu entwickeln vermochte. Der Roland, ein Wahrzeichen der Stadt, steht nach wie vor mit steinernem Gesicht dem Dome zugewandt, während die alte Apotheke teilweise und manches andere Gebäude am Rande des alten Marktplatzes der Katastrophe zum Opfer gefallen sind.

Bremen hat für sich keinen großstädtischen Charakter, liegt aber ziemlich auseinandergezogen, sodass die pünktlich und zahlreich verkehrenden Straßenbahnen eine angenehme Einrichtung sind. Sehr im Gegensatz zu Frankfurt sind die Bahnen nicht überfüllt, und die freundliche Schaffnerin kündet immer die nächstfolgende Station voraus. Dadurch kann jeder Fahrgast sich rechtzeitig zum Aufbruch rüsten, und das Einsteigen und Aussteigen erfolgt reibungslos. Die weiblichen Polizisten sind für mich neuartig. Wie auch ihre männlichen Kollegen in saubere, blaue und mit einem silberglänzenden Stadtwappen geschmückte Uniformen gekleidet, versehen sie auf den Straßen wie in den Dienststellen einen verantwortungsvollen Posten. – Die Auslagen der Verkaufsgeschäfte gefallen durch die Vielseitigkeit, und wenn das Rationierungssystem wegzudenken wäre, möchte man des öfteren eine Ladentüre in die Hand nehmen. In den Bäckerläden wird blütenweißes Brot verkauft und lediglich der Mangel an Bezugsberechtigung ist es, was den Bürgern von Bremen so wie überall einiges Kopfzerbrechen bereitet.

In the course of these reflections, the sky has clouded over again and rain is hitting the window panes. Brother Heinz is resting in bed, Dorwood, since he's only sixteen,, can still participate in the children's meal from 3.30 to 4 p.m. and has just gone there, which leaves only me as the remnant of the original group here in the recreation room. Other emigrants are seated at neighboring tables, some studying magazines or books. Still others are together and embroiled in lively conversations with their visitors. A loudspeaker attached to the ceiling is transmitting a program from Radio Bremen at an almost uncomfortable volume.

I've just borrowed a Bible from the library. After searching for a while I found the text of today's sermon in the tenth chapter of the Gospel of Matthew, verses 16-22. What are you doing with a Bible? That's what Hans Schmitt asked me. It's a significant question for one who tries to impress at every opportunity with a dirty joke or a shameless way of talking, one whose inane and silly chatter finds no resonance in our company.

Während dieser Betrachtungen hat sich der Himmel wieder mit Wolken bedeckt, und Regenschauer schlagen die Scheiben. Bruder Heinz ruht im Bett, Dorwood kann mit seinen 16 Jahren noch an den Mahlzeiten der Kinderküche von 15.30 bis 16.00 Uhr teilnehmen und ist gerade nach dort gegangen, so bin ich der Rest unserer anfänglichen Tischgesellschaft im Recreation-Room. An den Nachbartischen sitzen andere Emigranten, die teils Zeitschriften oder Bücher studieren; wieder andere sind untereinander und mit ihren Besuchen in lebhaften Gesprächen verwickelt, und ein an der Decke befestigter Lautsprecher überträgt in einer fast unangenehmen Lautstärke das Programm von Radio Bremen.

Soeben habe ich mir in der Bibliothek eine Bibel entliehen. Nach einigem Suchen fand ich den Predigttext von heute morgen im 10. Kapitel des Matthäus-Evangeliums in den Versen 16 bis 22 verzeichnet. Was willst du denn mit einer Bibel? So war die Frage von Hans Schmitt, eine bezeichnende Frage für einen, der wie er bei jeder Gelegenheit mit einem zotigen Witz oder einer schamlosen Redensart zu imponieren glaubt, dessen geistlos albernes Gerede jedoch in unserer Gemeinschaft keinen Widerhall findet!

June 9

There's something new every day! That's what Mr. Petzinger in my Frankfurt office used to say, and he would be able to repeat it almost daily if he were here in my stead.

Today we succeeded in contacting the lady from ACCR. She was very nice and particularly happy about Heinz's language ability. She then explained the actual purpose for the conversation, showed us a form, which by signing, meant we agreed to repay the $311 for the passage to America. ACCR puts the money up front and places no pressure at all on the sponsored individuals for repayment within a given time period. The committee leaves repayment up to the individual's means and discretion. I hope not to remain a debtor for too long, so that I can feel inner freedom, for I'm convinced that no pressure will be exerted on me.

I have to take a moment now to recollect how long it has been since we left home. Barely a week has passed but it seems like an eternity. Our mother must often think of her two boys. How will the two girls help ease her daily work-load? Today, or at least at the moment, I don't feel any homesickness at leaving. No doubt that's because of all the daily new impressions which first have to be digested. But when the daily grind sets in again, then my thoughts will cross the great water and my heart will engage in silent dialogue with mother. Perhaps at that time the words I said a few years ago will be prophetically fulfilled, when I wrote in my journal: 'If tomorrow the weapons should cease their work and everyone were to embrace one another with joy, I would nonetheless remember that precious time, for I shared it with my mother!'

9. Juni

Jeden Tag was Neues! So sagte auch Herr Petzinger in meinem Frankfurter Büro, und er würde es fast täglich wiederholen können, wenn er an meiner Statt hier wäre.

Heute gelang es uns, die Dame vom ACCR zu erreichen. Sie war sehr nett und über Heinz' Sprachkenntnisse besonders erfreut. Den eigentlichen Zweck der Rücksprache erläuterte sie alsdann, unterbreitete ein Formular, und mit der Unterschrift haben wir anerkannt, dass wir die 311 Dollar für die Überfahrt zurückzuzahlen haben. ACCR legt also den Betrag vor und drängt keinesfalls auf eine zeitgebundene Rückerstattung. Das Committee überlässt den Betreuten die Begleichung nach Können und Willen. Ich hoffe, nicht allzulang Schuldner zu bleiben, damit ich auch innerlich frei werde, und davon kann ich überzeugt sein, dass man keinen Druck ausüben wird.

In Gedanken muss ich erst einmal überschlagen, wie lange wir nun schon von zu Hause weg sind. Kaum eine Woche ist vergangen und doch dünkt mich es eine Ewigkeit. Oft wird unsere Mutter an ihre beiden Buben denken. Wie werden ihr die Mädchen die tägliche Last erleichtern? Heute oder augenblicklich empfinde ich noch keinen Abschiedsschmerz. Das kommt wohl von den täglich neuen Eindrücken, die erst alle einmal verdaut werden wollen. Wenn aber der Alltag wieder sein Regiment antritt, dann werden die Gedanken auch über das große Wasser schweifen, und das Herz wird sich in stummer Zwiesprache mit der Mutter auseinander setzen. Dann werden die vor ein paar Jahren gesprochenen Worte vielleicht ihre prophetische Erfüllung finden, als ich in mein Tagebuch schrieb: „Mögen dereinst die Waffen ruhen und alle Menschen mögen sich vor Freude in die Arme sinken, so werde ich dennoch jener köstlichen Zeit gedenken, denn ich habe meine Mutter gehabt!"

June 10

Yesterday afternoon also brought meaningful news. I received my boat ticket from the shipping company USL, i.e., United States Lines. Next to the departure date of June 12th is the name of the ship, the Ernie Pyle, and my cabin is also listed as C20-101. In my estimation there's nothing that can now stand in the way of our pending journey, and it's possible that by tomorrow we'll be moved to Bremerhaven.

Heinz was already complaining about a headache after lunch, and attributes this and the diarrhea that had begun earlier to the unappetizing canned fish that was served yesterday evening. So he went to bed and used the afternoon for a recuperative sleep. We were disturbed by the fever that nonetheless ensued, and this morning we were glad to find that the pills that a roommate had given him had driven away the annoying headache and fever.

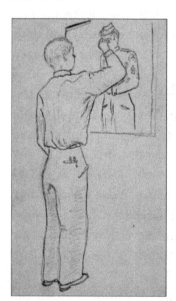

Yesterday afternoon, while Dorwood was practicing drawing a soldier on the chalkboard, I attempted to sketch him doing this. We spent the evening together with Traude Naumann playing an extremely interesting game called Bingo in the big room of Eisenhower Hall. This game, which is similar to a lottery, is won by the player who can demonstrate that he has a complete horizontal or vertical row of numbers from among those that have been called. Among the prizes being distributed were chocolate, combs, toothbrushes, toothpaste, and other objects. Since these were all things that were generally withheld from the emigrants, the money being collected (1 card for 1 mark, and almost 200 players per game) has to be seen as illegitimately gained money, and evidence of the extreme business sense of the organizers. For me, the most interesting part of the whole evening was studying the different players and their notion of fair play. Afterwards we three chatted for a while in the social room, and before that I'd also quickly checked up to ensure that Heinz was sleeping peacefully.

10. Juni

Auch der gestrige Nachmittag brachte Neuigkeiten von bedeutsamem Wert. Durch die Schiffahrtsgesellschaft USL, wörtlich United States Lines, erhielt ich meine Schiffskarte, auf der neben dem Abfahrtsdatum 12. 6.!, der Name des Schiffes „Ernie Pyle" und das Bordquartier mit C 20-101 angegeben sind. Nun kann sich nach meinem Ermessen der vorliegenden Reise kein Hindernis mehr in den Weg stellen, und möglicherweise werden wir schon morgen nach Bremerhaven befördert.

Schon nach dem Mittagessen klagte Heinz über Kopfschmerzen und führt dies mit dem vorher aufgetretenen Durchfall auf den Genuss der Fischkonserven zurück, die am Vorabend verabreicht wurden und wenig appetitlich waren. Deshalb begab er sich zu Bett und nutzte den Nachmittag zu einem erholenden Schlaf. Das trotzdem eintretende Fieber beunruhigte uns, und heute morgen waren wir recht froh, als die Tabletten eines Zimmergenossen ihm neben den lästigen Kopfschmerzen auch das Fieber ausgetrieben hatten.

Gestern Nachmittag war es auch, als Dorwood kreidezeichnend einen Soldaten an die Tafel praktizierte und ich ihn bei dieser Tätigkeit zu skizzieren versuchte. Den Abend verbrachten wir gemeinsam mit Traude Naumann bei einem überaus interessanten Gesellschaftsspiel „Bingo" im großen Saal der Eisenhower-Hall. Dieses lotterieähnliche Spiel bringt dem einen Gewinn, der auf seiner mit Ziffern versehenen Tafel nach den aufgerufenen Zahlen als erster in horizontaler oder vertikaler Anordnung eine vollständige Reihe aufweisen kann. Als Gewinne wurden Schokolade, Kämme, Zahnbürste und -paste sowie andere Gegenstände verteilt. Da es sich um Dinge  gehandelt haben dürfte, die man den Emigranten vorenthält, so sind auch die eingenommenen Beträge als unrechtmäßig erworbenes Geld anzusehen (1 Karte = 1 RM; ca. 200 Spieler) und ein Zeugnis von der rigorosen Geschäftstüchtigkeit der Veranstalter. Das Studium der verschiedenen Spieler und ihre Auffassung von „fair play" war für mich die interessanteste Seite des ganzen Abends. Nachher plauderten wir drei noch eine Weile im Unterhaltungszimmer, und ich hatte mich zuvor noch schnell vergewissert, dass Heinz ruhig schlief.

Today brought a particularly happy event: a visit from Fräulein Irene Jürgens, who had not balked at the trek from Eggese in order once again to wish us luck. The event of the day for Dorwood was a visit from his father, most especially because he brought an accordion with him. It's little wonder that Dorwood immediately fell in love with the instrument and couldn't get enough of its mellow tones.

Mr. Blumenschein, Dorwood's father, is now the only member of his family still remaining in Germany, for his wife and both younger children had already returned to their land of birth last year, and Dorwood is in the process of joining them, Mr. Blumenschein is waiting for an early decision which would allow him, as a former member of the German armed forces, to travel to his new homeland.

In the course of the afternoon I wrote to my friend, Werner. He was a dear friend to me, and I'll be glad if we can share our experiences through regular correspondence. My friend, Rico, still has no clue that I'm emigrating. Is it cowardice or fear that I'll get into an argument with him? It's also my own uncertainty as to whether we'll continue to understand each other as well, after believing that study was the right choice, an incentive and justification for both of us. It's quite clear to me that the desired goal of higher education could only have been achieved with a great deal of sacrifice, although I had reached the conclusion that it was certainly possible. And surely I showed that I was serious about it by sacrificing my vacation time, and, by dint of strong willpower, performed the labor detail that was a pre-requisite, only fourteen days before making this momentous decision.

Ein besonders freudiges Ereignis brachte der heutige Tag im Besuch von Fräulein Irene Jürgens, die den Weg von Eggese nach hier nicht scheute, um uns nochmals Lebewohl zu sagen. Für Dorwood war das Tagesereignis ein Besuch seines Vaters, das seine besondere Note in dem mitgebrachten Akkordeon hatte; kein Wunder, dass Dorwood sich sofort in das schöne Instrument verliebt hatte und an den vollen Klängen kaum satthören konnte.

Herr Blumenschein, Dorwoods Vater, ist nunmehr das letzte Glied seiner Familie hier in Deutschland, denn nachdem seine Frau und die beiden jüngeren Kinder bereits im letzten Jahr in ihr Geburtsland zurückgekehrt sind und Dorwood im Begriffe steht, ihnen nachzukommen, harrt Herr Blumenschein einer baldigen Entscheidung, die es auch ihm als einem ehemaligen Wehrmachtsangehörigen ermöglicht, in die Wahlheimat zu reisen.

Im Laufe des Nachmittags schrieb ich an Freund Werner. Er war mir ein lieber Kamerad, und ich bin froh, wenn wir in regelmäßigem Gedankenaustausch von unseren Erlebnissen berichten wollen. Freund Rico weiß noch immer kein Wort von meiner Auswanderung. Ist es Feigheit oder Angst von mir, mich mit ihm auseinanderzusetzen? Das ist auch meine eigne Ungewissheit, ob wir uns hinfort noch so gut verstehen können, nachdem wir einander im Studium Neigung, Ansporn und Bewährung wähnten! Es ist für mich ganz klar, dass diese gewünschte Entwicklung nicht ohne große Opfer durchzuführen gewesen wäre, wenn ich auch die Überzeugung gewonnen hatte, dass es durchaus möglich sei. Und da ich noch 14 Tage vor dieser richtungweisenden Entscheidung unter Opferung meines Erholungsurlaubes und mit festem Willen beseelt, den für das Studium notwendigen Arbeitseinsatz ableistete, beweist wohl, dass es mir ernst gewesen war.

It would have been very advantageous if I had considered emigrating only after completing my studies. Nonetheless, I chose the difficult and uncertain path, trusting my own strength, health, and my desire for external and internal freedom. For this reason, perhaps it's understandable that I say goodbye without any great difficulty to the civil service and more broadly to the circumstances of daily life, where a merciless egoism is disguised under the mask of bourgeois individuality. It might seem as if I'm trying to avoid this struggle against conventionality, but that's not true, for I know the same prejudices are to be overcome over there (*in the U.S.*) as well. But I hope to have an opportunity, through iron determination and personal ability and decency, to reach a level of life where one's eyes aren't so focused on the depths of human problems. I am not entertaining any illusions, and certainly expect a hard struggle for basic existence.

Those who think it incomprehensible that I am leaving my mother behind in this time of need should remember that the former times, which were so filled with hard work and ample worries, brought no visible improvement in life. The coming era, however, will give me the means to provide my mother tangible help in the form of Care packages. If I manage to do this, I'll have attained an intermediate goal and then I'll be happy that I dared take this step into a new life.

In the evening, the dance music lured Dorwood, Traude and Heinz, along with other happy dancers, into the big room of Eisenhower Hall, from where the sounds of waltzes and tangos reached to the recreation room, where I was able to continue my journal and write a letter to Rico undisturbed.

Von sehr großem Vorteil wäre es auch gewesen, wenn ich erst nach Beendigung des Studiums den Gedanken einer Auswanderung erwogen hätte. Trotzdem wählte ich den schweren und ungewissen Weg im Vertrauen auf die eigne Kraft, Gesundheit und den Willen der äußeren wie der inneren Freiheit. So ist es auch wohl verständlich, wenn ich ohne große Hemmung im besonderen dem Staatsdienst und im allgemeinen der täglichen Umgebung Lebewohl sage, wo man unter der Maske bürgerlicher Individuen einen erbarmungslosen Egoismus verbirgt. Es könnte mithin scheinen, dass ich diesem Kampf wider die spießbürgerliche Welt aus dem Wege gehe, doch ist dies irrig, weil ich weiß, drüben sind die gleichen Vorurteile zu bekämpfen. Ich erhoffe aber dort eine Möglichkeit, durch eisernes Beharren und persönliches Können im Verein mit Anständigkeit ein Niveau zu erreichen, das den Blick nicht zu sehr an die Tiefen der menschlichen Problematik fesselt. Ich geb mich keiner Illusion hin und erwarte mit Bestimmtheit einen harten Existenzkampf.

Wem es unverständlich erscheinen mag, wenn ich in dieser Notzeit meine Mutter zurücklasse, der halte sich vor Augen, wie die mit viel Arbeit und noch mehr Sorgen angefüllte rückwärtige Zeit doch keine sichbaren Lebenserleichterungen brachte. Die kommende Aera wird mir aber die Handhabe dazu geben, meiner Mutter tatsächliche Hilfe in Form von Lebensmittelsendungen spenden zu können. Nach diesem Gelingen habe ich ein vorläufiges Ziel erreicht, und ich werde mich dann freuen, dass ich diesen Schritt in ein neues Leben gewagt habe.

Am Abend lockte die Tanzmusik neben dem andern tanzlustigen Völkchen auch Dorwood, Traude und Heinz in den großen Saal der Eisenhower-Hall, von wo die Walzer- und Tangoklänge bis in den Recreation-Room kamen, in dem ich ungestört das Tagesjournal ergänzen und einen Brief an Rico schreiben konnte.

June 11

What Miss Gates was able to tell us today about the ACCR sounds quite confident; after all, there's no need to be paralyzed by fear at the last minute about the great unknown. The embarkation which was scheduled for tomorrow will not take place, so we'll be in Bremen for another day, or perhaps longer. Apparently the Ernie Pyle is undergoing repairs. But all of this doesn't change anything about the experience that will grant us a new life over there in America. Miss Gates told us, through an interpreter, that upon arrival in America we would be received, looked after, and also helped to find work. That piece of news took a burden from us. She further recommended that we not stay in New York, as there were representatives of the ACCR in all states, who were keen to take us under their wing, just as a father cares for his children. In conclusion, candy was bestowed on the children, which was a very nice gesture; no doubt Miss Gates had brought the candy along for this express purpose.

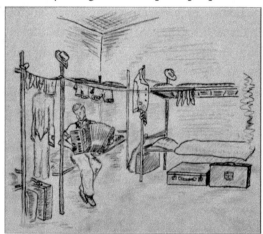

Now that we've completed all the requisite formalities, life is starting to become boring here. As a consequence of the cold and unfriendly weather, no one has much interest in going outside, and no doubt the lack of interest in doing something different can be ascribed to the lack of exercise and of appetite. Dorwood plays around on his accordion to the point of insanity, or tries not to fall prey to lethargy by using his gramophone, and I write in my journal or write letters as if I've never done anything else in my life. The orchestra rescued us for two hours, and yet none of this makes the golden cage bearable in the long run. Despite its good quality, even the daily sameness of the food doesn't please me any more; rather my thoughts go longingly to the boiled potatoes and green salad of home.

11. Juni

Was uns heute Miss Gates vom ACCR mitteilte, klingt recht zuversichtlich, und es braucht einem nicht noch in letzter Stunde die Angst vor der großen Ungewißheit den Hals zuzusschnüren. Die ursprünglich für morgen vorgesehene Einschiffung kann noch nicht stattfinden, und wir sind einen Tag oder unter Umstanden noch länger in Bremen. Die „Ernie Pyle" soll sich in Reperatur befinden. All dies ändert ja nichts mehr an dem Erlebnis, das uns drüben in Amerika ein neues Leben vermitteln soll! Miss Gates ließ uns verdolmetschen, dass wir bei der Ankunft empfangen, betreut und auch in Arbeitsverhältnisse eingewiesen werden. Dadurch wurde uns eine Sorge genommen. Sie empfal weiter, nicht in New York zu bleiben, denn in allen Provinzen des Landes leben die Vertreter von ACCR, die für uns aufkommen wollen, wie ein Vater für seine Kinder sorgt! Eine schöne Geste war die anschließende Bescherung der Kinder mit Süßigkeiten, die Miss Gates wohl eigens zu diesem Zweck mitgebracht haben dürfte.

Nach Beendigung aller notwendigen Formalitäten fängt das Leben hier an, langweilig zu werden. Infolge des kalten und unfreundlichen Wetters hat keiner große Lust, außer Haus zu gehen, und der mangelnden Bewegung ist wohl auch neben der Appetitlosigkeit die Interessenlosigkeit an einem Abwechselung bringenden Unternehmen zuzuschreiben. Dorwood orgelt bis an die Grenzen der Vernunft auf seinem Akkordeon oder versucht durch die Betätigung seines Grammophons keiner apathischen Lethargie zu verfallen, und ich schreibe Tagebuch und Briefe, als hätte ich im Leben nie anderes zu tun gehabt. Für 2 Stunden erlöste uns das Unterhaltungsorchester, doch ist dies alles nicht dazu angetan, den goldenen Käfig auf längere Zeit erträglich zu gestalten. Auch das täglich gleichbleibende Essen erbaut mich trotz seiner hohen Qualität nicht mehr, sondern die Gedanken bewegen sich sehnsüchtig nach heimatlichen Pellkartoffeln und grünem Salat.

Starting a few days ago, a Mr. Henning, who claims to be a graduate trade school teacher and professor at Frankfurt University, has begun to show evidence of being quite a corrupt person. This is all the more regrettable for his nonsensical poetry is injurious to his nimbus as an intelligent person, and would be better not repeated in front of us young people. I'm at a loss to know how he can take pleasure in such crude sayings in the presence of the Poles, as a German and particularly as a representative of the educated social class. I might add that, in light of the Poles' anti-German attitude, there is no longer any prospect of reciprocal respect occurring.

However if I were to identify this as the reason for the unpleasantness, it means that I'm not willing to remain aloof from the matter. Dorwood, despite his almost presumptuous arrogance, is not so neutral, and his stubborn persistence is a personal peculiarity, and can be ascribed to the inexperience of his youth.

June 14

Now that I'm aboard the "Ernie Pyle," I'm once again finding the time to make my journal entries; and I want to look back and recall recent events.

When it first became known that the ship would, in fact, not be departing on June 12th, rumors flew from all kinds of absolutely "reliable" sources. However, the rumor that our ship would not put to sea until the 30th of this month could not be outdone by any others.

Seit einigen Tagen offenbart sich ein Herr Henning, der Diplom-Handelsschullehrer und Dozent an der Frankfurter Universität gewesen sein will, als ein ganz verdorbenes Individuum. Dies ist umso bedauerlicher, da seine perversen Knittelverse nicht nur seinem Nimbus als intelligentem Menschen abträglich sind und besser nicht vor uns jungen Leuten deklariert würden. Es ist mir unverständlich, wie er sich vor den anwesenden Polen als Deutscher und gar als Repräsentant der akademisch gebildeten Volksklasse in solch ordinären Aussprüchen gefallen kann. Ich konnte daraufhin beobachten, dass bei der deutschfeindlichen Einstellung der Polen ohnehin von einer gegenseitigen Achtung nicht mehr die Rede sein kann.

Wenn ich dies jedoch als einen Anlass des Ärgernisses bezeichnen würde, so bedeutete es, dass ich nicht gewillt bin, über der Sache zu stehen. Dorwood ist trotz seiner fast anmaßenden Überheblichkeit nicht so überparteilich, und sein eigensinniges Beharren ist eine persönliche Eigenart, und der Unerfahrenheit seiner Jugend zuzuschreiben.

14. Juni

Erst an Bord der „Ernie Pyle" komme ich wieder zur Eintragung, und in rückschauender Betrachtung will ich mir die Ereignisse wieder in die Erinnerung rufen.

Als erst einmal bekannt wurde, dass das Schiff tatsächlich nicht am 12. Juni fahren kann, überstürzten sich die Parolen aus den unbedingt „sicheren" Quellen. Das Gerücht, dass unser Schiff erst am 30. dieses Monats in See stechen könne, dürfte dabei aber nicht übertroffen worden sein.

In this atmosphere of uncertainty the announcement posted on the afternoon of June 12 put an end to all the speculation. It displayed clearly the check-in times for the following day. That evening, we went to bed early, and, despite the unreasonable noise of the Poles, were well rested the following morning. Breakfast was from 6:30 on; our linens were returned and the remaining formalities were accomplished so early that we were seated in the train a full hour before the scheduled departure time.

After being shunted around a bit, we set off for Bremerhaven without any particular delays. The rails ran all the way to the pier and barely twenty meters from our stopping place, the "Ernie Pyle" lay alongside the dock. We had a very good impression of this clean ship, though as landlubbers we viewed the voyage across the ocean with some trepidation. Holding their landing cards in their hands, each person was shown inside. We first crossed the gangway, then walked down three stairways, and arrived at our cabin. Heinz, Dorwood, and I are once again together, not far from Hans Schmitt. All this happened at about 2 o'clock in the afternoon, and it was a disappointment to learn that, contrary to the needs of our stomachs, dinner was announced for six o'clock.

Directly behind us, the larger troop carrier, the "William Alexander," lay at anchor, though our "tub" with its 12,000 gross tonnage is also a sizeable ship. The passengers had disappeared quickly into its voracious stomach, but stowing the luggage took much longer. It was interesting to watch the well-functioning teamwork of a specialized vehicle (caterpillar crane) on the loading dock with the cargo derrick on our ship. The boxes and suitcases swayed from the train to the quay, like in a housewife's huge shopping net; once there, they were carried again as if by strong arms, high above our heads, and also disappeared through a loading hatch into the hold of the ship.

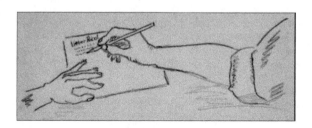

In dieser Ungewissheit berichtigte der Anschlag am Nachmittag des 12. Juni alle Vermutungen. Auf diesem standen in klarer Folge die tags darauf einzuhaltenden Abfertigungszeiten. Abends legten wir uns zeitig ins Bett und waren, trotz des ungebührlichen Lärms der Polen, morgens gut ausgeruht. Bereits von 6.30 Uhr an war Frühstückzeit, die Wäsche abzugeben und die restlichen Formalitäten waren so früh beendet, dass wir eine ganze Stunde vor der planmäßigen Abfahrt im Eisenbahnzug saßen.

Nach einigen Rangierbewegungen eilten wir dann ohne besondere Aufenthalte nach Bremerhaven. Dort verliefen die Gleise bis zum Kai und keine 20 Meter seitlich von unserer Haltestelle lag die „Ernie Pyle" im Wasser. Der Eindruck von diesem sauberen Schiff war denkbar gut, wenn wir auch als Landratten dem Ozeanfahrzeug mit einigem Misstrauen gegenüber standen. Mit der Schiffskarte in der Hand wurde jeder in das Innere verwiesen. Zunächst ging es über einen Laufsteg hinauf, dann 3 Treppen hinunter und wir hatten unsern Schlafraum erreicht. Heinz, Dorwood und ich sind wieder beieinander, dazu unweit Hans Schmitt. Dies geschah etwa um zwei Uhr mittags und es war eine Enttäuschung, als die Zeit des Abendessens entgegen den Bedürfnissen unserer Mägen für sechs Uhr kund war.

Gleich hinter uns lag der größere Truppentransporter „William Alexander" vor Anker, doch auch unser „Pott" ist mit seinen 12.000 Bruttoregistertonnen ein ansehnliches Schiff. Die Passagiere waren schnell in seinem gefräßigen Leib verschwunden, mehr Zeit nahm das Verstauen des Gepäcks in Anspruch. Hierbei war die Beobachtung der gut funktionierenden Zusammenarbeit eines auf der Ladestraße stationierten Spezialfahrzeuges (Raupenkran) mit dem Ladebaum unseres Schiffes interessant. Wie in einem riesigen Einkaufsnetz unserer Hausfrauen schwebten die Kisten und Koffer vom Zuge zum Kai, wurden dort nochmals wie von starken Armen erfasst, hoch über unseren Köpfen bewegt und verschwanden dann gleichfalls durch eine Ladeluke im Innern.

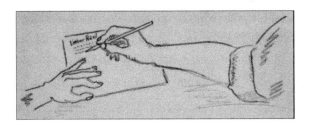

When some harbor tugs came alongside shortly thereafter and a pilot climbed aboard from one of them, we knew that the voyage was about to begin. At the signal of a ship's officer, the hawser on land was cast off and pulled in. The tugs towed the Ernie Pyle into deeper water and when she was able to move under her own power, they returned to the harbor. After a sun-deprived week, the warming sun shone from a bright blue sky and white and grey seagulls circled the ship. To the supposedly superstitious seamen, this Friday the 13th did not seem unlucky enough to delay our departure. Sounding her horn three times, the ship left the harbor. The shore retreated more and more and we knew our homeland was disappearing from the visible horizon. But the same was not true in our hearts, for there our home-loving youth lives on in our memories. We sent greetings with all ships traveling landward.

At first, everyone found the lightly swaying movement quite unaccustomed, and none of the passengers could accept the thought that it really wasn't anything to worry about. Nonetheless, we admired the fishermen passing by in their nutshells, as their work demands more sheer courage than just once going on board a large ship.

I thought that staying out in the fresh air was the best remedy for sea sickness. Little wonder then, that mistrusting the bad air of our swaying sleeping quarters, I stayed on deck till the early morning hours, and again returned to the fresh air after a brief sleep. More than a hundred people are accommodated in bunk beds in the big dormitory room of the former troop carrier. The almost unbearable atmosphere is improved somewhat through the ongoing hum of the ventilators.

At eight o'clock, breakfast is served in the "cafeteria." Previously unfamiliar dishes are served on the trays we've become familiar with since Bremen. Two eggs, boiled, baked or scrambled, are the main ingredient. In addition, the morning soup and a pat of butter are put on the tray by the Negro servers. The special item of the day is usually the fruit; grapefruit and oranges represent unfamiliar or long-denied pleasures. Then you proceed to one of the many tables, where coffee, milk, and tea, freshly baked white bread and orange marmalade are offered in unlimited quantities.

The same could be said of the midday meal served around one p.m., but staying with this topic of food might be seen as proof of how meager or how humble our former life was.

Als wenig später einige Hafenschlepper beilegten und von ihnen ein Lotse überstieg, wußten wir, dass die Fahrt beginnen würde. Auf den Wink eines Schiffsoffiziers wurden die Taue an Land gelöst und eingeholt; die Schlepper zogen die „Ernie Pyle" in tieferes Wasser, und nachdem sie sich durch eigene Kraft fortbewegte, kehrten die Schlepper in den Hafen zurück. Seit einer sonnenentwöhnten Woche schien von strahlend blauem Himmel die wärmende Sonne, und die weißen und grauen Möven umkreisten das Schiff. Auch die angeblich abergläubigen Seeleute maßen dem auf einen Freitag fallenden 13. Monatstag nicht jene unselige Bedeutung zu, dass die Ausfahrt etwa verschoben hätte werden müssen. Nach dreimaligem Aufheulen der Sirene verließ das Schiff den Hafen. Immer weiter wich das Land zurück und wir wußten, dass unsere Heimat am sichtbaren Horizont verschwand. Nicht so im Herzen, denn dort wohnt mit der Erinnerung die ganze heimatgebundene Jugend. Allen landwärts fahrenden Schiffen geben wir Grüße mit.

Zunächst kam jedem die leicht schlinkernde Bewegung sehr ungewohnt vor, und keiner der Passagiere konnte sich mit dem Gedanken befreunden, dass dies eben noch „gar nichts" sei. Immerhin bewunderten wir die vorbeifahrenden Fischer auf ihren Nußschalen, deren Beruf mehr Wagemut erfordert als das einmalige Besteigen eines Großschiffes.

Ich hielt den Aufenthalt an der frischen Luft für die beste Medizin gegen Seekrankheit. Kein Wunder, dass ich infolge großen Misstrauens wider die schlechte Luft unseres schaukelnden Schlafraumes bis in die frühen Morgenstunden an Deck blieb und dann nach kurzem Schlaf an die frische Luft zurückkehrte. Über einhundert Personen sind in der Großkabine des ehemaligen Truppentransporters auf zweistöckigen Betten untergebracht. Die fast unerträgliche Atmosphäre wird lediglich durch immerwährendes Arbeiten der Ventilatoren etwas gebessert.

Um acht Uhr wird in der „Cafeteria" das Frühstück ausgegeben. Auf den seit Bremen bekannten Tabletts werden allerdings bisher unbekannte Genüsse dargereicht. Zwei Eier, gekocht, gebacken oder in Form von Rührei, bilden den Hauptinhalt. Dazu werden von den bedienenden Negern die Morgensuppe und ein Stückchen Butter auf das Tablett geladen. Als besondere Zutat kann gleichfalls das verabreichte Obst gelten, wobei Grapefruit und Orange unbekannte oder doch langentbehrte Genüsse darstellen. Damit begibt man sich zu einem der vielen Tische, und dort bieten sich Kaffee, Milch und Tee sowie stets frisch gebackenes Weißbrot und Apfelsinenkonfitüre in unbeschränktem Umfange an.

Von der Mittagsmahlzeit ab ein Uhr könnte gleiches gesagt werden, doch wäre das Verweilen bei diesem Thema lediglich als ein Beweis dafür zu erachten, wie armselig oder doch bescheiden das bisherige Leben geführt werden musste.

June 18

I had actually wanted to write in this book every day, but I had neither desire nor time to do so because of the energy I expended combating sea sickness. By now, my body has gotten more or less used to the rocking motion, since today is already our fifth day underway.

After the English coast with its steep chalk cliffs became visible on the afternoon of the second day of the voyage, and the cape of Norfolk was passed the following morning, only the restless sea will be visible until our arrival in New York. For lack of anything better to do, I spent hours each day watching the foaming waves chase one another. In doing so, I often enjoyed the company of a young Greek woman who is traveling to New York to join her bridegroom. For the first time, Dorwood came up on deck again today and ate heartily at mealtimes, after the restless sea had condemned him, like most other passengers, to the sufferings of seasickness and confined him to bed. During this time I supplied him with the necessary "munchies." Heinz and I were affected far less by it, and our excellent appetites even currently demand that we go for seconds at every meal. In the meantime I received my three dollars of ship's money, and, feeling like a rich man, allowed myself to make a loan to Dorwood, who had not received any ship's money. With it, you can buy cigarettes, chocolate, and drinks at a canteen that's open every night.

The weather leaves much to be desired, for, other than for a few hours now and then, the sun remains hidden behind thick veils of clouds. Spending time on deck allows one to observe an interesting drama. For it often seems as if the ship is about to shoot into the sea, when, after continual rocking up and down, the bow is lifted up by a particularly mountainous wave. Other than that, the Ernie Pyle is a good ship and has already completed half of the voyage. The engines work unceasingly and the churning spray of the wash comes together again and again with the foam-topped waves formed by the bow. We draw closer to America by about sixteen to eighteen knots per hour. Our goal will be realized by Sunday or Monday, so the ship's crew tells us.

18. Juni

Eigentlich wollte ich jeden Tag in dieses Buch schreiben, doch hatte ich durch die Energieleistung gegen die Seekrankheit weder Lust noch Zeit hierzu. Nunmehr hat sich der Körper wesentlich auf die Schaukelei eingestellt, sind wir doch auch heute den fünften Tag unterwegs.

Nachdem am Nachmittag des zweiten Reisetages die englische Küste mit ihren steilen Kreidefelsen sichtbar wurde und am folgenden Morgen das Kap von Norfolk umschifft war, bleibt bis zur Ankunft in New York nur das unruhig wogende Meer sichtbar. Mangels einer besseren Beschäftigung beobachte ich täglich stundenlang das jagende Spiel der schäumenden Wogen. Dabei genoß ich oft die Gesellschaft einer jungen Griechin, die zu ihrem Bräutigam nach New York fährt. Dorwood war heute erstmals wieder an Deck und nahm mit gutem Appetit an den Mahlzeiten teil, nachdem ihn die unruhige See wie die meisten Passagiere zu den Leiden einer Seekrankheit verurteilt und ans Bett gefesselt hatte. In dieser Zeit versorgte ich ihn mit den notwendigen „Fressalien". Heinz und ich wurden weniger davon betroffen und unser ausgezeichneter Appetit verlangt zuweilen sogar eine Wiederholung der betreffenden Mahlzeit. Inzwischen erhielt ich meine dreieinhalb Dollar Bordgeld und, immerhin schon ein vermögender Mann, kann ich mir gestatten, Dorwood, der kein Bordgeld erhielt, ein Darlehen zu gewähren!! In einer allabendlich geöffneten Kantine kann man Zigaretten, Schokolade und Getränke erwerben.

Das Wetter lässt sehr zu wünschen übrig, denn außer wenigen Stunden hält sich die Sonne hinter dichten Wolkenschleiern verborgen. Ein interessantes Schauspiel offenbart der Aufenthalt an Deck. Denn oftmals hat es den Anschein, als wolle das Schiff ins Meer schießen, wenn nach ständigem Aufundab der Bug von einem besonders großen Wellenberg emporgehoben wurde. Ansonsten ist die „Ernie Pyle" ein braves Schiff und hat schon die Hälfte des Weges zurückgelegt. Unaufhörlich arbeiten die Maschinen und die wirbelnde Gischt des Heckwassers vereint sich immer wieder mit den schaumgekrönten Wellen der Bugseen. Sechszehn bis achtzehn Knoten kommen wir in der Stunde Amerika näher. Bereits am Sonntag oder Montag wird das Ziel erreicht sein, so sagen auch die Leute von der Schiffsmannschaft.

When we arrive, this carefree life will be over, with its bell calling us to ample meals at eight, one, and six o'clock. On the other hand, this situation only has limited appeal. Without any duties and responsibilities this life would succeed only in turning us into lazybones. Nighttime movies offer some change of pace, but not for me, since I have as little interest in these as I do in the card games that most of the passengers indulge in.

Yesterday, when I received my visa at the counter of the Purser's Office, after handing in my custom's declaration form, there was an old man standing there helplessly with his blank forms. As it turned out, as an ethnic German he had been brought back from Bukowina before the war and could neither read nor write. I completed his forms on his behalf, and since he couldn't even write his signature, signed his name at the bottom, "Johann Ackermann."

The little lover's quarrel between Dorwood and Traude is a comical intermezzo. Dorwood is sixteen, Traude, eighteen. It's funny because Dorwood, who otherwise tries to be so serious, and Traude, who's so shy, are acting like children. The whole business is unimportant to me, and moreover I doubt their seriousness. Heinz, on the other hand, is uncomfortable, almost indignant, that the two of them have something going on beyond the usual norms of a friendship. Now all three of them have gone to watch a movie together, and I've jotted down a few thoughts so that there won't be too large a gap in these pages.

Dann hört das sorglose Leben auf, in dem jeweils um acht, eins und sechs Uhr eine Glocke zu den reichhaltigen Mahlzeiten ruft. Allerdings hat dieser Zustand nur bedingt seine Reize. Ohne Pflichten und ohne Verantwortung ist dieses Leben dazu angetan, uns zu Faulenzern zu erziehen. Abends bieten Filmvorführungen einige Abwechselung, doch nicht für mich, der diesen ebensowenig Interesse entgegenbringen kann wie dem stark gepflogenen Kartenspiel.

Als ich gestern nach Abgabe der Zollerklärung das Visum am Schalter des „Purser's office" erhielt, stand ein alter Mann ratlos vor seinem unausgefüllten Vordruck. Wie sich dann ergeben hat, ist jener vor dem Kriege als „Volksdeutscher" aus der Bukowina rückgeführt worden und verfügt weder über Lese- noch Schreibkenntnisse. Ich habe ihm das Formular ausgefüllt und da er sogar zu einer Unterschrift unfähig war, für ihn seinen Namen darunter gesetzt „Johann Ackermann".

Ein possierliches Zwischenspiel mit einer komischen Seite ist das kleine Liebesgeplänkel zwischen Dorwood und Traude. Dorwood ist 16 Jahre und Traude ist 18 Jahre alt. Komisch deshalb, weil der sonst so ernst sein wollende Dorwood und das zurückhaltende Fräulein sich dabei wie die Kinder benehmen. Mir ist die Sache unwichtig, außerdem bezweifle ich jede Ernsthaftigkeit. Heinz hingegen ist unangenehm berührt, ja fast empört, dass diese beiden sich außerhalb der kameradschaftlichen Gepflogenheiten bewegen. Nun sind die drei gemeinsam zu einer Kinovorstellung gegangen und ich habe einige Gedanken niedergeschrieben, damit keine allzugroße Lücke in diesen Blättern entsteht.

June 19

To many passengers, the voyage seems unbearably long. But for even more people, the time spent on board will never be forgotten. For where will such a comfortable life be possible again, along with such indolence? I'm not thinking so much of domestic comforts as of the ample kitchen, which has become the focal point of all daily happenings here. For example, today I ate four eggs at breakfast, for lunch had two helpings of the delicious dish of chicken thighs, and at dinner two pairs of sausages with sauerkraut. God knows, we're all becoming greedy gluttons! Dessert is a particular delicacy, especially when apples, oranges, grapefruit, pudding, or cakes are distributed; ice cream is also a luscious discovery.

Today the weather was totally calm. The ocean lay as if sleeping. Not a single swell disturbed the peaceful picture, and I saw a whale dive up and down for the first time. An exercise performed by the ship's company offered a diverse and entertaining sight. The siren sounded repeatedly and the alarm bells called the sailors to their stations. Fire extinguishers were tested and the lifeboats unfastened and swung out. In the course of these exercises, everyone, from the captain to the ship's cook, wore a lifejacket. Dorwood and I stayed out on deck for a while longer. Not so Heinz, who was suffering from a stomach ailment and stayed in bed.

Only three days to go to New York. Only a little while longer, then new problems will present themselves, and the solving of them will determine my daily routine. It's useless to fantasize about things that are hidden behind the curtain of the future and cannot be revealed. In one sense I'm even looking forward to it, for succeeding through my own abilities will help fulfill my dream of being able to provide for much of my dear mother's support. The day after tomorrow, she will celebrate her fifty-first birthday without any visible sign that I am with her in spirit. But surely she must feel and know that I'm thinking of her with special affection. I hope she isn't too affected by being so far away and that she isn't grieving over it. And I hope my sisters are easing her daily burden. A particular petition to God is that he'll spare her for me for a long while yet, for in all my memories of home, it is to her that I owe the most gratitude.

19. Juni

Vielen Passagieren scheint die Reise unerträglich lang. Aber noch mehr Leuten wird die Zeit an Bord unvergessen sein. Denn wo wird bei aller Untätigkeit ein derart komfortables Leben möglich sein? Ich denke nun nicht an häusliche Bequemlichkeit, sondern an die reichhaltige Küche, die nun einmal hier der Mittelpunkt aller Tagesereignisse bildet. Heute aß ich zum Beispiel beim Frühstück vier Eier, beim Mittagmahl gleich zweimal die köstliche Platte mit den Hühnerschenkeln und bei dem Abendmahl zwei paar Würstchen mit Sauerkraut. Weiß Gott, man wird noch zum Vielfraß! Eine besondere Delikatesse stellt der Nachtisch dar, wenn er in Äpfeln, Apfelsinen, Grapefruits, Pudding oder Kuchen zur Verteilung kommt; auch Eiscreme ist eine köstliche Erfindung.

Heute war es vollkommen windstill; die See lag wie schlafend. Keine Furche störte das friedliche Bild, und erstmals sah ich einen Walfisch auf- und niedertauchen. Eine Übung der Schiffsleute bot ein abwechselungsreiches Bild. Mehrmals ertönte die Sirene, und die Alarmglocken riefen die Mannschaften auf ihre Stationen. Löschgeräte und das Lösen und Ausschwenken der Rettungsboote wurden probiert. Dabei war jeder vom Kapitän bis zum Smutje mit einer Schwimmweste bekleidet. Dorwood und ich lagerten noch einige Zeit an Deck. Heinz dagegen litt unter Magenbeschwerden und hütete das Bett.

Noch drei Tage bis New York. Nur eine kurze Spanne noch, dann werden sich neue Probleme aufwerfen und deren Lösung den Alltag bestimmen. Es ist unnütz, über Dinge zu spinnen, die hinter dem Vorhang der Zukunft nicht zu entschleiern sind. Einesteils darf ich mich sogar darauf freuen, denn das Behaupten durch eigene Kraft wird dem Wunsche eine erstmögliche Erfüllung bringen, meiner lieben Mutter weitgehende Unterstützung zu gewähren. Übermorgen begeht sie ihren einundfünfzigsten Geburtstag ohne ein sichtbares Zeichen meiner Teilnahme. Aber sie muss es doch fühlen und wissen, dass ich ihrer in besonderer Herzlichkeit gedenke. Hoffentlich geht ihr das Fernsein nicht allzunahe und sie grämt sich nicht darob. Und hoffentlich erleichtern meine Schwestern ihr die tägliche Last. Ein besonderes Anliegen an den Herrgott ist, daß er sie mir noch recht lange erhält, denn in aller Erinnerung an die Heimat gebührt ihr die größte Dankbarkeit.

The first fruits of my garden must be approaching harvest about now, and they will be a significant help in alleviating housekeeping concerns. I wonder if my apple trees will bear fruit this year. Of one thing I'm sure: that my friend, Werner, will be of great help in the garden.

Oh! From what a perspective I can already view the daily difficulties of life in Germany! Without basic subsistence, the human spirit remains confused, in a fog, under an illusion of what might be the ideal. There is hunger and deprivation throughout the land, and yet a glance cast beyond the borders dispels the notion of a hungry world. I observe daily how any superfluous food is dumped into the sea!! The knowledge that people are finding jobs at home is a consolation. A new path is being sought and will be found, for with a good attitude a selfless frame of mind can only be a plus.

Nun müssen auch die ersten Früchte meines Gartens zur Reife gelangen und eine wesentliche Hilfe zur Behebung der hausfraulichen Sorgen sein. Ob wohl meine Apfelbäume einen Ertrag bringen? Eins weiß ich, im Garten wird mein Freund Werner ein braver Helfer sein!

Ach! Unter welchen Blickpunkten kann ich schon heute das tägliche Plagen in Deutschland betrachten! Ohne die nötigste Nahrung irrt der menschliche Geist im Wahne idealer Haltung im bedenklichen Zwielicht. Hunger und Not im ganzen Land; ein Blick über die Grenze aber zerreißt schon die Phrase von einer hungernden Welt. Täglich gehört es zu meinen Beobachtungen, wie die überflüssigen Speisen in das Meer geschüttet werden!! Ein Trost bleibt das Wissen, dass in der Heimat gearbeitet wird. Es wird ein neuer Weg gesucht und gefunden werden, weil bei gutem Willen eine selbstlose Haltung nur ein Plus bedeuten kann.

Friday, June 20

Warm thoughts of my mother today. Quite a distance still separates us from the American continent, but we'll have reached our destination in two days. Now we're on the threshold of the New World, and there's no doubt that a new life will soon begin. At first it will certainly be simpler and not as comfortable as regards domestic life. And it will be difficult at times, as long as I don't have a good command of the language. But this means future. The time that's gone before is behind me as one stage in my life. And it will always be a blessing for me and for everyone if I can see in this past stage of life an inexhaustible source of strength to keep friendly memories and gratitude toward those who were true friends, teachers and counselors, and thus helped prepare the way for these new possibilities.

And whom do I thank more than my mother? Subordinating all her own desires, she remained our only true friend through all the trials and tribulations. I'm sure I'll never be able to repay her in like measure, but I can act with true Christian love in faithfulness to her example by not glorifying myself in egoistic slavery. Was it right to leave her back home? I'm sure the leave-taking wasn't easy for her, and when she said, "My best goes with you!" they were no empty words. I hope her domestic peace can continue.

How will little Christel understand the absence of his uncles? I hope he'll grow up to be a good, useful man. And as for Hannele and Martin, the dear Dorfmarker children, I hope soon to have an opportunity to send the two little satellites some "treats" of which they've long been deprived, for how else can they be convinced that an Uncle Paul lives in America?

Last night I dreamed of Rico, and took this to mean that he'd now received my news, news that will probably cause him a headache or two. I would be terribly sad if I were to lose this comrade.

Actually, for a few days now I've only noticed from time to time that I'm living on a ship, my body has so accustomed itself to the rocking motion. The sky is still overcast, the sea is quiet, the meals as excellent and plentiful, and the card games every evening are still repulsive. The ship's money had barely been distributed when several rowdies were playing passionately for dollars. Since then, the community of card players has grown daily; some of the players will step onto American soil with gambling debts.

20. Juni

Meiner Mutter auch heute ein herzliches Gedenken. Noch trennt uns eine große Wegstrecke vom amerikanischen Kontinent, doch in zwei Tagen werden wir am Ziel sein. Wir stehen nun vor der Schwelle der „Neuen Welt", und dahinter wird ohne Zweifel ein neues Leben beginnen. Zunächst gewiss einfacher und nicht so bequem in Bezug auf die Häuslichkeit. Und, solang ich die Landessprache nicht beherrsche, auch zuweilen beschwerlich. Doch all dies bedeutet Zukunft. Hinter mir liegt die rückliegende Zeit als Etappe. Und ein Segen für mich und jeden wird es immer sein, wenn man in dieser Etappe einen unerschöpflichen Born der Kraft zur Bewährung, der freundlichen Erinnerung und der Dankbarkeit gegenüber denen besitzt, die in jener Zeit wahrhaft Freund, Lehrer, Berater und somit Wegbereiter zu diesen neuen Möglichkeiten waren.

Und wem danke ich mehr als meiner Mutter? Sie ist unter Hintansetzung aller persönlichen Wünsche durch alle Nöte und Stürme unser einziger, wahrer Freund geblieben. Ich kann ihr dies wohl nie in gleichem Maße vergelten, aber ich kann getreu ihrem Vorbild in wahrhaft christlicher Liebe wirken, indem ich nicht als Sklave meiner selbst das eigene Ich verherrliche. War es richtig, sie in der Heimat zu lassen? Ihr war der Abschied gewiss nicht leicht, und sie sagte: Mit euch geht mein Bestes!, so war das keine Phrase. Hoffentlich bleibt ihr die häusliche Frieden erhalten.

Wie wird Klein-Christel die Abwesenheit der Onkels begreifen? Hoffentlich wird er ein braver brauchbarer Mann. Und Hannele und Martin, die lieben Dorfmarker Kinder. Recht schnell wünsche ich mir die Gelegenheit, den kleinen Trabanten langentbehrte „Kostbarkeiten" zu entsenden, denn wie anders können sie überzeugt werden, dass ein Onkel Paul in Amerika lebt?

Vergangene Nacht träumte ich von Rico und deute dies so, dass er meine Nachricht nunmehr erhalten hat, die ihm wohl manchen Kopfschmerz bereiten wird. Mir wäre sehr leid darum, wenn ich diesen Kameraden verlieren müsste.

Eigentlich merke ich seit einigen Tagen nur noch gelegentlich, dass ich auf einem Seeschiff lebe, so sehr gewöhnt sich der Körper an die Schaukelei. Noch immer ist der Himmel bedeckt, das Meer ruhig, die Mahlzeiten sind ausgezeichnet und reichlich, sowie die abendlichen Kartenspieler widerlich. Kaum dass seinerzeit das Bordgeld ausgegeben war, spielten schon einige Rowdies leidenschaftlich um Dollars. Und seitdem wuchs die Kartenspielergemeinde täglich; mancher wird schon mit Spielschulden den amerikanischen Boden betreten.

June 21

Only a few hours separate us from New York. Meantime, night is falling once again. The suitcases are packed and ready to go, and must be submitted for customs inspection tomorrow. Tension is reaching a fever pitch; people are excited, and out of this situation arose the bad scene between Dorwood and Heinz. They got into an argument by a quibble about nothing. Typically, the instigator, Schmitt, was behind the business. A pity that such a bad mood should arise on the last day. As if we couldn't have exercised some judgment and backed down, which in any event is the only way to reach a peaceful resolution with the extremely opinionated Dorwood. We'll soon lose sight of him and should neither allow nor trouble ourselves to correct him in things that his own parents failed to inculcate in him and which he will simply have to learn from his own experiences.

Today was a gloriously beautiful day and everyone was enjoying the sun. The sea showed itself in a steel blue color, and the fish that occasionally appeared were visibly enjoying the good weather. My thoughts were often with my mother. She will have thought of us just as much as we her. Dear, good mother. I wish you all the best, particularly health and sun in your heart!

A huge passenger steamer passed us that morning, going in the opposite direction. Unfortunately it was too far away to be able to make out its name. Based on the enormous size and the two smokestacks, I would guess that we had met the German ship, the Europa, which was now in French service. Like this former representative of the German nation, we, too, are sailing under a foreign flag, as we must suffer throughout the world because of the bad reputation that we personally did least of all to create. It's no surprise if people encounter us with a strong sense of mistrust. However, I could also imagine that this doesn't necessarily have to be a disadvantage.

21. Juni

Nur noch wenige Stunden trennen uns von New York. Inzwischen wird es gerade noch einmal Nacht werden. Die Koffer sind aufbruchfertig gepackt und müssen morgen für die Zollrevision abgegeben werden. Die Spannung erreicht den Höhepunkt, die Gemüter sind erregt, und aus dieser Situation entstand auch die üble Szene zwischen Dorwood und Heinz. Sie gerieten sich um eine Wortklauberei in die Wolle. Typisch war hier wieder der stichelnde Inszenator Schmitt im Hintergrund. Schade, dass am letzten Tag so eine Misstimmung aufkommen konnte. Als hätte man nicht in klügerer Weise nachgeben können, was sowieso das einzige Mittel zur friedlichen Auseinandersetzung mit dem anmaßend rechthaberischen Dorwood darstellt. Wir werden ihn bald aus den Augen verlieren und sollten uns weder das Recht nehmen noch der Mühe unterziehen, ihn dort zu berichtigen, wo es seine Eltern versäumt haben und er selbst erst seine Erfahrungen sammeln muss.

Heute war ein strahlend schöner Tag und das Volk genoss die Sonne. Das Meer zeigte sich in stahlblauer Farbe, und selbst die zuweilen auftauchenden Fische hatten sichtlich ihre Freude daran. Meine Gedanken waren oft bei Mutter. Und nicht weniger wird sie an uns gedacht haben. Liebe, gute Mutter! Ich wünsche dir alles Gute, vor allen Dingen Gesundheit und Sonne im Herz!

Entgegen unserer Fahrtrichtung passierte am Vormittag ein mächtiger Passagierdampfer. Leider war die Entfernung zu groß, um den Namen erkennen zu können. Aus dem enormen Umfang und den zwei Schornsteinen lässt sich vermuten, hier dem nun in Frankreichs Dienst fahrenden deutschen Schiff „Europa" begegnet zu sein. Ähnlich diesem früheren Repräsentanten der

deutschen Nation fahren auch wir unter fremder Flagge, weil wir in der ganzen Welt unter dem Misskredit zu leiden haben, den wir persönlich am allerwenigsten heraufbeschworen. Kein Wunder, wenn man uns mit starkem Misstrauen begegnen wird. Ich könnte mir allerdings denken, dass dies nicht unbedingt ein Nachteil zu sein braucht.

For every young German who is somewhat conscious of his responsibilities should make a special effort to do his part to restore the name of his fatherland to a place of honor. This is a general human duty and one shouldn't turn it into a nationalist issue. It's precisely the Poles who, though an object of scorn, demonstrate through their attitudes the questionableness of such prejudice, while the arrogant Germans still are not inclined to learn from their past mistakes. As for me, I will be able to learn many a lesson from the future, and also from the past, in order to achieve that which I expect from others. The fact that I have the possibility of becoming an American citizen one day doesn't change a thing. For it's arrogant to be proud of something without contributing to that good reputation by one's own actions. Children are often conceited if their parents are wealthy. But how helpless they often are when they have to stand on their own two feet and experience how difficult life is. At that juncture what's decisive is not the parental bank account but one's own abilities.

Denn jeder etwas verantwortungsbewusste junge Deutsche sollte sich deshalb besondere Mühe geben, um für seinen Teil den Namen des Vaterlandes wieder zu Ehren zu bringen. Das ist eine allgemein menschliche Pflicht, und man darf daraus keine nationale Angelegenheit machen. Gerade die verrufenen Polen beweisen manchmal durch ihre Haltung die Fragwürdigkeit eines Vorurteils, während die überheblichen Deutschen immer noch nicht aus begangenen Fehlern zu lernen gewillt sind. Ich selbst werde aus der Zukunft noch manche Lehre gewinnen können und aus der Vergangenheit gleichfalls lernen müssen, um in allen Dingen selbst jenes zu leisten, was ich bei anderen zur Voraussetzung machen möchte. Daran ändert auch nichts die Möglichkeit, dass ich amerikanischer Staatsbürger werden kann. Denn es ist ein törichter Dünkel, auf etwas stolz zu sein, ohne durch eignes Zutun zum guten Rufe beizutragen. Kinder haben oft einen Dünkel, wenn ihre Eltern begütert sind. Aber wie hilflos sind sie oft, wenn, auf eigene Füße gestellt, an sie die Härten des Lebens herantreten. Dann entscheidet nicht der elterliche Geldbeutel, sondern das persönliche Können.

June 24

New York, the largest city in the world, is now my hunting grounds. I think I can express it this way because, other than a hotel room near Broadway, I don't have a fixed address. With my $2.50, or rather with $5.00 (including my brother's money) we try to venture further and further afield from Hotel Alvin, 223 West 52nd Street at Broadway. Yesterday we managed to get to Long Island, where Traude Naumann is now living with in her parents' home, having been denied it for almost her entire life. Traude was still a young child when her parents emigrated to America, leaving her in the care of her grandparents. Because of the disruptions of the war, a reunion was not possible for so long that Traude is only now, at the age of eighteen, getting to see her parents again.

Our final day on the boat was very strenuous. Those most desperate to be on terra firma were up in the wee hours of June 22, and their noise prevented further sleep. I was also up on deck at 4.30 a.m. and thus witnessed our arrival in New York from the start. To begin with, the beacon buoys and lighthouses announced the proximity of the shore. Then the lights from rows and rows of houses betrayed the position of the city, and it was just a pity that the morning fog deprived us of any long-distance view. A fast motorboat brought a pilot on board, and more and more arriving and departing ships enlivened the area. Shortly thereafter we anchored outside the harbor along with other steamers, waiting with engines stopped for permission to enter. A small boat belonging to the health department visited every other ship, but it never came to us. Other small craft belonging to the coast guard patrolled the area continuously.

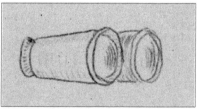

24. Juni

New York, die größte Stadt der Welt, ist mein derzeitiges Jagdgebiet. So kann ich wohl sagen, denn außer einem Hotelzimmer nahe dem Broadway habe ich keinen festen Platz. Mit meinen zweieinhalb Dollar oder vielmehr fünf mit denen meines Bruders versuchen wir täglich größere Kreise um den Punkt Hotel Alvin, 223 West 52nd Street at Broadway zu ziehen und gelangten gestern schon nach Long Island, wo nun Traude Naumann im elterlichen Hause wohnt, nachdem sie solches fast zeitlebens entbehren musste. Traude war noch ein kleines Kind, da wanderten die Eltern nach Amerika aus und überließen sie der großelterlichen Obhut. Die Kriegswirren vereitelten die Wiedervereinigung so lange, dass Traude nun erst mit 18 Jahren ihre Eltern wiedersieht.

Der letzte Tag auf dem Schiff war sehr anstrengend. Schon in den ersten Morgenstunden des 22. Juni waren die Landhungrigsten auf den Beinen und ihr Lärm verhinderte die weitere Nachtruhe. Auch ich war schon um halb fünf Uhr auf Deck und somit Augenzeuge der Ankunft in New York vom frühesten Zeitpunkt an. Zuerst kündeten die Leuchtbojen sowie die Leuchttürme das Nahen der Küste. Dann verriet der Lichtschein vieler Häuserzeilen die Lage der Stadt und es war nur zu schade, dass der Morgendunst jede Fernsicht nahm. Ein schnelles Motorboot brachte einen Lotsen an Bord und immer mehr ein- und ausfahrende Schiffe belebten die Umgebung. Wenig später lagen wir mit andern Dampfern vor dem Hafen und mit abgestoppten Maschinen darauf wartend, dass die Einfahrt gestattet würde. Ein kleines Boot der Gesundheitsbehörde besuchte Schiff um Schiff, nur zu uns kam es nicht. Andere Fahrzeuge der Küstenpolizei patrouillierten fortgesetzt an uns vorbei.

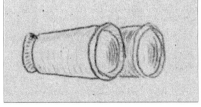

After a significant period of waiting, the ship slowly entered the harbor. We were now able to admire to the full the Statue of Liberty and the gigantic skyscrapers of New York. Boats large and small crossed our path. Ferries with entire trains on board were particularly noticeable. The ocean-going giants anchored at the enormous warehouses of the various shipping lines, and, although it was Sunday, were partially loaded.

The "Ernie Pyle" tied up at Pier 51, and with that our ocean voyage had come to an end. It had certainly been an interesting voyage and, until our arrival in New York, also a pleasant one. However, after that came the martyrdom, which lasted for several hours. All 900 passengers had to go into a room in the inner part of the ship to be processed by the health and customs officials. By this point, everyone just wanted to get off the ship quickly, and those who had become boxed in by the crowds soon found that the long wait in the sticky atmosphere was becoming unbearable. We therefore hung back and didn't get the all-important stamp on our landing card until around 4 p.m. This allowed us to pass through customs and leave the ship. Outside, the ladies of the committee welcomed us warmly and assisted us with the necessary formalities regarding luggage control. After a short rest, we and our luggage were transferred to a taxi and passed through the streets of Manhattan on to our hotel. I'd never seen such traffic in all my life. Cars, often in three lanes, race forward like wild dogs to the next street corner, where they are restrained by the next traffic light. These automatic traffic regulators take the guesswork out of the question of right-of-way, and when the green light appears, the mad dash begins all over again.

There's nothing easier than finding your way in downtown New York. The broad avenues all run north-south, and all the streets run east-west, with the street numbers rising from downtown to uptown. Fifth Avenue is pretty much the axis of the city. All streets east of Fifth Avenue have the suffix "East" and the same streets on the other side of Fifth Avenue have the suffix "West." We live at 223 West 52nd Street and the ACCR office is located at 147 West 42nd Street.

Nach geraumer Wartezeit fuhr das Schiff langsam in den Hafen ein. Nun konnten wir zur Genüge die Liberty-Statue neben den Riesenbauwerken der New Yorker Wolkenkratzer bewundern. Große und kleine Schiffe und Fähren kreuzten unsern Weg. Fährschiffe mit ganzen Eisenbahnzügen fielen besonders ins Auge. An den verschiedenen riesigen Lagerhallen der Schiffahrtslinien ankerten die Ozeanriesen und wurden trotz des Sonntags teilweise beladen.

Die „Ernie Pyle" wurde am Pier einundfünfzig befestigt, und somit war unsere Seereise beendet. Eine interessante Reise war es gewiss gewesen und bis zur Ankunft in New York auch angenehm. Dann allerdings für wenige Stunden ein Martyrium. Alle 900 Passagiere mussten zur Abfertigung durch die Gesundheits- und Zollbehörde einen Raum im Innern des Schiffes betreten. Jeder wollte jetzt schnell von Bord, und wer sich in der Menge eingekeilt hatte, dem steigerte sich der stundenlange Aufenthalt in der stickigen Atmosphäre bis zur Unerträglichkeit. Wir hielten uns deshalb zurück und erhielten erst gegen vier Uhr nachmittags den wichtigen Stempel auf die Landekarte. Damit konnten wir am Zollposten vorbei das Schiff verlassen. Draußen empfingen uns die Damen des Committees sehr herzlich und halfen bei den noch notwendigen Formalitäten in der Gepäckrevision. Nach einer kurzen Rast verfrachtete man uns samt den Handkoffern in ein Taxi, und durch die Straßen von Manhattan gelangten wir zum Hotel. So einen Verkehr habe ich mein Lebtag noch nicht gesehen. Auto an Auto, oft in drei Reihen nebeneinander schießen sie wie wildgewordene Hunde vorwärts, bis sie an den Straßenecken von den haltgebietenden Stoplichtern zurückgehalten werden. Diese automatischen Verkehrsregler nehmen allen Grund zur Frage des Vorfahrtsrechts, und wenn das grüne Licht wieder aufflammt, beginnt von Neuem die rasende Jagd.

Nichts ist leichter, als sich im Stadtkern New Yorks zurecht zu finden. In nordsüdlicher Richtung verlaufen stets die breiten Avenues und in ostwestlicher Richtung liegen die Streets, die von downtown nach uptown fortlaufend numeriert sind. Die „Fifth Avenue" ist praktisch die Achse der Stadt. Alle von ihr ostwärts abzweigenden „streets" haben die zusätzliche Bezeichnung „east" und die selben Straßen nach der entgegen gesetzen Seite den Zusatz „west". So wohnen wir in der 52nd Street 223 West und das Büro von ACCR findet sich in der 42nd Street 147 West.

The Committee lady responsible for us is called Miss Krauss. The following day we received money from her for the current week and brother, Heinz, received an additional five dollars to buy a pair of shoes. She asked us all about our work experience and what we hoped to do in the future in terms of jobs. We have this friendly lady to thank for many a valuable tip. For example, it was at her suggestion that we bought a street map of New York, with which we dared to take a trip to Long Island one evening to visit Traude Naumann. It was an interesting undertaking, though to what extent the Naumann family was interested in it, I can't say. Mr. Naumann drove us back to the city in his elegant automobile. New York at night is a fantastical sight and the colorful splendor of Broadway is a special experience.

During the day we go on little outings. The store windows offer everything imaginable, ready for the taking if you have the requisite dollars. We bought ten pairs of socks from a street vendor for two dollars. Our daily shopping for groceries, which I do at a local deli, uses a surprisingly small amount of money. And yet I manage to buy bread, butter, sugar, cheese, cold-cuts, milk, and some fruit. A big bar of chocolate costs twenty-five cents; these round out our meals. It's simply impossible to describe all the goods that are on display. A comparison with the Germany of today is hopeless and impossible. Like me, neither Werner nor Rico could help being astonished. It's just surprising how quickly one can take it for granted. Even today, I add up the numbers and find myself wishing to purchase this or that, but delay doing so until the time when I have some dollars in my pocket which I've earned myself. Anyone with a regular income in this country who can budget sensibly has no need to deny himself any wish. You can have anything, from clothes to a car! For now I still don't have any income, so this thought will remain future music to my ears, but pleasant music.

Die für uns zuständige Dame bei diesem Committee heißt Miss Krauss. Von ihr erhielten wir tags darauf das Geld für die laufende Woche und Bruder Heinz noch besonders fünf Dollar zum Einkauf von ein Paar Schuhen. Sie erfragte alle beruflichen Daten und die weiteren Wünsche. Manchen wertvollen Tip verdanken wir der freundlichen Dame, und auf deren Anraten erwarben wir eine „street-map", eine Straßenkarte von New York, vermittels der am Abend ein Ausflug zu Traude Naumann nach Long Island gewagt wurde. Es war ein interessantes Unternehmen, doch inwieweit sich die Familie Naumann dafür begeisterte, kann ich ja nicht wissen. Herr Naumann brachte uns mit seinem eleganten Wagen nach der Stadt zurück. Im nächtlichen New York zeigt sich ein fantastisches Bild, und die Farbenpracht des Broadways ist ein besonderes Erlebnis.

Tagsüber gehören die Streifzüge zu unserm Programm. In den Schaufenstern der Geschäfte bietet sich alles Erdenkliche an; frei zu haben, wenn man die nötigen Dollars dazu hat. Von einem Straßenhändler erwarben wir zehn Paar Socken für zwei Dollars! Der tägliche Einkauf von Lebensmitteln, den ich in einem Delikatessenstore tätige, bedingt nur eine erstaunliche Mindestausgabe. Dann habe ich aber Brot, Butter, Zucker, Käse, Wurst, Milch und einiges Obst. Eine große Tafel Schokolade kostet fünfundzwanzig Cents; auch solche vervollständigen unsere Speisefolge. Die Fülle der dargebotenen Waren lässt sich einfach nicht beschreiben. Ein Vergleich mit dem heutigen Deutschland ist hoffnungslos und unmöglich. Werner wie auch Rico würden gleich mir nicht aus dem Staunen herauskommen. Und es ist nur verwunderlich, wie rasch man sich daran gewöhnen kann! Schon heute kalkuliere ich, wünsche diesen und jenen Einkauf zu tätigen und verschiebe das Vorhaben lediglich bis zu der Zeit, da die ersten selbstverdienten Dollars in der Tasche liegen. Wer hier im Lande regelmäßig verdient und dazu vernünftig haushalten kann, der braucht sich keinen Wunsch unerfüllt zu lassen. Von Kleidern bis zum Auto nicht! Noch habe ich keinen Verdienst und somit bleibt es eine Zukunftsmusik, aber eine schöne.

June 27

We've already sent two airmail letters home and one to Buenos Aires. An aunt, father's sister, Susy, lives there. She is the only one of my father's family line who survived the Nazi terror. And she only did so because she managed to emigrate in 1936. Now we've become emigrants ourselves and our experiences are just as interesting to her as her suggestions are good for us.

I will begin all correspondences seriously only when, along with a fixed address, I can report I have a job. A visit to the Meixner relatives in Elmhurst on Long Island turned out quite nicely. In particular, fourteen-year-old Hermi made great efforts to explain the rules of baseball to me. Today we rode what's called the subway for the first time. This mode of transportation speeds from station to station in the blink of an eye. It's wise, therefore, to keep a look-out for the names of the stations, so as not to miss your stop. Mr. Ruppert wasn't at home, and so we want to repeat the visit tomorrow if Clement Caralunas doesn't call to invite us to Plymouth for the weekend. But I need to report that in greater detail.

After lunch yesterday we took the subway downtown to visit the lower west side. At the same time, we wanted to send one of the familiar grocery packages to Frankfurt from the CARE organization's office. It didn't take a lot of doing, for one simply has to fill out a form at 50 Broad Street and pay ten dollars.

27. Juni

Schon zweimal haben wir Luftpostbriefe nach Hause gesandt und einen nach Buenos Aires. Dort lebt eine Tante, meines Vaters Schwester Susy. Sie ist die einzige Verwandte der väterlichen Linie, die den Naziterror überlebte. Und dies nur, weil sie bereits im Jahre 1936 emigrieren konnte. Nun sind wir selbst Auswanderer geworden, und unsere Erfahrungen sind für sie ebenso interessant als ihre Ratschläge gut sind für uns.

Ich werde alle Korrespondenz erst dann ernstlich eröffnen, wenn ich neben einer festen Adresse auch von einer Beschäftigung berichten kann. Ein Besuch bei den Meixner'schen Verwandten in Elmhurst auf Long Island gestaltete sich recht nett. Besonders der vierzehnjährige Hermi bemühte sich geflissentlich, mir die Regeln des Baseballspiels verständlich zu machen. An diesem Tag benutzten wir erstmals die U-Bahn, hier „subway" genannt. In Gedankenschnelle eilt dieses Verkehrsmittel von Station zu Station. Da ist es angebracht, auf die großen Ankündigungstafeln zu achten, um nicht über das Ziel hinaus zu fahren. Herr Rupert war nicht zu Hause gewesen, und wir wollen morgen den Besuch wiederholen, wenn nicht Clement Caralunas noch anruft, um uns übers Wochenende nach Plymouth einzuladen. Doch das soll ausführlicher berichtet werden.

Gestern nach dem Mittagsmahl begaben wir uns per Subway nach Downtown und wollten die untere Stadt besichtigen. Gleichzeitig hatten wir die Absicht, vom Büro der CARE-Gesellschaft eines der bekannten Lebensmittelpakete nach Frankfurt zu schicken. Das hat keine Umstände gemacht, denn in der Broadstreet 50 braucht man lediglich ein Formular ausfüllen und 10 Dollars bezahlen.

The harbor area is like a huge building site; old buildings disappear and foundations are blasted into the rock for what will certainly be bigger new buildings. One could put a whole house into the foundations alone, they're so huge. Powerful jack hammers ram the strong metal bars into the earth, in the process of which the hammer hits the iron again and again. One gets thirsty just by watching, and a cold glass of beer for 10 cents is a pleasant drink.

That's how we spent the afternoon, and the evening brought us an unexpected surprise, a visit by Clem and his younger brother. Clem had been an American soldier in Germany and Heinz had met him there. A friendship developed between them. Heinz had continued their correspondence when he reached New York and Clem responded by visiting us. We were all, particularly Heinz, quite delighted. At the moment, Clem is working in New Jersey, so it was just a short trip for him. And yet he considers the job market in the New York area bad and intends to move to the city of Cleveland in Ohio soon, to take a job on a ship. Since we were also considering traveling further to the inland states, we were interested in hearing this and hope also to find employment soon. As we were saying goodbye, he mentioned the possibility of taking us to his mother's place in Pennsylvania from Friday till Monday. It would be nice if it were possible, and now we're just waiting for him to call and let us know.

Das Hafengelände gleicht hier und da einem riesigen Bauplatz; alte Baulichkeiten verschwinden, und für neue, gewiss größere Bauten werden Fundamente in den Fels gesprengt, in die man gut und gern ein ganzes Haus hineinstellen könnte. Gewaltige Presslufthämmer rammen starke Doppel-T-Träger in die Erde, wobei der Bär immer wieder dröhnend auf das Eisen niederfällt. Auch vom Zusehen wird man durstig, und ein kühles Glas Bier für 10c ist ein angenehmes Getränk.

So verging der Nachmittag, und der Abend brachte uns die unerwartete Überraschung: Ein Besuch von Clem und seinem jüngeren Bruder. Clem war amerikanischer Soldat in Deutschland gewesen und da begegnete ihm mein Bruder Heinz. So hat sich eine Freundschaft entwickelt. Seinen Briefverkehr hat Heinz dann auch von hier aus fortgesetzt und Clem brachte seine Antwort in Form eines Besuches zu uns. Wir und ganz besonders Heinz waren sehr erfreut. Clem arbeitet augenblicklich in New Jersey, also war es nur ein kurzer Weg für ihn. Doch er hält den Arbeitsmarkt in der New Yorker Gegend für schlecht und beabsichtigt, demnächst nach Ohio in die Stadt Cleveland zu übersiedeln, um auf einem Schiff einen „job" anzunehmen. Da auch wir unter Umständen in das Innere der Staaten weiterfahren werden, war uns dies recht interessant zu hören, und wir hoffen, dann auch bald einen Arbeitsplatz zu finden. Beim Abschied sprach er von der Möglichkeit, uns ab Freitag bis Montag nach Pennsylvanien zu seiner Mutter mitzunehmen. Das wäre schön, wenn sich dies einrichten ließe, und nun warten wir auf seinen entscheidenden Anruf.

June 30

Even though friend Clem didn't call, our visit to the Rupperts' home on Saturday evening was a nice change. Mrs. Ruppert had invited us to have dinner with them and surprised us with a good German meal. This couple emigrated nineteen years ago and now have a lovely house, an elegant car, and the two children are offered everything that they could wish in terms of their personal and vocational desires. Fourteen-year-old Hermann is about to start high school, and will then be sent to college. Attending high school here (which is akin to a Gymnasium at home) doesn't cost anything; tuition is charged only for college or university. That evening we talked a great deal about our common homeland and the strange paths people took when they allowed themselves to be dominated by the Hitler loyalists.

Whereas in Germany need and suffering hold sway, here, someone who over there would be considered an average worker, can attain a comfortable standard of living in a relatively short time, as represented by Mr. Ruppert, who owns both a house and a car. Of course we also spoke of our relatives in Germany, of their troubles and the constraints on the necessities of life. The Rupperts would very much like to take in each one of their brothers and sisters for a while in their hospitable house, but the distances are too great and in addition these days the borders are closed to travel. Because of this, the only possible way to help is by sending food packages to Germany. And when one considers that these people regularly send packages to each of their twelve relatives, it must be acknowledged that their commitment entails considerable financial sacrifice.

30. Juni

Auch wenn Freund Clems Anruf ausblieb, so war der Besuch bei Rupperts am Samstagabend eine schöne Abwechselung. Frau Ruppert hatte uns zum Essen eingeladen und mit einer gutdeutschen Mahlzeit überrascht. Schon vor neunzehn Jahren ist dieses Ehepaar nach hier eingewandert, und heute verfügen sie über ein schönes Haus, einen vornehmen Wagen, und den beiden Kindern wird alles geboten, was sich an ihren persönlichen und beruflichen Wünschen erfüllen lässt. Der vierzehnjährige Hermann wird nun die Highschool besuchen und dann auf ein College geschickt werden. Hier wird für den Besuch der gymnasiumähnlichen Highschool allerdings kein Schulgeld erhoben, und erst das Studium auf dem College oder einer Universität ist direkt mit Unkosten verknüpft. Wir sprachen an diesem Abend viel über unsere gemeinsame Heimat und die sonderbaren Wege, welche die Landsleute beschritten hatten, als sie sich unter die Pantoffeln der „führertreuen" Clique stellten.

Während nun drüben Not und Elend das ganze Land beherrscht, vermag hier einer, den man dort nur als „gewöhnlichen" Arbeiter bezeichnet, in verhältnismäßig kurzer Zeit zu einem Wohlstand zu gelangen, wie ihn auch Herr Ruppert als Haus- und Autobesitzer repräsentiert. Natürlich war auch von den Anverwandten in Deutschland die Rede, von ihrer Plagerei und der Beschränkung lebensnotwendiger Dinge. Rupperts würden gerne jeden ihrer Brüder und Schwestern eine Zeitspanne in ihr gastliches Haus aufnehmen, doch sind die Entfernungen zu groß und die Grenzen heutzutage außerdem noch für einen Reiseverkehr geschlossen. So sind die Lebensmittelsendungen nach Deutschland die einzig mögliche Abhilfe. Und wenn man bedenkt, dass diese Leute in regelmäßigen Abständen an jeden ihrer zwölf Anverwandten Pakete schicken, so ist dies schon mit geldlichen Opfern verbunden und anzuerkennen.

It's also laudable how much Mr. Ruppert is willing to do to help us get ahead. Probably Mrs. Meixner, our subtenant in Frankfurt, had asked her brother to do so. As we had agreed on Saturday, we met with him at his work site on Monday morning. He's a foreman in a shoe factory that belongs to a German Jew. From there, we searched for a blacksmith he knew, who was to set up a job for us. After the Italian had shown me a sketch of an elevator in order to gauge whether I was able to understand it, we agreed to start work the following morning at eight.

At least, that would have been our start, if our Miss Krauss of the ACCR hadn't called to tell us about a telegram from Cincinnati. So we have to meet with Miss Krauss tomorrow morning and I will miss this chance to earn my own dollars for the first time.

Auch ist es lobenswert, wie sehr sich Herr Ruppert für unser persönliches Fortkommen einsetzt. Wahrscheinlich hat Frau Meixner, unsere Frankfurter Untermieterin, ihren Bruder darum gebeten. Wie bereits am Samstag verabredet, trafen wir uns heute am Montagmorgen an seinem Arbeitsplatz. Er ist Vorarbeiter in einer einem deutschen Juden gehörigen Schuhmaschinenfabrik. Von dort suchen wir eine ihm bekannte Schmiede auf, um für uns einen Job auszumachen. Nachdem mir der Italiener eine Zeichnung von einem Aufzug vorgelegt hatte, um zu sehen, ob ich sie zu lesen imstande sei, vereinbarten wir für morgen früh um acht Uhr den Arbeitsbeginn.

Das wäre immerhin ein Anfang gewesen, wenn nicht unsere Miss Krauss vom ACCR angerufen hätte und von einem Telegramm aus Cincinnati berichtete. Darum müssen wir morgen früh aber zu Miss Krauss, und somit komme ich um meine ersten selbstverdienten Dollars.

July 3

From the moment Miss Krauss told us about the answer from Cincinnati and we had reached agreement on the details, only a few hours had passed. A good possibility had perhaps developed for our future well-being in this short time. Today we are living in a boarding house in Cincinnati. The house is located in a green, natural setting on one of the seven hills surrounding the city. Our comfortable room has a double bed as well as a couch on which a third person could sleep. The washstand and chest of drawers accommodate our underwear, the rather old-fashioned wardrobe houses our other clothing. In all we pay $30 for this room which has checkered linoleum, and faded pink and green rose-patterned wallpaper. So, each of us pays fifteen dollars, and that isn't expensive for a week when you consider three meals a day are included in the rent.

But I must return briefly to New York. We entered the ACCR offices shortly after nine in the morning on the first of July. That's where we learned about Cincinnati from Miss Krauss, and received our instructions and travel money. Then we returned to our hotel, collected the big suitcases we'd already packed that morning, and took a taxi to Penn Station. Tickets to Cincinnati cost $43. We checked our luggage for delivery to Cincinnati. After that, we informed Mr. Ruppert of the change of plans. After eating for the last time in our hotel room, it was time to say good-bye to Broadway.

People who come to the station too early must wait until ten minutes prior to departure time before access to the platforms is permitted. So I had some free time to watch what was going on. Some passengers arrived at the last minute, rushed down the steps and possibly might have reached their trains on time. Stairs to the platforms below lead off right and left from the main concourse. Displays visible even from a distance and loudspeakers announce the time and location of departing trains. When it was our turn, we boarded a coach that in Germany might have been considered third class. By contrast, here the accommodations were comfortable. Every passenger has his own comfortable seat, which can easily be turned into a lounge chair by moving a lever.

3. Juli

Von der Stunde an, in der uns Miss Krauss von der Antwort aus Cincinnati berichtete und wir mit den Abmachungen einverstanden waren, sind wiederum nur wenige Stunden vergangen. In dieser kurzen Zeit hat sich für unser ferneres Wohlergehen vielleicht eine gute Entwicklung eingeleitet. Heute wohnen wir schon in einem „boarding house" in Cincinnati. Auf einem der sieben die Stadt umgebenden Hügel liegt diese Villa ganz im Grünen eingebettet. In unserm comfortablen Raum bietet neben einem doppelschläfigen Bett eine Couch die dritte Schlafgelegenheit. Der Waschtisch und die Kommode dienen zum Unterbringen der Wäsche, der etwas altmodische Schrank beherbergt die anderen Kleider. Für diesen Raum, dessen Fußboden mit buntgewürfeltem Linoleum belegt ist und dessen Wände von einer verblassten, rosa und grün gestreiften Rosenmustertapete begleitet sind, zahlen wir zusammen dreißig Dollars. Also jeder Teil beträgt fünfzehn Dollars, und das ist für eine Woche nicht zu teuer, da hierin täglich drei Mahlzeiten inbegriffen sind.

Aber nochmals nach New York zurück! Kurz nach neun Uhr am Vormittag des ersten Juli betraten wir das Büro von ACCR. Dort erfuhren wir von Miss Krauss die Sache mit Cincinnati und von ihr erhielten wir Instruktionen und das Fahrgeld. Alsdann begaben wir uns zum Hotel zurück, nahmen die bereits am Vortag gepackten großen Koffer und ließen uns von einer Taxe zur Pennsylvania-Railroadstation befördern. Zwei Tickets nach Cincinnati kosteten dreiundvierzig Dollars. Unsere Koffer übergaben wir der Bahnspedition. Anschließend daran informierten wir Herrn Ruppert von der neuen Situation, und nachdem wir letztmals in unserm Hotelzimmer gespeist hatten, hatte die Abschiedsstunde vom Broadway geschlagen.

Wer zu früh in die Halle des Bahnhofs kommt, der muss warten, bis zehn Minuten vor Abfahrt der Züge der Zutritt zu den Bahnsteigen gestattet wird. Auch ich hatte so einige Muhe, die Geschehnisse zu beobachten. Auch kamen die Fahrgäste erst in letzter Minute, stürzten die Treppen hinunter, und vielleicht haben sie ihren Zug noch erreicht. In der großen Halle des Bahnhofs führen links und rechts Treppen zu den tiefer gelegenen Bahnsteigen. Weithin sichtbare Tafeln im Verein mit einem Lautsprecher künden Zeit und Ort der abfahrenden Züge. Als wir dann an die Reihe kamen, bestiegen wir eine Coach; in Deutschland wäre es etwa dritte Klasse. Hier hingegen sind es angenehme Wagen. Jeder Passagier verfügt über einen bequemen Sessel, der sich durch Umlegen der Lehne leicht in eine Liegestatt verwandeln lässt.

A pity that the journey took place during the night. Only in the evening light that remained and again the next morning could we admire the landscape that was flying past. However, our train did have the undeniable advantage that we were able to reach our destination without changing trains. We left New York at 5.25 p.m. and the next station we reached was Newark in New Jersey. I was delighted already by the fresh greenness I could see here, which in New York itself could only be found in the artificially created parks. The famous city of Philadelphia and the smaller station of Paoli followed. The train was powered by electricity until Harrisburg near Lancaster. From there, a steam engine picked up the speeding train. During the night we passed the stations of Pittsburg, Newark in Ohio, and Columbus. Next morning the train stopped briefly in Xenia, Norwood, and Winton Place. Then we reached our destination. As agreed, we were met at the station by a Miss Blick, who drove us to one of the seven hills in her luxurious car and delivered us to Miss Bärwald's boarding house. So, now I'm back to the beginning of today's report, but also at the end of it, because I still want to write a letter home to Germany today.

My dear friend!

Today I arrived in Cincinnati, a town in the south of the state of Ohio. Everything's very new to me and I can't make any judgment about it yet. I simply hope the best for the future. My thoughts are again in New York, and that's what I want to tell you about.

Zu schade, dass sich die Reise während der Nacht vollzog. Wir konnten nur in wenigen Abendstunden und dann am anderen Morgen die vorbeifliegende Landschaft bewundern. Demgegenüber hatte unser Zug den unbestreitbaren Vorteil, wir konnten ohne Umsteigen das Ziel erreichen. Wir verließen New York um 5:25 PM (past meridian) und erreichten als nächste Station Newark in New Jersey. Schon hier erfreute mich das frische Grün, das New York nur in seinen künstlich angelegten Parks zeigte. Dann folgte die bekannte Stadt Philadelphia und die kleinere Station Paoli. Bis Harrisburg, das wir über Lancaster streiften, war die Strecke elektrisch betrieben worden. Dann übernahm eine Dampflokomotive den schnellfahrenden Zug. Während der Nacht passierten wir die Stationen Pittsburg, Newark in Ohio und Columbus. Am andern Morgen pausierte der Zug noch in Xenia, Norwood und Winton Place. Dann hatten wir das „destination" erreicht. Wie vereinbart, war eine Miss Blick auf dem Bahnhof, die uns dann mit ihrem feudalen Auto zu einem der sieben Hügel fuhr und in Miss Bärwalds Boarding House ablieferte. Nun bin ich wieder am Anfang des heutigen Berichts, aber auch am Ende, denn ich will noch einen Brief nach Deutschland schreiben.

Mein lieber Freund!

Heute bin ich in Cincinnati, einer südlichen Stadt im Staate Ohio, angekommen. Alles ist für mich sehr neu und lässt sich jetzt noch nicht beurteilen. Ich erhoffe für die Zukunft nur das Beste. Meine Gedanken sind nochmals in New York, und von dort will ich Dir berichten.

I'm sure you can recall the last few days at the Brentano pool complex. It was so terribly hot. The climate here is almost more unbearable, for it should be noted that New York lies on the same latitude as Naples. The weather makes for a sunny shadow-side of the much-praised land of America. Basically, I have no real reason to complain, and besides, I wanted to come here. For here the half-starved European can easily believe he's been transported into a fairy tale of a land of milk and honey. Everything that the heart desires is available here. Without rations, stamps, or a black market! The only limitation that I'm facing is that I lack the necessary funds. I'll first have to earn a few dollars of my own. But even so, things aren't going badly for me. Together with my brother, I have a nice hotel room right on the famous Broadway and in addition, five dollars a day between us. All this is at the Committee's expense, the same people who helped us leave Germany. We rarely need more than three dollars for daily subsistence, and so with the money we've saved we've already been able to send our mother one of the familiar CARE packages. Since taking care of her was our primary goal in coming here, we've at least had this initial success.

The Americans have hardly a clue about the hardships in Europe and have a hard time imagining the situation there. A person here who is willing to work and thus has a steady income has the means to establish his life and home so comfortably that he cannot imagine those kinds of limitations. As I've already reported once, no one here would think of keeping an allotment garden, unless it were just for the fun of it. No housewife cans fruit or vegetables in the summer because both are available in her store at any time of year. The same goes for preserving eggs. A dozen eggs costs about 75 cents.

Even if Americans are indignant about inflation--prices have doubled since before the war--I still regard circumstances here as ideal. One is almost blinded by the rich selection in every store and now that wartime restrictions have been lifted, no housewife even gives a thought that something might not be available.

Du kannst Dich gewiss noch der letzten Tage im Brentanobad erinnern; es herrschte eine Bruthitze. Hier ist das Klima fast noch unerträglicher, denn es ist zu beachten, dass New York auf dem gleichen Breitengrad wie Neapel liegt. Das ist eine sonnige Schattenseite des gelobten Landes. An und für sich habe ich gar keinen Grund zum Klagen und außerdem habe ich es ja so gewollt! Denn hier kann sich der halbverhungerte Europäer leicht in eine Szene des Märchens vom Schlaraffenland versetzt denken. Es gibt alles, was das Herz begehrt! Ohne Punkte, Marken und Schwarzen Markt! Die einzige Beschränkung, die mir naturgemäß noch auferlegt ist, es mangelt an den nötigen Barmitteln, und ich muss erst einmal einige Dollars selbst verdienen. Aber es geht mir auch so gar nicht schlecht. Mit meinem Bruder verfüge ich über ein nettes Hotelzimmer, direkt am berühmten Broadway und daneben zusammen über täglich fünf Dollars. Dies geht alles auf Kosten des Kommittees, das uns auch von drüben fortgeholfen hat. Für den täglichen Unterhalt benötigen wir selten über drei Dollars, sodass wir mit den ersparten Mitteln schon eines der bekannten CARE-Pakete an unsere Mutter abschicken konnten. Wenn man bedenkt, dass dies unser erstes Ziel darstellt, so ist immerhin schon ein Anfang bewerkstelligt.

Die Amerikaner haben fast keine Ahnung von der europäischen Not und können sich schlechtweg nichts darunter vorstellen. Wer hier arbeiten will und somit ständig verdient, der kann sich sein Leben und sein Heim derart komfortabel einrichten, dass ihm derartige Einschränkungen unvorstellbar sind. Wie ich schon einmal berichtete, denkt hier kein Mensch daran, einen Schrebergarten zu unterhalten, es sei denn eine sportliche Marotte. Keine Hausfrau macht im Sommer Obst oder Gemüse ein, weil beides zu jeder Jahreszeit in ihrem Store erhältlich ist. Dasselbe gilt für das Einlegen der Eier; ein Dutzend davon kosten etwa fünfundsiebzig Cents.

Wenn die Amerikaner auch empört sind über die Teuerung, die Preise sind gegen das Vorkriegsniveau um das Doppelte gestiegen, so erachte ich die hiesigen Verhältnisse als ideal. Man ist schier geblendet von der Fülle der Auswahl in jedem Geschäft, und nachdem heute wieder jede kriegsbedingte Einschränkung weggefallen ist, denkt auch keine Hausfrau mehr daran, dass irgend etwas vielleicht nicht zu haben wäre.

In the short time that I've been here, I haven't yet been able to grasp what a typical American way of life is like, although people who have been here for some time claim that they're always content if there's enough to eat and drink and they can watch a movie. One fact that seems pretty clear is that almost all immigrants from Europe have a good standard of living. They have their own homes and their own cars. Every third worker here has a car, by the way.

The kinds of concerns German children and youth face are for the most part utterly unknown to American youth. Whether that's construed as superficiality or whatever, the fact is that life here is better, nicer, easier, and more desirable for young people. School attendance is mandatory until the age of sixteen, and you can't leave before eighteen without the express consent of your parents. Most people enjoy sports most of all, and the most popular sport is baseball, which is little known in Germany. There are playgrounds for children throughout the cities. They do not lack for swings, slides, sand-boxes, sprinklers, and much more besides. At the edge of world-class metropolitan areas, wherever there's a green space, the bigger boys practice catching and throwing the small leather balls, and the grownups delight in watching.

What the girls like doing best is hard to say from my perspective. As everywhere, they like looking pretty, and from the variety of their wardrobe it's evident that getting a new dress never presents a problem. A well-known lady said of her daughter that she couldn't find quite the right pair of shoes from among the twenty pairs she owns. Now those are really some problems!

Today is a sun-drenched work day and it was a hellishly hot day that lent my entry into New York such a festive air about ten days ago! Perhaps you've experienced something similar so you can sympathize with how I felt when most of the emigrants were being heartily welcomed by their relatives and I, the prodigal son, envied them for it.

Eine typische amerikanische Lebensart konnte ich in der kurzen Zeit meines Hierseins noch nicht feststellen, wenn auch verschiedene schon länger ansässige Landsleute behaupten, jene seien immer zufrieden, wenn sie gut zu essen und zu trinken haben und daneben ihre Movies (Kino) besuchen können. Eine Tatsache scheint mir allerdings, dass fast alle eingewanderten Europäer über einen gewissen Wohlstand verfügen. Sie haben ein eigenes Heim und ein eigenes Auto. Ein Car besitzt hier überhaupt jeder dritte Arbeiter.

Was bei uns drüben für die Kinder und die Heranwachsenden an Sorgen existiert, ist der amerikanischen Jugend größtenteils unbekannt. Mag das als Oberflächlichkeit oder sonstwie ausgelegt werden, auf jeden Fall ist dieses Leben besser, schöner, leichter und für die Jugend wünschenswert. Die Schulpflicht geht hier bis zum sechzehnten Lebensjahr und kann nicht vor dem achtzehnten beendet werden, wenn nicht die Eltern ausdrücklich damit einverstanden sind. Sport ist das größte Vergnügen und das bei uns weniger bekannte Baseball das meist ausgeübte Spiel. In jedem Viertel der Stadt sind hier für die Kinder Spielplätze erbaut worden; es fehlt darin keine Schaukel, Rutschbahn, Sandkasten, Brause und vieles mehr. Am Rande des Weltstadtverkehrs üben auf jeder grünen Insel die größeren Jungens ihre Fertigkeit im Werfen und Fangen des kleinen Lederballs. Die Erwachsenen ergötzen sich dabei am Zusehen.

Was den Girls am meisten Vergnügen macht, lässt sich von meiner Warte aus schlecht beurteilen. Sie lieben es, so wie überall, gut auszusehen und haben in der Mannigfaltigkeit ihrer Garderobe den besten Beweis, dass die wiederholte Neuanschaffung eines Kleides kein Problem bedeutet. Eine bekannte Dame sagte von ihrer Tochter, dass sie aus ihren zwanzig Paar Schuhen zuweilen nicht die richtigen herausfinden kann. Das sind natürlich auch Sorgen!!!

Heute ist ein sonnenbeschienener Werktag, und etwa vor zehn Tagen war es ein bruteißer Sonntag, der meinem Einzug in New York das festliche Gepräge gab?! Vielleicht hast Du schon ein ähnliches Gefühl kennengelernt, und dann kannst Du mir nachfühlen, wie mir zumute war, als die meisten Auswanderer von ihren Angehörigen stürmisch begrüßt wurden und ich verlorener Sohn sie darum beneidet habe.

Of course, the first few years will often witness such situations until one gets to know and love a new circle of friends based on mutual esteem. In this situation it's good to know that I have friends at home who think of me on occasion. In my mother I have left the most valuable friend at home, and if I succeed in bringing her over here, I will once again have a big piece of home with me. Fortunately my brother is still here, and we complement one another well. I likewise expect to hear from you; write and tell me about life and changes back home. I'm sorry I can't send greetings right away to all my sports friends. So I'm asking you please to tell them that I am thinking of them, and let them know I promise to write. I have no idea if I'll ever get back into playing sports, particularly since soccer is almost unknown over here.

I also believe that for the time being I especially have to remind myself of the German saying: first work, then play. In this respect I always had the right attitude, only now, free will has to yield somewhat to coercion. But I'm not afraid of any work nor any kind of dirt, and if some good comes of this in the end I'll consider myself as the cleverer one compared to my comrades who, blinded by their prejudices against the outside world, prefer to daydream away their youth in the constricted world of home. After all, not everyone can emigrate from Germany today, but again, only a few could overcome their narrow-minded views and dare to cross this narrow bridge to a new beginning.

What use were the phrases about home and fatherland if it wasn't possible to help my mother or serve my friends in an honest way? You could eke out a living without having so-called connections if you upheld an ideal that was incomprehensible to most people, so as not to be sucked into the dirty web of corruption. I'm sure I would have had opportunities to get ahead; after all, I was always full of plans and ambitious to learn new skills. But I would have had to keep seeking a distance from what makes life comfortable. And in addition, I would have needed a lot of time, time that I'm using here to attain similar goals but despite that to have some life. But in so doing, as before, I place no value on silly amusements or on possessing pompous things. But it's certainly an honest need of mine to be equal in every respect to the task of being head of a family one day. And for this, as well as a sensible attitude, I need the maturity of manhood and, obviously, a corresponding income. Once again I've searched for and found myself a task to do by setting myself this goal. I hope it will be realized, for my own satisfaction and for the blessing of all who have to live around me.

Die ersten Jahre werden gewiss noch oft eine solche Situation mit sich bringen, bis man einen Kreis von Freunden kennen und lieben gelernt hat und eine gegenseitige Wertschätzung entsteht. Dafür ist nun die Gewissheit gut, dass ich in der Heimat einige Freunde besitze, die meiner zuweilen gedenken. Besonders in meiner Mutter habe ich den wertvollsten Freund drüben gelassen, und wenn es mir gelingt, sie nach hier zu holen, dann habe ich auch wieder ein großes Stück Heimat bei mir. Zum Glück ist ja noch mein Bruder hier, und wir ergänzen uns gut. Von Dir erwarte ich natürlich ebenfalls Lebenszeichen, indem Du mir von dem Leben und Wandel aus der alten Heimat berichtest. Mir ist leider nicht möglich, gleich an alle Sportfreunde Grüße zu senden. Ich bitte Dich deshalb, ihnen mein herzliches Gedenken zu übermitteln und dazu das Versprechen, dass ich an sie gelegentlich schreiben werde. Ob ich noch einmal zur Ausübung eines Sportes komme, weiß ich heute nicht zu beurteilen, zumal der Fußballsport hier kaum bekannt ist.

Ich glaube auch, dass ich mir für die nächste Zeit das gutdeutsche Sprichwort: Erst die Arbeit, dann's Vergnügen – besonders einprägen muss. In dieser Hinsicht war ja meine Einstellung schon immer richtig gewesen, nur muss jetzt die Freiwilligkeit der Unfreiwilligkeit etwas das Feld räumen. Nun, ich fürchte keine Arbeit und auch keinen Schmutz, und wenn am Ende etwas dabei herauskommt, dann betrachte ich mich als der Klügere gegenüber den Kameraden, die, voller Vorurteile wider die äußere Welt, ihre Jugend lieber in der engen Heimat verträumen. Heute kann ja nicht jeder von drüben auswandern, aber auch nur wenige könnten sich über ihren beschränkten Horizont hinwegsetzen, um über diese schmale Brücke einen neuen Anfang zu wagen.

Was nutzten mir die Phrasen von Heimat und Vaterland, indem es mir dort unmöglich war, auf ehrlichem Wege meiner Mutter zu helfen oder meinen Freunden zu dienen? Man konnte doch ohne die sogenannten Beziehungen lediglich sein Leben fristen, wenn man einem allgemein unverständlichen Ideal huldigte, um nicht in das schmutzige Netz der Korruptionen eingesponnen zu werden. Auch hätte ich gewisslich Chancen gehabt, ein Vorwärtskommen zu finden; war ich doch immer voller Pläne und bestrebt, Neues hinzuzulernen. Aber ich hätte immer größeren Abstand von vielem suchen müssen, was das Leben angenehm macht. Außerdem hätte ich viel Zeit gebraucht, die ich nun hier anwende, um einem ähnlichen Ziel zuzustreben und trotzdem etwas vom Leben zu haben. Dabei lege ich nach wie vor keinen Wert auf irgendwelche Amüsements oder den Besitz pomphafter Dinge. Doch es ist mir ein gewiss ehrliches Bedürfnis, dereinst einer Aufgabe als Familienoberhaupt in jeder Beziehung gewachsen zu sein. Und hierzu gehört neben einer vernünftigen Einstellung die Reife eines wirklichen Mannes und, wie überall, der entsprechende Verdienst. Mit dieser Zielsetzung habe ich auch wieder eine Aufgabe gesucht und gefunden. Möge es in Erfüllung gehen, mir zu Genugtuung und allen, die um mich herumleben müssen, zum Segen.

It's probably too early to regard these views and thoughts as final, since I've so far only spent a short time since discovering this "New World." Nonetheless, I would wish every young person to have this opportunity, for the coming generation will place less importance on confused theories than on a happy future. And here every decent and hardworking person is assured of such a future.

Now that our paths have separated and only the good Lord knows where they will lead, I can do no better than to wish you the best from my heart and please promise me also to think of me from time to time.

Yours,
Paul Mayer

Long-Lost Friend
Many suns and moon have vanished
Since our paths together joined.
The bright sunshine shone upon us
Young companions, he and I.
All his planning, all his daring
His bold youth inspired me,
But I had a premonition
Of darkness that could come his way.
So his pathway took him from us
Led him to a wider world.
Where at last he finds himself now
Where his home is, none can say.
Never will these memories leave me
An autumn leaf falls from the tree
In evening's stillness I remember
What our friendship meant to me.

Es ist vielleicht noch zu früh, diese Ansichten und Auslegungen als endgültig anzusehen, da erst eine kurze Zeitspanne seit der Entdeckung dieser „Neuen Welt" meinerseits vergangen ist; trotzdem würde ich jedem jungen Menschen die Wahrnehmung dieser Chance anraten, denn die kommende Generation wird weniger Wert auf verworrene Theorien legen als auf eine glückliche Zukunft. Und die ist jedem anständigen und tüchtigen Menschen hier gewährleistet.

So sich nun unsere Wege getrennt haben und nur der gütige Herrgott weiß, wo sie hinführen, kann ich nichts Besseres tun, als Dir von Herzen alles Gute zu wünschen, und Du gibst mir das Versprechen, dass Du auch meiner zuweilen gedenken wirst.

Dein
Paul Mayer

Verschollener Freund

Längst sind Zeiten hinverflossen,
Seit uns unser Weg vereint.
Mir und ihm, dem Weggenossen,
Hat die Sonne oft geschient.
Mich begeisterte sein Planen,
Seiner Jugend Ungestüm,
Doch ich glaub, es war ein Ahnen
Dunkler Zukunft über ihm.
Dann hat sich sein Weg gewendet,
In die weite Welt hinaus.
Keiner weiß, wo er geendet
Oder wo er heut zu Haus.
Niemals kann ich ihn vergessen,
Herbstlich fällt vom Baum ein Blatt,
Und am Abend denk ich dessen,
Was uns einst verbunden hat.

July 4

Since my first journal entry on the American continent, I've been making an effort to write in an acceptable Latin script. It's evidently going to take more practice to be at all successful. We have now found our first relatively permanent home on American soil. With regard to our living situation, our comfort and the service at meals, it must be said that we've probably never had it so good. And yet everything is still so unfamiliar; even today, on the American national holiday, we don't feel much like celebrating. Yesterday we went downtown in the morning and afternoon. There's a tram stop right outside our door. Along with the buses, the tram maintains the connection to the city center. The fare here is $0.10.

Yesterday afternoon, Miss Hartocollis, a Greek woman who immigrated here in 1939 and who is Heinz's case worker for the "Family Service", took us around to various places in order to deal with the necessary paperwork. First we received our social security cards at the post office; I think this is a kind of social insurance. Then Miss H. took us to an office where we turned in our first papers to apply for citizenship. This also necessitated having our passport photos taken in a photography studio. On the way home we bought a copy of the Staatszeitung und Herold, which contained a surprise for me as it had a report on the status of the soccer leagues in Hesse— though I had long since been aware of the facts themselves. I clipped the article and enclosed it for Werner with my nightly letter home.

We slept late today and have no idea how to spend the afternoon. I'm in favor of a trip that was recommended to us, but Heinz is very much opposed to it, for reasons of frugality. Maybe we'll go for a walk. This boredom is the result of the unaccustomed lack of anything to do. Usually, every free minute would be welcome, but today precious time is passing by unused. I'm quite annoyed at this inability to take advantage of this free time which will soon be over. I would so much like to go into the garden or to the ball park with Werner once again. At least I'll take a look at my technical books again today so that I don't lose my ability to think, on top of everything else.

4. Juli

Seit meiner ersten Eintragung auf amerikanischem Kontinent bemühe ich mich nun, in der lateinischen Schrift einen annehmbaren Stil zu schreiben. Es bedarf wohl einer weiteren Übung, um einen Erfolg zu erzielen. Nun haben wir ja den ersten festeren Wohnsitz auf dem amerikanischen Boden gefunden. Was die Wohnlage, die Bequemlichkeit sowie die Aufwartung bei den Mahlzeiten anbelangt, ist uns solches wohl kaum vorher widerfahren. Aber es ist halt noch alles so fremd, und selbst heute, an dem amerikanischen Nationalfeiertag fühlen wir wenig feierliche Impulse. Gestern waren wir morgens und nachmittags in der Stadt drunten gewesen. Gerade vor unserem Haus ist eine Haltestelle der Straßenbahn, die im Verein mit Autobussen die Verbindung mit dem Zentrum aufrechterhält. 10c kostet hier die Fahrgebühr.

Miss Hartocollis, eine 1939 nach hier eingewanderte Griechin, welche nun im Dienste des „Family Service" Heinz's Sachbearbeiterin ist, führte uns gestern nachmittag zu verschiedenen Stellen, um notwendige Formalitäten zu erledigen. Zuerst erhielten wir im post office unsere Social Security Account Card; ich denke, das ist so eine Sozialversicherung. Dann brachte uns Miss H. in ein Büro, wo wir unser „1st paper" einreichten, um ein Citizenship zu erhalten. Dafür war es auch notwendig, dass wir in einem Photogeschäft Passbilder machen ließen. Auf dem Heimweg kauften wir uns noch die „Staatszeitung und Herold", die für mich in dem Bericht über den Stand der hessischen Fußball Ligen eine Überraschung enthielt, auch wenn mir das lang bekannte Tatsachen waren. In dem abendlichen Brief nach Hause habe ich diesen Ausschnitt für Werner beigelegt.

Heute haben wir lange geschlafen und wissen auch nicht, was wir mit dem Nachmittag anfangen sollen. Während ich für einen anempfohlenen Ausflug bin, ist Heinz aus Sparsamkeitsgründen sehr dagegen. Möglicherweise werden wir einen Spaziergang unternehmen. Diese Langeweile ist das Ergebnis des ungewohnten Nichtstuns. Während ansonsten jede freie Minute willkommen war, vergeht heute manche kostbare Zeit ungenutzt. Ich bin recht ärgerlich über dieses Unvermögen, aus dieser bald entflogenen Freizeit so wenig Nützliches gewinnen zu können. Recht gerne ginge ich wieder einmal mit Werner in den Garten oder zum Sportplatz. Heute will ich wenigstens wieder einmal in meine technischen Bücher sehen, damit man nicht überdies auch noch an Verstand einbüßt.

July 7

In keeping with this plan, I pretty much spent the last few days refreshing my mathematical and English language skills. The importance of having a good grasp of the English language is obvious, for you can only take advantage of the various opportunities for further education if you actually understand the material. Heinz certainly has a bit of an advantage here, because for a long time he was focused on the fulfillment of his plan to emigrate. I, however, focused on my technical studies, along with my work in the garden. It is certainly not out of the question to return to the studies that I had earlier chosen and now have given up. That would be nice. But first I've got to attend to my English!

What our case worker, Miss Hartocollis, had predicted turned out, in fact, to be true, as a Mr. and a Mrs.…. picked us up in their car for a short tour of the town on Saturday evening. We admired Cincinnati's splendid location, the lovely parks, wide streets, and other attractions. I must also mention that we were treated to ice cream. It was a very nice evening, and in addition the couple invited us to go swimming with some other young people the next day. The rendezvous was supposed to be the Methodist Church in Clifton, because we were to go with a church youth group.

Unfortunately it rained the next day at the appointed time and we stayed home, assuming the event was canceled. At three o'clock, just as we were sitting down to dinner as we always did on Sundays and holidays, Miss Koti, who was covering for Mrs. Barwald who was traveling to Europe, came to tell us that the youth group had asked why we had not shown up and after some discussion had promised to pick us up shortly to go to a party. This is the prelude to what happened that lovely Sunday afternoon in Cincinnati.

A car stopped outside, a lady stepped out and asked for the Mayer boys. She was the aunt of a member of the Wesley Foundation, a church youth group, mainly composed of students. She drove to the suburb of Clifton through streets as yet unfamiliar to us, and took her leave after introducing us to her niece. We walked through the front garden and entered a room just off the porch; ten young people of both sexes were already gathered there, entertaining themselves playing bridge, with which we were unfamiliar.

7. Juli

Die letzten Tage habe ich gemäß meines Vorsatzes auch weitgehend mit Wiederholen mathematischer wie auch englischsprachiger Kenntnisse ausgefüllt. Wie wichtig das Beherrschen der englischen Sprache ist, geht daraus hervor, dass man an den mannigfach gebotenen Gelegenheiten zur Weiterbildung naturgemäß dann einen Vorteil gewinnen kann, wenn man den gebotenen Stoff zuerst sprachlich versteht. Heinz hat hier gewiss einen großen Vorsprung, weil er schon längere Zeit nur noch der Erfüllung dieses Auswanderungsplanes lebte, während ich neben der Wahrnehmung der gärtnerischen Arbeiten meinen technischen Studien den Vorrang gab. Es ist hier unter Umständen noch nicht einmal ausgeschlossen, wenn ich den früher gewählten und nun aufgegebenen Weg des Studiums letztenendes doch wieder beschreite. Schön wäre das. Aber zuerst das Englische!

Was uns schon unser Caseworker Miss Hartecollis in Aussicht gestellt hatte, bewahrheitete sich insofern, als am Sonnabend eine Mrs. und ein Mr. uns zu einer kurzen Stadtrundfahrt mit ihrem Auto abholten. Hierbei konnten wir Cincinattis herrliche Lage, die schönen Parks, breiten Straßen und sonstigen Schönheiten bewundern; dass man uns ein ice cream spendierte, soll natürlich hier nicht unerwähnt bleiben. Das war ein sehr netter Abend, an dem uns diese Leute außerdem zu einem Schwimmbadbesuch mit anderen jungen Leuten für den folgenden Tag einluden. Treffpunkt wäre die Methodist Church in Clifton gewesen, denn es handelt sich hier um eine kirchliche Jugendgruppe.

Leider regnete es anderntags zur verabredeten Zeit und wir wähnten das Rendezvous als hinfällig, blieben also zu Hause. Um drei Uhr, wie jeden Sonn-, Feiertag begaben wir uns zum dinner, als Miss Koti, die Vertreterin für die nach Europa reisende Mrs. Barwald, uns mitteilte, dass dieser Kreis um den Grund unseres Fernbleibens nachgefragt und nach abermaliger Rücksprache versprochen hatte, uns wenig später zu einer Party abzuholen. Dies ist die Vorgeschichte des schönen Sonntagnachmittags in Cincinati.

Draußen stoppte ein Wagen, eine Lady entstieg ihm und fragte nach den Mayer boys. Sie war die Tante einer Angehörigen der „Wesley Foundation", einer kirchlichen Jugendgruppe, die sich größtenteils aus Studenten zusammensetzt. Durch bisher unbekannte Straßen brachte sie uns in den Stadtteil Clifton und verabschiedete sich wieder, nachdem sie uns ihrer Nichte vorgestellt hatte. Dann betraten wir durch den Vorgarten ein an die Veranda des Hauses angrenzendes Zimmer, in dem bereits zehn junge Leute beiderlei Geschlechts versammelt waren und sich mit dem uns unbekannten Bridge amüsierten.

When we were introduced, I must admit I didn't remember a single name and only caught on to a few first names over the course of the evening. These young people were really nice, were interested in many things, and despite our linguistic clumsiness, whenever possible each of our questions received an intelligible response. Our hosts wanted to introduce us to the rules of bridge, which was clearly an important game here, but they had no success with me at all. A glass of Pepsi Cola did me good not so much because of the temperature of the room as the linguistic difficulties I encountered, which made me break out in a sweat.

When the party began to break up, we thought the group was about to go to church. In order to catch the streetcar, we had to run a short stretch from the corner of the street. Our friends pointed out the most significant buildings of the city to our right and left: the university, various high schools, factories, hospitals, and so forth. A 25 cent pass which the leader of the group bought for us allowed us to transfer to various streetcar lines, which took us to the west end of town. Up to this point, Georg, a tall lanky youth, had been my companion, and, as a student of technology, he was familiar with an area of knowledge that interested me as much as it did him.

Then the group meandered down the street and headed for a nearby family residence. Suddenly we were once again surrounded by new faces, new rounds of introductions, embarrassed again at being unfamiliar with the local customs. With considerable gratitude I recall the young high school teacher (whose name escapes me) who went to great lengths to have a lively conversation with me. Someone was playing one of the latest hits at the grand piano, surrounded by other friends joining them in song; at little card tables some were devoting themselves to bridge, and the table settings and rattling of plates in the open adjoining room also left no doubt that we were guests at a genuine American party.

Wann wir auch der Reihe nach vorgestellt wurden, ich muss gestehen, keinen Namen behalten zu haben und erst im Laufe des Abends den einen oder anderen Vornamen wieder zu erlauschen. Diese jungen Leute waren wirklich nett, interessierten sich für vieles und trotz unserem sprachlichen Ungeschick wurde nach Möglichkeit jeder Frage unsererseits eine verständliche Antwort erteilt. In die Regeln des hier anscheinend wichtigen Bridge wollte man uns einführen, ohne jedoch bei mir irgendeinen Erfolg zu erzielen. Ein Glas Pepsi Cola tat mir weniger wegen der Zimmerwärme gute Dienste als der zuweilen auftretenden Sprachschwierigkeiten wegen, die mir den Schweiß auf die Stirn getrieben haben.

Als abermals ein Aufbruch erfolgte, glaubten wir eben, es würde ein genugsamer Kirchenbesuch unternommen. Von der nächsten Ecke mussten wir ein kurzes Stück rennen, um die Straßenbahn noch zu erreichen. Rechts und links wurden uns die repräsentativen Gebäude der Stadt gezeigt: die Uni, verschiedene High Schools, Factories und Hospitäler u.a.m. Ein Pass für 25c, den der Präses dieser Gruppe für uns erworben hatte, gestattete das wiederholte Umsteigen in verschiedene Straßenbahnlinien, die uns dann ans W.E.-Ende der Stadt brachten. Bis hier war mir Georg, ein lang aufgeschossener Junge, Gesellschafter gewesen, und als technischer Student hatte er ein mich ebenso interessierendes Wissensgebiet.

Dann ging die Gruppe zwanglos durch die Straße und steuerte einem naheliegenden Einfamilienhaus zu. Plötzlich waren wir wieder inmitten neuer Gesichter, neuerliches Vorstellen, neuerliche Verlegenheit, ob der Unkenntnis hiesiger Sitten, und nur mit Dankbarkeit gedenke ich der für mich wieder namenlosen jungen High-School-Lehrerin, die sich so viel Mühe gab, mit mir eine angeregte Unterhaltung zu führen. Am Flügel spielte einer die neuesten Schlager, umgeben von andern mitsingenden Kameraden, an kleinen Tischen huldigte man dem Bridge, und auch die Gedecke und das Tellergerassel im offenstehenden Nebenzimmer ließ keinen Zweifel mehr daran, wir waren Gast bei einer echt amerikanischen „Party".

Soon everyone was seated around the extended table, and the two grown daughters of the house assumed the role of hostess. Soup was offered in small bowls decorated with a flower pattern. Next, bread, butter, cheese, cold cuts, bean salad, and wafer thin French fry-like potato slices were passed around. An ice-cold glass of orange juice stood at each person's place, and to top it all off, slices of delicious chocolate cake were handed out. As the new guests from half-starved Europe we even received a second slice of cake.

It was still light outside, and the garden behind the house offered a welcome opportunity to play ball. Meanwhile, the table was cleared and the dishes were washed, so that when darkness fell, the rooms with the light blue wallpaper beckoned anew to the continuation of the unavoidable game of bridge. Just to be nice to us, a smaller group played a game akin to gin rummy. The fact that I actually emerged as the winner surely confirms that we had a lot of fun playing this easier game.

It was a nice experience to be in the midst of carefree, happy young people, and I'm sure that the sincerely meant farewell of, "Come again, boys", shows that we're not considered strangers, and that by being part of this group we have an opportunity to turn a new page in our book of life. On the way home, nine people squeezed into the small car, so it's no wonder that despite the nice evening I was glad to say goodbye at our door and be relieved of the weight on my lap. Our alarm clock, which indicated midnight, didn't seem to reproach us. The clock alone knows how the time after that passed, for we slept very soundly.

This afternoon we visited the Bollmann family, immigrants from Berlin, who had invited us. In general I got the impression of an educated and well brought-up family, and, though the wife seemed to have become a bit hysterical because of all they'd been through, she, her untiring husband and the two pretty children comprised a harmonious little community. Although after a mere six months they have their own home,—albeit rather primitive and perhaps different from their previous standard of living—they complain about how badly they have been treated by the ACCR which, they claim, sent them here under false pretenses! Why did they emigrate from Germany if they shy away from the effort involved in starting over? Today they mock the helpfulness of earlier immigrants who are now nicely settled in, although they expect extensive support from them. How will the Bollmanns react to new immigrants a few years hence?

Bald saßen alle um den ausgezogenen Tisch, und die beiden großgewachsenen Töchter des Hauses hatten die Rolle der Hausfrau übernommen. Auf kleinen, blumengemusterten Schüsseln wurde Suppe angeboten, hernach gingen Brot, Butter, Käse, Wurst, Bohnengemüse und hauchdünne, Pommes frites ähnlich zubereitete Kartoffelscheiben reihum. Währenddessen stand für jedermann ein eisgekühltes Glas Orangensaft auf dem Tisch, und abschließend wurde eine Schnitte köstlichen Schokoladenkuchens verteilt. Wir als die neuen Gäste aus dem halb verhungerten Europa erhielten sogar ein weiteres Tortenstück.

Noch war es draußen hell und der Garten hinter dem Hause bot willkommene Gelegenheit zu einem kurzen Ballspiel. Inzwischen wurden Tisch und Geschirr gereinigt und geordnet, so dass nach anbrechender Dunkelheit die Räume mit den hellblauen Tapeten erneut zur Fortsetzung das obligatorischen Bridge einluden. Uns zuliebe spielte eine kleinere Gruppe ein Rommee-ähnliches Spiel, und dass ich sogar als Sieger hervorging, bestätigt wohl, dass uns dies leicht begreifliche Spiel manchen Spaß bot.

Es war ein schönes Erlebnis inmitten unbesorgter fröhlicher Jugend, und das gewiss aufrichtig gemeinte „Come again, boys" beim Abschied beweist, dass wir einmal nicht als Fremde gelten und überdies durch den Verkehr mit dem Kreis eine neue Seite in unsrem Lebensbuch aufschlagen können. Neun Personen saßen heimwärts in dem viersitzigen Auto, kein Wunder, dass ich trotzdem froh war, als wir vor unserer Haustür good bye sagten und ich persönlich von der meinem Schoß aufgebürdeten Last entledigt war. Unser Wecker schien mit seinem Mitternacht zeigenden Antlitz auch keine Vorwürfe zu erheben, und wie die Zeit bis heute vergangen ist, hat er ganz allein bemessen, denn wir haben prächtig geschlafen.

Heute Nachmittag besuchten wir die Berliner Emigranten-Familie Bollmann, die uns zuvor eingeladen hatten. Im allgemeinen gewann ich den Eindruck einer gebildeten und wohlerzogenen, aber durch die Erlebnisse etwas hysterisch gewordenen Frau, die mit einem unermüdlichen Mann und zwei hübschen Kindern dennoch eine harmonische Gemeinschaft bilden. Obwohl sie schon nach halbjähriger Anwesenheit über ein eigenes Heim verfügen, primitiv noch und vom früheren Niveau vielleicht verschieden, so jammern sie über die ungebührliche Behandlung seitens der ACCR, welche sie unter falschen Voraussetzungen nach hier gesandt hätten! Warum sind sie aus Deutschland ausgewandert, wenn sie die Mühen eines neuen Anfangs scheuen? Heute spötteln sie über die Hilfsbereitschaft der bereits wohlsituierten Einwanderer früherer Jahre und erwarten darüberhinaus von denen weitgehende Unterstützung. Wie werden Bollmanns in wenigen Jahren den weiterhin Neuankommenden gegenüberstehen?

1947

July 9

I just finished a letter to my friend, Werner, and let him know that my thoughts are often with him. I wonder if my friend, Rico, thinks of me. In the near future I'll try to gather together the events of this year as recorded in my journal entries and share with my friends my reflections and motivations regarding the path I've taken. My searching has not stopped, as I reflect every day on how I can best take advantage of the opportunities offered me. Will I be able to continue my studies? Where there's a will, there's a way! Other common sayings as well as my own inner conviction leave me in no doubt that the attainment of any goal is completely dependent on pursuing it systematically and taking the necessary steps. But will I recognize what's necessary at the right time?

My thoughts return to Frankfurt am Main, to my former job, to my former friends and colleagues. With gratitude I recollect the decency of my supervisor, Mr. Kreussler, the helpfulness of Max Meusel, and many others, whose books first gave me the opportunity to study on my own and today still comprise part of my library. But more important still is mastering the English language. That is the primary and decisive step to be taken in the near future. Only with that skill can I take advantage of the many opportunities available for further education. High school, college, and university are available and, God willing, for me as well.

I wonder what my former colleague, Eifert, is doing. Before falling asleep last night I spent a long time thinking about him. He's a very forgettable type of person, a person of pathogenic arrogance, a person completely without ambition, and well suited to fall into oblivion as an undifferentiated member of the mass of humanity. And what if the opposite were the case?

9. Juli

Soeben beendete ich einen Brief an Freund Werner und ließ ihn wissen, dass meine Gedanken oft bei ihm weilen. Und was wird mein Freund Rico z.Zt. für Gedanken über mich haben? Ich werde in nächster Zeit versuchen, die Geschehnisse dieses Jahres getreu meinen Tagebuchaufschreibungen zusammenzufassen, um meinen Freunden die Gedanken und Beweggründe des eingeschlagenen Weges mitzuteilen. Mein Suchen ist nicht irgendwie beendet, sondern täglich will es überlegt sein, wie man am besten die gebotenen Lebenschancen ausnützen kann. Werde ich noch studieren können? Wo ein Wille, ist auch ein Weg! Auch andere oft gebrauchte Sprichwörter im Verein mit meiner eigenen inneren Überzeugung lassen keinen Zweifel daran, dass das Erreichen irgendeines Zieles ganz allein von der systematischen Verfolgung und Ausführung notwendiger Schritte abhängt. Und werde ich das Notwendige rechtzeitig erkennen?

Meine Gedanken schweifen nach Frankfurt am Main zurück, zur früheren Arbeit, zu den früheren Kollegen und Kameraden. In Dankbarkeit gedenke ich der Anständigkeit meines Vorgesetzten, H. Kreußler, der Hilfsbereitschaft von Max Meusel und vieler anderer, deren Bücher mir erst die Möglichkeit zum Selbststudium gaben und heute sogar z.T. den Bestand meiner Bibliothek ausmachen. Noch wichtiger ist das Erlernen der englischen Sprache. Das ist der erste und entscheidende Schritt in naher Zukunft. Dann erst kann ich Nutznießer der vielfach gebotenen Gelegenheiten zur Weitebildung werden. Highschool, College und Universität sind offenstehende Möglichkeiten, und so Gott will, auch für mich.

Was wird wohl Kollege Eifert machen? Gestern vor dem Einschlafen habe ich lange über ihn nachgedacht. Er ist doch recht eine Type zum Vergessen, ein Mensch mit krankhafter Arroganz, ohne jeden anderen Ehrgeiz und recht dazu geeignet, als undefinierbares Glied des Begriffs Masse in Vergessenheit zu geraten. Und wie wird es umgekehrt der Fall sein?

There are only a very few people in the professional and sports circles I joined to whom I ascribe a good heart by overlooking their common human failings. These few would have understood my striving, would have respected my decisions, and therefore I will honor their memory. Those people to whom all this seemed foolish or who mocked my ambitions are in the final analysis people without tact or spirituality. It was my interior life that first gave me the strength to travel lonely paths and which, thanks to a positive outlook on life, keeps me from being lonely. Only my true friends, and most of all, my journal, are told the things I can't talk about openly. Later on I'll have an opportunity to describe this or that necessary step with a good conscience, free of all the mistakes that are part of me today.

Nowadays, I'm not fully in favor of my whole family moving here because I'm skeptical about this viewpoint, which Heinz is in favor of. Of course it's mother's decision, because she's the one who would have to leave behind all her belongings. I have personal reasons for not wishing a reunion with my sisters, because quite honestly I want to avoid any depressing unpleasantness. Furthermore, I think that it will not be possible to undertake such a responsibility until Heinz and I have paid our debts and can make the necessary purchases with savings and a steady income. After all, look at the Bollmann family and others. Our family members can get enough to eat in Germany as well, if we continue to send assistance, and if at some point we want to see each other again, there will be plenty of opportunities to do so.

July 10

Yesterday evening we went to the Wesley Foundation's weekly meeting and witnessed how, in an open discussion, these young people made plans for the next party. Unfortunately I only understood bits and pieces of the conversation. Afterwards we played table tennis. My partner, Julian, and I were an unbeatable team. Because it was raining, one of the young men drove us home, but not before we'd been invited to the swimming excursion planned for next Sunday. Today was a rainy day, and only when I came down at mealtimes did I poke my nose out of doors. Other than that I designed a few illustrations for the record of my experiences that I'm planning to assemble and write down.

Wie in der durch den Beruf bedingten und in der sportlichen Gemeinschaft gesuchten Umgebung sind nur wenige Menschen, denen ich durch Außerachtlassung allgemein menschlicher Schwächen einen guten Kern zuschreibe. Diese werden auch meine Bestrebungen verstanden, meine Haltung anerkannt haben und dafür ein bleibendes Andenken bewahren. Denen dieses etwa töricht erschien oder auch ob meiner Eigenschaften verspottet haben, sind letztenendes Leute ohne Takt und seelische Impulse. Mein Innenleben gab mir erst die Kraft zur Beschreitung einsamer Wege und bewahrt mich trotzdem dank einer glücklichen Fantasie vor der Vereinsamung. Worüber ich nicht allgemein sprechen kann, erfahren nur meine wirklichen Freunde oder in ganzer Offenheit nur mein Tagebuch. Darin wird sich mir selbst in späteren Tagen die Handhabe bieten, mit gutem Gewissen diesen oder jenen Schritt als notwendig darzulegen, geläutert von allen heute anhaftenden Irrtümern.

Heute bin ich auch gar nicht so rückhaltlos für die Übersiedlung der ganzen Familie nach hier, weil ich bei dieser von Heinz verfochtenen Anschauung mit skeptischen Beweisen operiere. Mutter obliegt natürlich die Entscheidung, denn sie ist es ja, die sich von allem Hausrat zu trennen hat. Gegen die Wiedervereinigung mit den Schwestern führe ich persönliche Motive ins Feld, denn ich möchte diesen deprimierenden Gehässigkeiten aus dem Weg gehen. Außerdem halte ich diese Last der Verantwortung erst für tragbar, wenn Heinz und ich mit unsern Schulden ins Reine gekommen und den notwendigen Anschaffungen mit Ersparnissen und geregeltem Verdienst begegnen können. Denn siehe Fam. Bollmann und andere. Sattessen kann man sich auch in Deutschland, wenn wir laufend Unterstützungen senden, und wollen wir uns einmal wiedersehen, dann sind Wege genug offen.

10. Juli

Gestern Abend waren wir der Wesley Foundation zu ihrer wöchentlichen Besprechung gefolgt und waren Zeuge, wie diese jungen Leute unter freier Diskussion den Plan zu der nächsten Partie entwarfen. Ich selbst habe leider nur Bruchstücke der Gespräche verstanden. Anschließend spielten wir noch Tischtennis, wobei mein Partner Julian und ich eine ungeschlagene Mannschaft bildeten. Wegen des Regens brachte uns einer der jungen Leute mit dem Auto nach Hause, ohne dass man vorher versäumt hätte, uns für den am Sonntag geplanten Schwimmausflug einzuladen. Heute war ein regnerischer Tag, und lediglich zu den Mahlzeiten bin ich vor die Haustür gegangen. Im übrigen entwarf ich einige Illustrationen für die geplante Zusammenstellung und Niederschrift meiner Erlebnisse.

July 19

Today the completed book lies before me. I experienced it myself, wrote it down and illustrated it myself, even bound it myself; it is definitely all my own work. Everything that occurred to me at the time and that I was able to relate is embedded in these 44 typed pages. This little book is dedicated to and intended for my friends, although I have no idea at the moment how I could send it to them. There is one clean original and I have two carbon copies in my drawer. I've somehow got to bind these loose pages as well in order to be able to send the complete story to Rico and Werner.

We still don't have jobs. However, another agent named Mr. Paul Lane promised he'd help us find work soon. For me, time never dragged, and often I didn't leave the typewriter for days at a time. Yet something that happened is of great significance. Last Thursday, the Family Service bought us new clothes. Miss Hartcollis and another nice lady showed good taste as they helped us make our selections. That same afternoon we proudly carried a package home. Per person it contained two shirts, two undershirts, and two pairs of (short!) underwear. In addition, the package also contained a pair of swimming trunks especially for me. The tailor is putting the finishing touches to our two new pairs of pants and we can pick them up today.

The whole business cost a total of $34, thus not overly expensive. Of course, it didn't cost us a penny personally, but nonetheless it's good to be thrifty with every purchase. Each of us might still receive a pair of shoes in the coming week, at which point we would be fully acclimated, at least outwardly. We will feel more comfortable when we are able to wear lighter clothing, and other than that, getting accustomed to this climate is simply a matter of time. We've received the first communication from Mother, and I must also note here that a second care package was sent off.

19. Juli

Endlich liegt das fertige Buch vor mir. Selbst erlebt, selbst niedergeschrieben und illustriert, dazu sogar selbst gebunden, ist es unbestreitbar mein Werk. Was mir die Momente eingegeben und was ich wiederzugeben fähig war, liegt in diesen 44 Maschinenseiten verankert. Ich habe dieses Büchlein meinen Freunden zugedacht und gewidmet, ohne heute zu wissen, wie ich es ihnen übermitteln könnte. Ein Original ist perfekt und zwei Durchschläge liegen in meiner Lade. Diese losen Blätter muss ich auf irgendeine Art und Weise ebenfalls einbinden, um die zusammenhängende Geschichte Rico und Werner übersenden zu können.

Noch immer haben wir keinen „job". Mr. Paul Lane, ein anderer Agent, versprach uns jedoch bald dazu verhelfen zu wollen. Mir wurde die Zeit inzwischen nicht zu lang, und oft tagelang bin ich nicht von der Maschine weggegangen. Eine zwischenzeitliche Begebenheit ist allerdings von großer Bedeutung. Am vergangenen Donnerstag verhalf uns das Family Service zu neuen Kleidern. Miss Hartecollis und eine andere nette Dame halfen uns mit gutem Geschmack bei der Auswahl. Am selben Nachmittag zogen wir stolz mit einem Paket nach Hause. Darin waren für jeden je zwei Oberhemden, zwei Unterhemden und zwei Unterhosen (kurze!). Für mich speziell enthielt es noch eine Badehose. Die beiden neu gekauften Hosen erhielten erst vom Schneider den notwendigen Schliff und können heute abgeholt werden.

Der ganze Aufwand betrug 34 Dollar und bewegt sich so in erträglichen Grenzen. Uns kostete dies nun ja nichts, doch ist trotzdem die Wirtschaftlichkeit jedes Einkaufs zu beachten. In der nächsten Woche bekommt jeder vielleicht noch ein Paar Schuhe, womit wir äußerlich dann akklimatisiert wären. Das leibliche Wohlbefinden wird sich mit dem Tragen leichterer Kleider auch bessern, und das restlose Gewöhnen an dieses Klima ist doch eben eine Frage der Zeit. Auch das erste Lebenszeichen von Mutter erhielten wir schon, und die Absendung eines zweiten Lebensmttelpaketes ist zu verzeichnen.

July 22

Today we were able to send a third package to Mother, and there's a similar one ready to be sent to Aunt Jeanne—but today we don't have enough money for the postage. We're still unemployed. The situation is a cause for some anxiety. Heinz has inquired about work at various companies, but without success. Unfortunately there's been no action. Nonetheless, I have kept busy working on my book and have not been plagued by boredom.

We've been in the States exactly four weeks today and have experienced quite a bit. All the old ways that we used to prize so greatly have long since lost their value and significance. Even though I regard athletic activities as a hobby, I must say I've enjoyed many a pleasant hour on account of it; however, my lack of activity in this area doesn't concern me at all. But my studies are altogether different. For the time being I've lost sight of the goal and don't yet see any possibility of getting back on track. I imagine that in most of the schools here I would not encounter the same difficulties I had in Frankfurt, where I applied in vain for two years to be admitted. But a new obstacle has arisen, since the basic requirement here is fluency in the language. So that's at the top of the list.

Recently, when we were guests at the home of Phil, a member of the Wesley Foundation, he gave me two technical text books as we were leaving. One dealt with trigonometry, the other was a very valuable book on technical drawing. I can pretty much understand these technical books, but my lack of knowledge of English is disturbingly obvious. Therefore, I'll devote the coming time exclusively to reading English; there's no better alternative to actual employment.

22. Juli

Heute konnten wir ein drittes Paket an Mutter absenden, und ein solches liegt zur Absendung an Tante Jeanne bereit; heute fehlt uns das Geld für das Porto!! Noch immer sind wir ohne Arbeit. Das ist eine besorgniserregende Begebenheit. Heinz hat allerdings verschiedene Male bei Arbeitgebern nachgefragt, aber ohne Erfolg. Leider hat sich noch nichts gerührt oder geregt. Immerhin hatte ich bis zur Fertigstellung meines Buches genügend Beschäftigung und wurde von keiner Langeweile geplagt.

Heute sind wir datummäßig genau vier Wochen in den Staaten und haben mancherlei erlebt. Alle früheren hochgeschätzten Gepflogenheiten besitzen längst nicht mehr den Wert und die Bedeutung. Wenn ich in der sportlichen Betätigung auch eine Liebhaberei erblicke, so habe ich dadurch manche schöne Stunde erlebt; die nunmehrige Untätigkeit auf diesem Gebiet bereitet mir keine Sorgen. Anders ist es mit meinen Studien. Zunächst habe ich das Ziel aus den Augen verloren und sehe noch keine Möglichkeit, den Faden wieder aufzunehmen. Wohl sind in der Vielzahl der hiesigen Schulen nicht die Frankfurter Schwierigkeiten zu suchen, weil ich dort bald zwei Jahre vergeblich um Aufnahme nachgesucht habe. Aber eine neue Barriere hat sich in den Weg gelegt, denn Grundbedingung ist hier das Beherrschen der Landessprache. Also ist dies der erste notwendige Schritt.

Als wir kürzlich Gast bei Phil, einem Mitglied von Wesley Foundation, waren, schenkte er mir zum Abschied zwei technische Lehrbücher. Eines über Trigonometrie und ein weiteres wertvolles Buch über das technische Zeichnen. Diese Bücher mit technischer Grundlage kann ich schon leidlich lesen und verstehen, doch macht sich der Mangel an Sprachkenntnissen störend bemerkbar. Also werde ich die kommende Zeit nur der englischen Lektion widmen und besser gibt es keinen Ersatz für eine werktätige Arbeit.

July 24

Today, Miss Hartocollis called and asked us to come over once again as she thought she had located a job for us. But it turned out that the plumbing company on Eastern Avenue wasn't hiring today. On the way over there I noticed a sign from the streetcar that said "Ironworker Wanted." And so we made our way there to ask about jobs. It so happens that they were Germans, and the boss's son who was on site suggested that we come back the next day, i.e., today, to speak with his father.

And so this morning we went back and inquired about the situation. The father, an old man, told us a great deal about his past successes and complained about present-day problems. He showed us many wrought iron products which comprise the production line of the business, although they have now been superseded by cast iron and press work. Lamps, tables, graveyard items and church furniture as well as cast iron garden furniture are produced. By the end of the interview the good man believed he could hire one of us for 60 cents an hour. I think that we will not make good on our provisional acceptance of the job.

August 24

The prediction expressed in the last few entries was based on an erroneous assumption, because today marks my fourth week with this company. Thanks to my skill level, however, I'm already being paid 80 cents an hour. With overtime, I make $45 a week.

Well, four weeks have passed since my last entries, and a number of vivid impressions have been forgotten. We received our first mail from Germany and a confirmation that the situation back home remains unchanged. I also received a communication from Rico in the last letter. It pleased me greatly. Always moving ahead, he's finishing up his studies and then it's up to him to shape his life in whatever way he wants. Is that right? Will he not enjoy different freedoms than I, who have chosen a different path? Time will tell, and down the road I'll look back on my youthful worries with an indulgent smile.

Earlier I sent a letter to Frankfurt. And now I'll make an effort to renew contact with my friend, Rico.

24. Juli

Wieder einmal rief uns gestern Miss Hartecollis zu sich und glaubte einen „job" ausfindig gemacht zu haben. Aber auch die Plumbing Co. in der Eastern Ave. brauchte heute keine Arbeiter. Unterwegs sah ich von der Straßenbahn aus ein Schild: Ironworker wanted. Also bemühten wir uns zu diesem Platz, um einen job zu erfragen. Zufälligerweise handelt es sich wieder einmal um Deutsche, und der anwesende Sohn des Chefs stellte die Möglichkeit in Aussicht, wenn wir anderntags, also heute, mit seinem Vater verhandeln wollten.

So fuhren wir heute morgen wieder zu diesem Platz und erkundeten die Lage. Der Vater, ein Greis, erzählte viel von seiner erfolgreichen Zeit und klagte über den Mangel der heutigen Tage. So zeigte er uns viele schmiedeeiserne Arbeiten, die heute durch Guß- und Stanzarbeiten längst überholt worden sind und die Produktion des Betriebes darstellen. Es werden Lampen, Tische, Grab- und Kirchengeräte, sowie gußeiserne Gartenmöbel produziert. Am Ende des Interviews glaubte der gute Mann, einen von uns zu einem 60c Stundenlohn engagieren zu können. Ich glaube, dass wir unsere vorläufige Zusage nicht einhalten werden.

24. August

Die bei den letzten Eintragungen geäußerte Vermutung beruhte auf einer irrigen Annahme, denn heute arbeite ich bereits die vierte Woche in dieser Firma. Dank meiner Fähigkeiten wird mir allerdings heute schon 80c in der Stunde gezahlt. Mit einer Anzahl Überstunden komme ich auf 45 Dollars in der Woche.

Also vier Wochen sind seit der letzten Eintragung vergangen, und eine Menge lebendiger Eindrücke sind wieder erloschen. Inzwischen erhielten wir die erste Post aus Deutschland und die Bestätigung der unveränderten Lage. Mit dem letzten Schreiben erhielt ich auch ein Lebenszeichen von Rico. Das hat mich sehr gefreut. Immer fortschreitend beendet er einmal sein Studium, und ihm ist dann die Handhabe gegeben, sein Leben nach eigenem Ermessen zu gestalten. Ist das richtig? Wird er nicht andere Freiheiten genießen können als ich, der einen anderen Weg gewählt hat? Die Zeit wird es lehren, und in späteren Tagen werde ich meine Jugendsorgen belächeln können.

Vorhin sandte ich einen Brief nach Frankfurt. Und nun werde ich mich bemühen, Kontakt zu Freund Rico zu finden.

January 4

For quite a while now I've been regretting this intermission or gap in my journal entries. I will give it another try with the start of the New Year.

It's less noteworthy that I slept through New Year's Eve than that I was a guest at Ray's house with H. till after midnight the next day. Ray and his wife, Velma, and also their little son, Garry, are our only friends. But the Ziegler family is also quite interested in us. Velma does our laundry and also likes to host us at her dinner table. All this without any type of compensation.

I continue to work at Cinti Artistic Wrought Iron Works Co. After all, why should I release the bird in my hand to reach for two in the bush? Although I get no intellectual satisfaction from my work, I am able to attend evening classes, and regular attendance at church services also provides a certain balance. All of this keeps alive my longing for a true vocation and strengthens my will and my knowledge.

Regrettably, I have neither a male nor a female friend, and Brother Heinz's interests tend to be quite materialistic. He's always tired, sleeps whenever he has an opportunity, and possibly dreams of better times to come.

The postal connection with home is quite good, even if none of Aunt Jeanne's letters arrived, probably because of an incorrect address. The arrival of almost all the Christmas packages we sent was confirmed, which resulted in many a happy celebration at home. It's very interesting and worth mentioning that we even received various packages from Germany. Mother once again sent me a Duden (*German dictionary*). My English is improving, and I got a grade of 95 in class. Of course that's an exaggeration, but nonetheless it's encouraging.

We have long since paid our debts to the ACCR, and each of us once again has $100 in the savings bank.

04. Januar

Schon lange bereue ich die Pause oder Lücke in meinen Tagebuchaufzeichnungen. Mit dem Beginn des neuen Jahres will ich wenigstens wieder einen Versuch machen.

Dass ich Sylvester verschlafen habe, ist weniger beachtenswert denn dass ich mit H. anderntags als Gast bei Ray bis nach Mitternacht weilte. Ray und seine Gattin Velma und nicht zuletzt noch Söhnchen Garry sind unsere einzigen Freunde. Aber auch Familie Ziegler zeigen reges Interesse. Velma wäscht unsere Wäsche und sieht uns noch gerne als Gäste an ihrem Tisch. Alles ohne Gegenleistung.

Noch immer arbeite ich in Cinti Artistic Wrought Iron Works Co. Warum sollte ich denn auch den Sperling fliegen lassen und nach den Tauben auf dem Dache langen? Es ist wohl wahr, dass ich keine geistige Befriedigung in meiner Arbeit finden kann, doch dafür gehe ich zur Abendschule und der regelmäßige Besuch der Gottesdienste bringt einen gewissen Ausgleich. Das alles hält auch meine Sehnsucht nach wirklichem Wirken wach und stärkt Wille und Wissen.

Bedauerlicherweise habe ich weder einen Freund noch eine Freundin, und Bruder Heinz' Interesse ist zu sehr materialistisch orientiert. Auch ist er immer müde, schläft, wenn er irgend Zeit hat und träumt womöglich von Zeiten, da er es noch bequemer hat.

Die Postverbindung mit der Heimat ist denkbar gut, wenn auch alle Briefe von Tante Jeanne wahrscheinlich infolge falscher Adresse nicht ankamen. Fast alle Weihnachtssendungen wurden bestätigt und mit diesen wurde manches Fest froher gestimmt. Dass wir aus Deutschland sogar verschiedene Sendungen erhalten haben, ist sehr interessant und erwähnenswert. Mutter sandte mir auch wieder einen Duden. Meine englischen Sprachkenntnisse machten gute Fortschritte, und der Schulbericht zeigt 95. Das ist natürlich übertrieben, immerhin jedoch eine Aufmunterung.

Unsere Schulden bei ACCR sind längst bezahlt, und jeder von uns hat bereits wieder 100- $ in der Sparkasse.

January 6

Yesterday marked the start of the second half of the first semester of evening classes. To round out my schooling, I'm now going there on Mondays and Wednesdays as well. Subject: American history. I actually wanted to take an algebra class or some other technically oriented course. But for lack of opportunity and in line with my decision not to take a beginner course in algebra, I had to take American history. Typing would have been another possibility. Well, now that I've made this decision, I also believe that it's necessary and also valuable to learn about the development of my new homeland.

Yesterday I wrote to Uncle Hermann to tell him I'd purchased some sports jerseys. No doubt he'll be greatly surprised and may even require a handkerchief. No word yet from Werner or Kreussler with regard to the Christmas packages. I've not heard a thing from Rico since his first two letters. But that's not quite true! He did after all explain to my mother and sent his apologies. We'll soon have more points of contact again.

Last Sunday Brother H. and I signed up for a $1,000 life insurance policy. My annual premium is $51.20, and has to be paid for 20 years. At that point I'll either be able to get the $1,000 back or pay taxes and leave the money in the account. Should one of us die, the other will receive the insurance. So it's pretty much a precautionary measure.

January 7

With midnight approaching, another work day is over. I've just reread a number of unanswered letters and stowed them in the drawer again. It was especially nice to receive confirmation of the arrival of the Christmas gifts I sent to the children. But the kind regards of Franz Eifert, Helma Mausolfs, and many others are worth noting.

We have not received any mail for 3 days or so. I'm sure it will all come at once.

06. Januar

Gestern startete die Abendschule den zweiten Abschnitt des ersten Semesters. Zur Ergänzung meines Schulplanes gehe ich nun auch montags und mittwochs nach dort. Subjekt: Amerikanische Historie. Eigentlich wollte ich eine Algebra- oder sonst eine technisch orientierte Klasse besuchen. Doch mangels einer Gelegenheit und gemäß meinem Vorsatz, keinen Anfänger-Algebra-Kurs aufzunehmen, nahm ich notgedrungen Amerikanische Historie. Typing wäre noch eine andere Möglichkeit gewesen. Nun, da ich mich entschieden habe, glaube ich auch, dass das Wissen um die Entwicklung meiner neuen Heimat notwendig und auch wertvoll ist.

Gestern schrieb ich an Onkel Hermann und berichtete ihm von meinem Kauf der Trikots. Er wird gewißlich Augen machen, womöglich muss er ein Taschentuch zu Hilfe nehmen. Werners wie auch Kreußlers Bestätigung der Weihnachtssendung ist noch nicht angekommen. Von Rico hörte ich seit seinen beiden ersten Briefen nichts mehr. Oder Doch! Er hat sich ja bei meiner Mutter beschwert und entschuldigt. Bald werden wir wieder mehr Berührungspunkte bekommen.

Vergangenen Sonntag haben Bruder H. und ich ja eine Lebensversicherung über 1000 $ abgeschlossen. Mein jährlicher Beitrag ist 51,20 und muss 20 Jahre lang entrichtet werden. Dann kann man seine 1000 $ entweder zurückbekommen oder sie unter Verzinsung in der Gesellschaft belassen. Wenn einer sterben sollte, wird dem andern der Versicherungsbetrag ausgehändigt. Er ist praktisch also eine Vorsichtsmaßnahme.

07. Januar

Wieder einmal nahe an Mitternacht liegt ein arbeitsreicher Tag hinter mir. Soeben habe ich eine ganze Anzahl unbeantworteter Briefe durchgelesen und wieder im Schubfach verstaut. Besondere Freude bereiten mir die Bestätigungen der an Kinder gesandten Weihnachtsgaben. Aber auch das Gedenken Franz Eiferts, Helma Mausolfs und vieler anderer ist beachtenswert.

Seit drei Tagen oder auch länger haben wir keine Post mehr empfangen. Sicherlich kommt wieder alles auf einmal.

January 9

Yesterday I received a nice letter from the Kreussler family. Even Elfriede added a greeting in English. I'll respond to her in like fashion soon. Today I got a letter from Werner about receiving his Christmas package and to acknowledge receipt of the package sent to Mary Mensch.

In our first chemistry class after the holidays, we got our test back. I got the highest grade in the class with a 97. Then we had lab work on supersaturated solutions. I enjoy going to my Friday classes and chemistry is also an interesting subject. Whether I'll ever be able to make use of it professionally, I don't know.

January 25

Today is Sunday and the streets are covered in deep snow. With temperatures about 15-20 degrees below freezing, it really feels like winter. My physical well-being is presently suffering from a nasty cold. Work at the factory has more or less become a habit. Petty thoughts often give this work a humiliating character and serve no good purpose.

Generally my thoughts are occupied with working out mathematical problems. I'm hoping that the nightly evening classes will open the door for further studies. Whether or not this could happen by next semester depends on if I make sufficient progress with my English.

We've recently been looking for another apartment. Although our current one is anything but ideal, I'm not expecting a miracle from this change. After all, there would be no one who cleans professionally. Nonetheless it will be a significant advantage if the toilet and bath are located nearby. For the time being, our plan of eventually buying a house remains just a dream.

Sooner or later we'll also have to deal with the problem of how to set about living together with our family, which will be arriving. Brother H's enthusiasm, while quite focused, is less far-sighted. Nothing is further from my mind than denying my relatives my aid. And yet it is an unnatural and perhaps even unreasonable idea to gather all the grown children together again. Once we've all taken our first independent steps into the future, once we have experienced the effort involved in being responsible for ourselves and have experienced the joy and satisfaction of managing on our own, it's a move backwards to return to mother's apron strings. This opinion should not imply that what I've stated up to this point should be recanted. I am very aware of how much we children have benefited by my mother's hard work. If today I can take care of myself, then this largely due to her.

09. Januar

Gestern bekam ich einen netten Brief von Familie Kreußler. Auch Elfriede sandte einen Gruß in englischer Sprache. So will ich ihr nächstens in gleicher Weise antworten. Heute schrieb Werner über den Erhalt seines Weihnachtspaketes und den Empfang der Sendung an Mary Mensch.

In der ersten Chemie-Stunde nach den Ferien bekamen wir den „Test" zurück. Mit 97 hatte ich die beste Arbeit in der Klasse absolviert. Dann hatten wir eine Lab-Arbeit über supersaturated solutions. Ich gehe gerne in die Freitag-Klassen und Chemistry ist auch ein interessantes Gebiet. Ob ich dies jemals beruflich gebruachen kann, ich weiss nicht.

25. Januar

Heute ist ein Sonntag, und die Straßen sind tief verschneit. Mit etwa 15 - 20 Grad unter „0" ist die Temperatur auch recht winterlich. Mein körperliches Wohlbefinden leidet lediglich unter einem heftigen Schnupfen. Die Arbeit im Fabrikbetrieb ist schon mehr oder weniger eine Gewohnheitssache geworden. Oft geben kleinliche Gedanken dieser Arbeit einen demütigenden Charakter und sind wenig zweckvoll.

Überhaupt bilden Problemstellungen den Hauptinhalt meiner Gedanken. Der allabendliche Schulbesuch soll mir die Chancen für weitere Studien eröffnen. Ob dies schon im nächsten Semester möglich sein wird, ist davon abhängig, ob ich genügende Fortschritte im Englischen mache.

Neuerdings suchen wir nach einer anderen Wohnung. Obwohl unsere jetzige alles andere als ideal ist, so verspreche ich mir von dem Wechsel auch keine Wunderdinge. Ist doch niemand da, der professionell sauber macht. Immerhin wird es ein bedeutender Vorteil sein, wenn das Klosett und ein Bad zur unmittelbaren Umgebung gehören. Unser Plan, eventuell ein Haus zu kaufen, ist zunächst ein fantastischer Gedanke.

Früher oder später stehen wir auch dem Problem gegenüber, wie das fernere Zusammenleben mit der ankommenden Familie vonstatten gehen soll. Bruder H's Begeisterung ist wohl recht zielstrebig, doch wenig weitschauend. Es ist mir nichts ferner, als meinen Angehörigen etwa meine Hilfe zu versagen. Doch ist es fast eine unnatürliche und vielleicht unvernünftige Ansicht, alle erwachsenen Kinder wieder zusammenzuführen. Nachdem wir die ersten selbständigen Schritte in die Zukunft getan haben, die Mühe der eigenen Verantwortung fühlen und die Freude und Genugtuung im Bestehen fanden, ist es ein Krebsgang, wenn man unter den mütterlichen Rockschoß zurückwandert. Diese Ansicht soll nicht den Anschein erwecken, dass meine bisher proklamierten Thesen widerrufen werden sollen. Ich weiß mit all meiner Überlegung, was meiner Mutter Werk an uns Kindern Gutes getan hat. Wenn ich mich heute bewähren kann, dann ist dies ihr größtes Verdienst.

But where does my path lead? What are the pathways of life and can a person help shape his destiny and intervene in a decisive way? Does God have a special plan for each individual? If such a plan exists, it must be within our power to discern our part. For it's my belief that God does nothing for us that we can do for ourselves. Perhaps we can compare human existence to mountain streams. By way of natural progression, despite many different twists and turns and direction, each waterway reaches the valley and then flows into the huge, unfathomable ocean.

January 28

Two significant events are upcoming. Next Sunday we will be able to speak with mother. And next week I'll commence my studies at the U.C. (*University of Cincinnati*) Evening College. I'm well aware that this is quite risky. May the kind Lord help me so that my good intentions suffice to bring this undertaking to a successful conclusion.

Eleven letters arrived today, after a full 21 letters arrived on one day recently. Mother gave us a detailed report on Christmas. As did Werner, Kreussler, and other friends. Christel was showered with a whole toy store full of gifts. Mother's report described a joyful celebration, a comfortable home, and happy, contented people. So why this impatience? They want to give up and give away everything they have. For what? We ourselves are like a boat without a harbor, so how can we become a harbor for the family?

January 31

It was an eventful day. Whether it was a victorious day the future will have to decide.

First of all I went downtown to Newman Bros. to apply for a job. After much discussion, it's possible that I might get a job in the technical area. After that I went to the U.C. and paid my student fees ($50.25) and am now entitled to attend evening college. Continuing on, I arrived at my old firm and quit my job, which was met with some consternation. I received my last pay of $7.36.

Doch wohin führt mein Weg? Was sind die Wege des Lebens und kann der Mensch zu seinem Schicksal beitragen und bestimmend eingreifen? Besteht für jedes Individuum ein bestimmter Plan Gottes? Wenn ein solcher Plan besteht, dann liegt es auch in unserer Macht, daraus unseren Teil zu erlesen. Denn es ist mein Glaube, dass Gott nichts für uns tut, wohin wir mit eigener Fähigkeit gelangen können. Vielleicht kann man das menschliche Dasein auch mit den Berggewässern vergleichen. Im natürlichen Ablauf, doch in den mannigfach verschiedensten Wendungen und Richtungen gelangt jedes Wasser zum Tal und weiter fort in den unermesslich großen Ozean.

28. Januar

Zwei bedeutsame Ereignisse stehen bevor. Am kommenden Sonntag können wir mit Mutter sprechen. Und dann werde ich nächste Woche mein Studium an dem U.C. (*Universität Cincinnati*) Abend-College aufnehmen. Ich bin mir vollauf bewusst, dass das ein rechtes Wagnis ist. Möge mir der gütige Herrgott helfen, dass mein guter Wille ausreicht, um das Beginnen zu einem erfolgreichen Abschluß zu bringen.

Heute kamen elf Briefe an, nachdem an einem der letzten Tage gar 21 Briefe angekommen waren. Mutter gab einen ausführlichen Weihnachtsbericht. Ebenso Werner, Kreußler und andere Freunde. Christel ist mit einem ganzen „Spielzeugladen" beschert worden. Dieser Bericht zeigte uns ein freudvolles Fest, ein gemütliches Heim und beglückte Menschen. Warum nur diese Ungeduld? Alles wollen die hergeben, aufgeben. Für was? Wir selbst sind ein hafenloses Boot und wie können wir zum Hafen für die Familie werden?

31. Januar

Heute war ein ereignisreicher Tag. Und ob auch ein Siegestag, das muss die Zukunft noch zeigen.

Zunächst fuhr ich zu Newman Bros., einer Firma downtown, um mich um eine Stelle zu bewerben. Nach allen Verhandlungen habe ich sogar die Chance, im technischen Büro beschäftigt zu werden. Daraufhin fuhr ich zur U.C. und bezahlte meine Studiengebühren (50.25 $) und bin nun berechtigt, das Evening College zu besuchen. Ein weiterer Weg führte mich zu meiner alten Firma, wo meine Kündigung einige Bestürzung hervorrief. Mit 7.36 $ erhielt ich meine letzte Löhnung.

I had to buy some drafting tools, and after that was able to go home. By now the hands of the clock were moving toward 2 p.m., and I still hadn't eaten anything. I might almost agree that one can summon more energy on an empty stomach, though a man who is always hungry is rarely able to do much work. — But now it's a matter of taking advantage of all available opportunities with all the energy I can muster. A position as draftsman means a cut in pay, at least to start. On the other hand, quitting time is always the same and you can go home without spending much time washing up. First and foremost, my task in the coming semester at evening school will simply be to maintain my level of knowledge. After all, algebra, trigonometry, analytical geometry and technical drawing aren't exactly new to me. What's most essential is concentration and energy.

April 13

I didn't have class tonight, so after studying for awhile I read an informative story about a Polish family. My job as a draftsman is quite satisfying. Going to school and the related courses are demanding, but nonetheless I'm managing to keep up. I went to concerts the last two weekends. Very nice.

Last Sunday I accepted an invitation from Velma's niece. Heinz has now got another job. We continue to receive good news from home. I expect mail from Rico any day now. I sent Werner a package today.

Der Einkauf einiger Zeichenwerkzeuge war noch notwendig, dann konnte ich wieder nach Hause fahren. Inzwischen rückten die Zeiger der Uhr nach 2.00 PM, und noch immer hatte ich nichts gegessen. Ob man mit nüchternem Magen mehr Energie aufbringt, möchte ist fast bejahen, wenn auch ein immer hungriger Geselle selten zu Taten aufgelegt ist. - Jetzt gilt es, mit aller Energie die vorhandenen Chancen auszunutzen. Eine Position als Zeichner bedeutet zwar ein Minus im Verdienst, zumindestens am Anfang. Dagegen aber ist mit dem Glockenschlag Feierabend, und ohne große Waschprozedur ist man reisefertig. Im kommenden Semester in der Abendschule gilt es zunächst ebenso die Position zu halten. Algebra, Trigonometrie, Analyt. Geometrie sowie technisches Zeichnen sind ja zuletzt keine fremden Dörfer. Konzentration und Energie sind die wichtigsten Faktoren.

13. April

Heute Abend hatte ich keine Schule und nach einigen Studien habe ich noch eine lehrreiche Geschichte über eine polnische Familie gelesen. Meine Arbeit als Zeichner ist recht befriedigend. Der Schulbesuch und die damit verbundenen Studien sind anstrengend, immerhin kann ich Schritt halten. Die letzten beiden Wochenenden war ich im Konzert. Sehr schön.

Letzten Sonntag folgte ich einer Einladung von Velmas Nichte. Heinz bekam inzwischen eine andere Arbeitsstelle. Von Zuhause bekommen wir gute Nachrichten. Ricos Post erwarte ich in den nächsten Tagen. Werner sandte ich heute ein Päckchen.

Paul's Original Illustrations

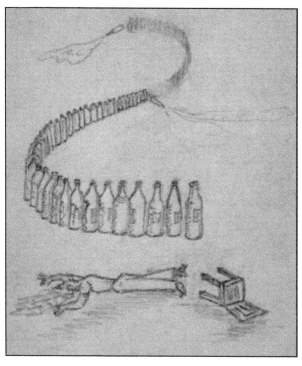

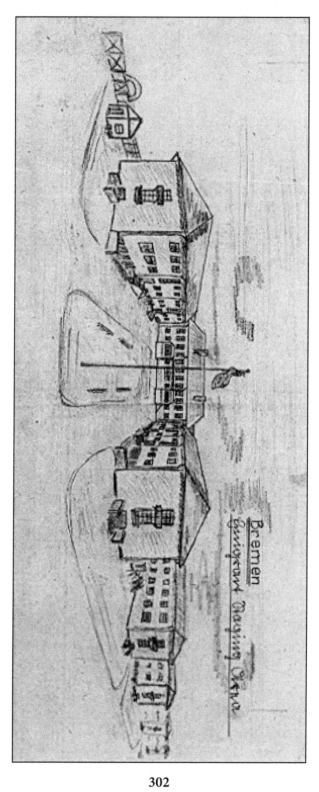

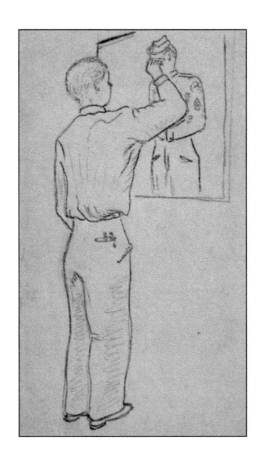

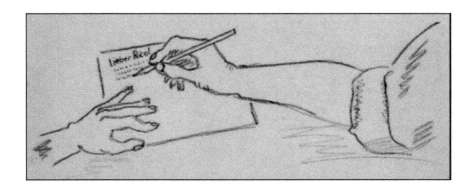

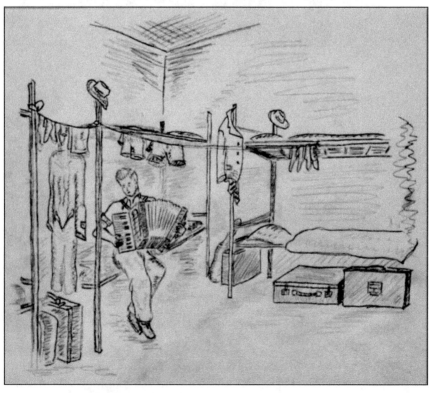

304

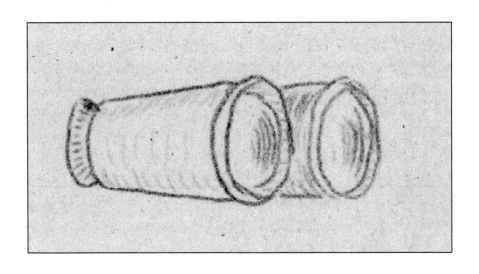

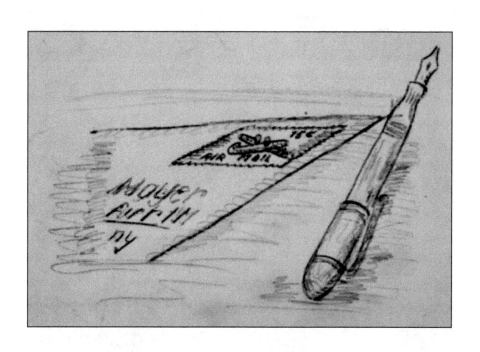

Part Three

August 1948-September 1950

A New Life in the United States

As Written in English

A Hymn of the Moon

What shines behind the cloud,
So gracious, pure and true?
Who offers people in the dark
A light for hope renewed?

It is the moon that's risen,
And guards us from on high!
I wish I could join in the flight
And shine throughout the night,

And could, like her, with gentle light,
Give help and comfort, peace of mind,
Soothe pain or even bring delight
To those who feel tormented.

To man in all his troubles
She is a silent friend,
Wants to enlighten all she finds
Caught up in dark intent.

No good to brood in darkened mood!
She comforts through the night.
She knows the way to inner peace
And keeps the watch alright.

Ein Lied vom Mond

Was scheint denn aus der Wolke
so huldreich, rein und wahr?
Wer reicht dem finstern Volke
sein Licht zur Labe dar?

Der Mond ist hochgestiegen
und hält am Himmel Wacht!
Ich wollt, ich könnt so fliegen
und leuchten durch die Nacht!

Und könnt wie es Elenden
mit seinem milden Schein,
recht Trost und Hilfe spenden
und lindern Seelenpein.

Dem Mensch in seinen Nöten
ist er ein stummer Freund!
Erleuchten will er jeden
den er im Finstern meint.

Nichts nützt im Dunkeln brüsten,
Er tröstet durch die Nacht,
er kennt den Weg zum Frieden
drum hält er treulich Wacht.

August 21

Tonight I have read two very interesting reports in the paper.

Queen Wilhelmina of Holland, who has reigned for 50 years will relinquish her crown to her daughter, Juliana, this month. The report praises mainly her great affections to her home country. During World War II she went to London and directed and strengthened the resistance of her people against the German conquerors. Now she is tired, physically as well as spiritually. Juliana, as her successor, has with her youth the energy and the better qualifications to lead the Dutchmen out of their postwar calamities (as they hope!)

The second story has stimulated a greater interest. When one might think the resignation of Queen W. is one of the subsequent incidents of our up to day history so is the report about Mr. Charles Bohlen a pointing career. Driven by his own desire to become a diplomat, he studied with earnest concern. While a Vice-consul in Prague (1930), he recognized the growing shadows of future implications. Since then, he studied the Russian language which he mastered within a few years. Especially during his assignment as Vice-consul in Paris, he joined the Institute for Oriental Languages to progress in Russian. It is said that B. has been able to write and to speak the R. language as well as English after two years only.

Nowadays, B. is the top advisor on R. affairs. With President FDR and Mr. Truman as well, he visited and interpretet all big meetings and to Mr. Marshal he is an indispensable advisor.

To me it seems the learning a foreign language, perhaps Russian, might be more advisable as the pure materialistically speculating study of engineering. Maybe there is one way to combine these two fields. Then whatsoever the future evolution might be, the knowledge itself will be determining in my case. Nothing shall be said about my own desires, how ever. For the sake of self determination it is of greatest importance to stimulate a similar response. The challenge of our days is rather to find a new jar for the new wine than trying to accommodate an growing organism within insufficient boundaries.

In a conversation with a young student, I discussed wether the possibilities of human progress for the individual lays in the spiritual or in the materialistic fields. His observation led him to the conclusion that men's progress is mainly limited to the secular sphere, whereas I did not agree. Surely, human interest is nowadays merely concerned in advance of earnings, gain of popularity and satisfaction of their own welfare but this does not count for the actual possibilities. It is one of my deepest convictions that this human response will lead and has led already in a spiritual dilemma, whereas for the way out the lack of responsibility and ability to readjust have caused far spread troubles.

Nations have fought to end a furious battle but have not won the abiding falue of peace. Nations as well as the individual and both as members of a society will continue to look in vain for an ideal solution of their problem unless they are looking for that new jar to accommodate the new wine.

Human destiny in my point of view is located on a superhuman level. It sounds rather like an utopy. However, consider the fact that human progress has led mankind from an animal like standard to the advanced standing of our civilization. The speedy progress of mechanical inventions does not as much determine the judgment where about we are standing. And it is not to be overlooked that the gain of an too convenient way of living causes a weakness in resistance against destruction physical as well as human environments. But in struggling for the liberty of all human beings we are entering a state of civilization which has not been entered by any society before our time.

September 2

Yesterday I have written a letter to Rico. In an easy time I have told him about how the chances are that I may be called for the selective service within the American Army. Though I'm not too much pleased in view of my studies I expect whatever may occur with a great patience and trustfulness. Mrs. D. who was working at the local board has been in charge of my registration, too. She seems to have an unusual interest for us boys because her recommendations are yielding to eliminate draft for both of us.

That same afternoon I went to see Mr. Bohm in M. K. Kenney Engineering Office in the Engineer Bldg., after I had made an appointment with him a few days ago. Although he was very friendly I could not get rid of a feeling that he was not so intensively interested to have me in his office. I'm doubtfully too whether or not I shall expect his call in one of these days. Some day, however, there will be a change as desired.

September 4

Today's actions were mainly influenced by the afternoon visit in Mr.

Potter's office. Potter, Tyler and Martin are the associates of an architects office at 6th St. in downtown of Cincinnati. Until 12 o'clock I worked in Neuman's as usual. Walt Schroer, another draftsman of N. drove me up to Mt. Auburn and in the shortest time I was home.

Heinz had prepared a good soup of lentils. After dinner I changed clothes. Though early in time I did not like to miss the arriving bus and a sprint was necessary to catch it. However, Mr. Potter was not in his office. An employee called somewhere and informed me afterward that Mr. Potter might be in at 2 o'clock.

Returning at 2 o'clock I found Mr. Potter in his office. A fast operating elevator needed just a few seconds for the way from the 1st floor to the eighth floor. Mr. P. is a very friendly man. He liked my drawings best. However, he does not have a job for me in his own office. He will try to place me somewhere this week. For reference he like to keep my drawings.

September 8

Preceding Sunday Heinz and I were invited to Zieglers. After Saturday's busy schedule I enjoyed to sleep for two more hours on Sunday morning. Zieglers live out in Boone County approximately 25 miles away from Cincinnati. Three different bus lines brought us there. First we used the Cincinnati Street Railway, second from the Dixie Terminal we traveled by a Green Line bus and finally an old shaky vehicle of the Hebros Bus Line served us over a beautiful country road to our destination.

Z. lived for years in the city. However they prefer the country life more. Their possessions include a small farm house, a barn and a few acres of land. Besides corn they raise beans, tomatoes and potatoes. This year the tomatoes are good and numerous but the potatoes are all taken ill.

Jack and Buddy are 14 and 13 years old. We had quite a nice time. Playing ball, pitching horse shoes, high jumping over cloth line, table and well as well as chasing one another were the main amusements. I met some of their relations too. Cliff, the older son of Z, took us home in his car.

September 11

This was the first "big" party in our home. Velma, Ray and Gary, also Mr. and Mrs. Wagner with Paul have been our guests. We all had a nice time. Mrs. Wagner brought a cake with her. Paul goes back to school next week for another year and we were glad to have had him with us.

February 5

Too bad for all the time and its events which have passed by, unrecorded for they are lost in respect of their originality. My life as a student at the U.C. is on the whole just a true discipleship of my consciousness which calls for an intensive struggle for self improvement. As I have said at an earlier date, before one goes out into the world one should be first very much concerned about his preparatory work in view of the job one will be called upon.

The opposing forces in life will especially be opposing at the very spot one fails to develop moral and mental strength. I will not try here to give myself a quick answer whether the non-resistant attitude of Gandhi or the aggressive militant philosophy of Nietsche promises to be the pass way towards the high neveau of living. All above is still the divine example of Jesus Christ. Surely not the mystified person of orthodox Christianity but the life near genius of humanity, the prophet and interpreter of God's will and the ever present fellow-traveler in life itself.

A problem can scarcely be said to have been solved until all factors have been honestly faced and completely reconciled. However, when there is a multitude of problems as in our days there are likewise many more chances of misunderstanding, confusion, discouragement and disillusionment.

At times when I am worried about the outcome of the periodical tests which are put up as a measurement of the students advancement. I'm also aware of the fact that the generally satisfactory results do not provide myself with any real satisfaction. Without question an engineer's education is bound up with the science of mathematics. My own talent did not require more than work and practice for the scheduled assignments. Thus I have been able to spend some time with friends and in reading and studying other than technical books.

My strife for knowledge is not determined by whether or not I will end up in a good paying position. In fact I am fully convinced that I will not have mountains of treasure other than real values as there are spiritual power mental strength and not at least a good bit of common sense. Often I'm very lonesome with such an attitude for most the fellow students live the life as if there does not exist other problems in this world other as within their narrow self-centeredness.

Yesterday I visited Ray, Velma and Gary. All of them are O.K. R's garage is almost finished now. I helped him to erect the outer door. Though it was not a very difficult job the low temperature and the dampness of that working place cause some discomfort.

February 19

The passed week or two have been very busy ones. At the end of another 7 week interval in school a depressing amount of work was thrown at me. Now its all over and as so often after very exhausting and exciting experiences I feel like having something accomplished. Unfortunately, however, one of my exams turned out to have a pittyful result. Always in Chemistry I have some trouble, though I like the subject.

One who does a lot at least accomplishes a little and so I am not depressed any longer. Also I have learned by means of new experiments which I was asked to undertake. The so-called "research paper" was a topic composed of freely chosen sources, as books from the library etc. Taking advantage of the free choice of the topic I worked on a non-technical subject. Thus I have read material about Tolstoy, Nietzsche, and other famous people; also my "study of history" has revealed itself once more as very valuable.

Last Wednesday I attented a Wesley party at church. W. is the only place I go to. Sometimes at Sunday nights I participate in their work in as far I function as the performer of a brief worship. This is besides being a subject in which I put in all my seriousness, also a good practice of public speaking. When I visited Mr. Olmsted last week he told me the very same thing namely to try to speak more distinctly. Since I have been able to increase my vocabulary it will be my chief concern to speak in a more correct manner.

An interesting story was told by Nancy Kellogg, the very amiable girl of W.F. In the course of the telling of everyone's life story in a "cell" group, a group of truth seeking students, it was her turn last Wednesday. Born and raised under good and harmonious circumstances she has developed a sunny attitude towards life. During the war her father left his "peace-serving job" as a soapmaker or better, engineer at P. and G. to become engaged with the filling of shells and bombs in some other city.

Thus N. went to high school away from her parents. When they returned to Cincinnati, Nancy was ready for her second year of college which she promptly began at U.C. She liked to play violin since she was a little girl. Today she is a member of the Civic Orcherster. Last year she graduated from U.C. and works at present as a caseworker for the Hamilton County Welfare Ass. Nancy has a lively sister 2 years younger than she. Susy has made a likewise good impression when I met her first. S. is a junior at the College of Dennison.

April 8

Today it is like having completed a tough job. Right now I'm sitting back and just wondering at myself how I could have done so well. After 28 weeks of "brain-crushing" studies I have now a break though I'm planning to work with Dolbey next week instead having a vacation. Still it will be purely physical work and I can relax. However, I have come to realize that one accomplishes things only when he tackles them with his full strength. The week after next will see me in my first co-op job. It will be with Nutting and Co. I do not know yet of what my duties will consist.

Supposingly on the coming Wednesday I will go there and introduce myself. I plan it for that specific day because then I will also meet Mrs. Dalzell. She is the president of the women organization of the Council of Churches. Last night she did invite me to be a guest at a luncheon at the Queen City Club. On her request I shall be giving a short talk at a Fellowship Dinner of her organization in the roof garden of the Hotel Gibson on May 6.

Probably on May the 8th, a Sunday, I will have a part in a television program featuring a panel discussion of foreign students. This all means that I will have ample opportunity to meet people and to observe the true aspects of the American way of living.

For next Sunday I have two tickets for the symphonic orchester. I have asked Helen M. for a date which was promptly accepted.

A event of lesser comfort took place today insofar Heinz did lose his job. Fortunately I'll start to work next week. On account of this I just don't feel free enough to tell him of the contract I have signed yesterday. Maybe it was rather foolish to do so but since I have done so there is not sense to regret it. For I have purchased a complete set of encyclopedias for a monthly payment of $10 and the total amount of $169. I just hope he'll find another job soon.

Things in school are going fine. Last Wednesday I'd have my final exam in Anal. Geometry. My grade of 96 gave me a final average of 94.3 which can be considered excellent. Thursday the final in Chemistry lasted also three hours. Though it was not too hard I'm not too sure of what the result will be. I just hope for the best. This morning we had a last quiz in vector algebra a course in which I did not too good. Then in the afternoon we had an enjoyable meeting in our English class. Mr. O'Connell asked every student to express his opinion of the class in a few word. Before the hour was over we were dismissed,

Since I have asked the Wesleyans for old cloth I have been rewarded to an unforeseen extent. Some of the things I have sent to Hansel Lofferts wife while others will go home for mother's disposal. Wesleyans also have shown their generosity in allowing me to send a package to Karl Eschmann in Fechenheim. Just today I did receive a check over $6.35 for which I bill them. This was obviously cheaper than buying a CARE package for $10.

April 10

When I woke up this morning, the sun was shining and the birds singing. I did feel fresh and ready to get up though it was just 7:30 a.m. and I did not go to bed before 1:00 this morning. For a long time I have not had such a enjoyable time with Velma, Ray and Garry. They sure are very nice people. Right after work I brought the laundry over to them and then stayed 'til late in the evening. For a while Ray and I worked on his radio hobby shop. Later on I was engaged in making potato pancakes which turned out very tasty.

Today I will join Clifton Methodist Church. There I have many friends and probably will gain more friends within the fellowship of the church. And this afternoon I plan on going to the Symphony. Helen will go with me.

Today is the forth anniversary of the escape out of the Camp-Derenburg. 4 years are gone since. The world seemed to have changed. How often can one hear the saying, "Oh, if I was born again I did live my life differently"? But only very few people actually realize what they mean by that. Often it is rather an expression of dissatisfaction or disillusionment which in turn does not generate any creative power to bring about the new birth. People never realize how close or how far away from their ideals they live.

To be born anew does not mean to return to the inabilities of an infant but to grow out of the narrow-gaged tracks of the habits. There is nothing more resisting ones own progress than his own habits. These things one thinks he can't get along without them, that personal comfort that when intruded awakens mighty forces of defense to regain it. But all the energy spent there, the amount of time involved, not to mention the money which almightily enslaves so many noble ambitions, all these things hinder the true progress. This world is not a place of untroubled existence or of such a high security which we search for. If it were so the contented cow might as well be our ideal.

Was I not reborn 4 years ago? One thing for sure, a new life began. A life of ambition for perception and truth. Out of the misery of earlier days I have grown out into a position from which I can see the horizon clear and golden. The pessimism of my soul has greatly gone and I became an optimist believing in my own strength; guided, as I hope, by the true stewartship of Christ. Now I will join the army of people who, like me, believe in Christ's guiding power. 4 years after I was reborn I will be received in the community of the saints. May God bless this hour that it may significantly determine my future ways.

April 16

Another week has passed by. I was working with the Ediphone Company. However, Tuesday I had taken off to go to the H.D. Nutting, the place where I will have my first coop job. Perhaps it is too early to give any impression of this job. I'll find out soon enough. The same day I was guest at a luncheon at the Queen City Club. It was a very enjoyable event. Also pictures were taken which will appear in the Cincinnati Enquirer on April 24, 1949. I like to see what face I did cut.

This new job might be very interesting and useful too for my engineering experiences. However, the pay is rather meager. $135 a month should hardly be enough for half as long a time. Especially since Uncle Sam will deduct some tax too. It will be a 40 hour week. Now I have tried to get a part time job beside it. For that reason I called Mr. Schaefer, the boss I worked for in my first job here in Cincinnati. He always wanted me to come back. Probably he can arrange that. I can work a few hours every night.

Heinz is laid off since last Monday. His boss told him he would call him back as soon as work and material come in.

I myself was spending the evenings of Monday, Tuesday and Thursday at Ray's house. There I was painting the part of the house underneath the roof. Right after work I did go to the Dixie Terminal to take a bus to Southgate. Though the days are still short and dark comes quickly I proceeded to work till late into the evening with artificial light. All kinds of bugs were flying toward the light and a few of them ended up in the pot or can of green paint which was hanging from gutter.

Every night Velma prepared an excellent meal. When I quit painting Velma had to clean my face from green paint by means of turpentine and a clean cloth. Then I took a bath. Velma prepared again a bite and Ray bought me home before he went to work in his radio station WCPO.

The other two nights I spent with Helen. Also last night I started a letter to Werner. His birthday is on April 25 and I shall not miss that.

June 14

And again back to school. After a 7 week working period it is rather hard to get readjusted. Today, mother wrote that probably Helga and Christel will undertake the trip first. The time factor plays an extensive part in this story.

Meantime I have received a scholarship in school and have also made the Dean's List. I have not seen Helen for a while. However, I had the pleasure to meet Rose Taschian and her family. Her parents are immigrants from Armenia. In order that I may understand these people better I have taken some books out of the U.C. library about Armenian history, fiction and actual questions. Arnold Toynbee's book was not at hand.

In school we started today with calculus and physics, Supposingly an easy section, it started rather stiff. Well, after one or two weeks I can say more about that.

August 29

Grant me the boon of a life
That is useful and earnest
The privilege of honest toil and well earned rest. Great hearted courage to
cheer each faithful soul that strongly strives and wins or fails.
Kind word and act for those who grieve
And eyes to see the beauties
That nature paints on land in sky and sea.
And ears to hear each music voice of life.
Senses to comprehend the meaning of the eternal plan
The confidence and trust of friends
More dear than wealth and laurels
Or soon forgotten praise
Grant me this, my father's God and mine
And when the summons call from out the sunset strip I'll go with
hastening feet and joyous heart to tell thee my gratitude, oh life!

- Richard Hardy
The Rotarian Magazine, June 1929

Since the beginning of this month I have not been in school. At first a 3 week vacation period lasted 'til the 21 of Aug. and was followed by a work section with the N.C. Nutting which will last to the early days in November. Registration day is Nov. 7, 1949

Meantime, mother's coming seems to become true, for on Aug. 30, that is tomorrow, she will leave home in order to come here. I do expect that Gretel, Helga and Christel will be also in the party. Especially the boy's growth in both physical stature and wisdom should be a surprise.

Without question, this undertaking requires an extensive amount of courage on mother's part because she will leave all her possessions behind, likewise many privileges. However she is just my mother and her children's welfare ranges far beyond her own security. That is what I would call Christian attitude. She has truly faith in the future and utmost confidence in God's goodness.

Recently, I was appointed treasurer for Wesley. This is a job which requires much attention as to accuracy and correctness. Besides that I will remain active in the worship committee. During the summer there we have a more or less "off season" program. Though we meet regularly every Sunday the attendance fluctuates considerably. In the first few meetings a devotional seems to be appropriate. However more and more this need was replaced by an "all-play" attitude.

The Sunday morning discussion groups exert a strong attractions on the Wesleyans. We have had some lively discussions. Even though I do not always agree with the conclusion arrived, it is very much an indication of the young people's attitude toward life.

I remember especially the discussion about the meaning and significance of the family from a religious point of view. At that morning Erwin Pauly was my guest. He was here during a furlough. His Station at the time present is Fort Bliss

Well, Dick asked the question as to experiences of ours in respect to family life. I started off with a description of the growing disunion of families due to a very loose bondage attacked by the strong challenges of political, industrial and other worldly influences.

Obviously, this challenge can not be met by simply reducing the size of the family as it was advocated by a number of persons. There the motive was conspicuously the lack of confidence in the future or more so the opinion that financial security is a prerequisite of a happy future. According to them the responsibility of parents towards the limit of the size of the family is directly proportional to the provisions they can make for the children

Probably nobody will ever ask my humble opinion to that matter but it seemed to me that my friends advocate a pessimistic defense policy. We surely do not gamble with the happiness of our children in displacing a yes attitude towards life. It is, however, a necessity to have faith in one's own ability, courage and the understanding that there is a God-father up above.

In any case the children of today are not more helpless as they have been at all times before. If the children of tomorrow are not born there can be no further argument for we have not even provided a bare chance for them.

September 9

Mother is on her way. The last letter written by Helga contained only a few short lines of her. Probably a natural reaction takes place within herself. After years of struggle her unbreakable spirit is tested anew. Her expression of tiredness is of less physical significance than the mental reaction to the sudden release of many stresses. As I have said before this newest action proves again her bravour.

Here on the local scene has been quite some activity. Dick Stevens returned from his vacation trip. Pleasant to see him again. So Wednesday night we resumed our delayed planning of the Wesley program. Dick was presiding. Bea, Nancy, Mickey, Rose, Dick Morgan and myself were there. Rose's conspicuous contribution helped largely to settle the matter. Nevertheless it was ¼ til midnight when I crossed my threshold.

Yesterday I worked some long hours so that I was not only too tired but also too late to go after things I intended to do. With my Black-Flag-Windex sprayer I cleaned Wesley's large mirror. To fasten a board as suggested by the house committee it was necessary to have a few tools. Joe Woodburn agreed to fetch them and thus I was enabled to complete the task. The two pieces of material previously used as background for the altar are supposed to undergo a dry-cleaning treatment.

September 12

Another weekend has passed and the summation of my experiences has been increased by it. Saturday I worked for Nutting before noon and for Roland in the afternoon. In between I stopped at Wesley to pick up the altar cloth to bring it to the Fenton Cleaners.

Sunday morning was too fair to stay in bed. So I rose, dressed myself and left for Sunday School. Dick was back to lead another successful discussion. We debated the significance of Old Testament scriptures, in starting with the Psalms; however, ending up with the general question: "Why is it that people do not use religious sayings in their conversations?"

Often it seems that they are ashamed of it. Nancy Kellogg was in our group and contributed effectfully. The following service upstairs had in N.'s consegration a significant part. In brief statements she spoke to the congregation. Rev. B.'s sermon was about the holiness of the Christian Sabbath. He quoted Emerson, saying, "To destroy Christianity you must destroy the Sabbath."

Juliana Story's invitation for dinner was a friendly gesture. Mrs. S. did prepare an excellent meal. When Mom has taken over here, I'll gladly bring some friends home.

October 8

To take the more recent incidents to start on a new diary section it is most conspicuous that Nancy Kellogg's disparture has caused a more personal touch. There has always been some sense of mutuality but any nearer approach seemed not appropriate on my part. Last Thursday, then, instead having a cell group meeting a general lack of interest on the side of the other members left Nancy and myself alone. Only Micky showed up for a short period of time. I was working at the construction of a bulletin board. But I did leave it to go to watch the eclipse of the moon. It was really an impressing picture as the moon, though apparently visible, was overcast by the earth's shadow.

Later on the "Kernschatten" swept across the surface of the moon, freeing little by little of its silvery disc. At that time, however, Nancy and I were on the way to her house, but only to pass by and to go on for a walk. Not a single star should have missed to convey our strides and to listen to the conversation because not many a cloud was blown across the nightly scenery. Later on the overcast was almost complete in the higher stratosphere.

The light of the moon and his heavenly companions was diffused such that an almost uniform distribution gave a fairy-land-like illumination. Rather to think of a romance I appreciate this experience as a revelation to myself and a very useful lecture as to the understanding of a worthy and faithful soul. May God give me the courage to cheer her, that my way of doing things and my prayers let her feel my warmth and affection, may strengthen her attitude as she will in turn devote herself to the fulfillment of the hopes and expectations which are held for her.

October 9

"And I do not say God bless you, because He will do it anyway. More as you deserve." These were the words, the very last ones of my friend Nancy. How true. But why is it that whenever something moves me very strongly I would like to do great things whereas in the many other times I'm happily engaged into trifles. Give me, oh Lord, the courage to cheer a faithful soul that strongly strifes! Should it be a matter of courage to make such a decisive resolution like hers, why for heavens sake am I not making my conscience my guide which tells me boastingly so many times, "If it is humanly possible, I can do it"?

Of course the reality is such that I do need to finish school before I can be accepted by the Board of Missions. Not so in God's sight. He gives me the chance every day of the week, every second breath. I should be more concerned about the things which are worthwhile doing, worthwhile speaking of. So often when I meet people I do not right know what to talk about or how to act. May I be of such concern that my whole life becomes my message, understandable to my neighbors but more so acceptable in my heavenly father's sight!

October 10

As soon as I arrived home I did call N. and told her how much I liked to see her again. So received permission to meet her and a friend of hers at Fred's place. That evening I spoke to N. about the conversation which Rev. Bright and I had had the evening before.

He asked me, "Have you ever thought to go into the ministry?" It sure struck me unexpectedly. For how many times have I thought of my future occupation as being one of a serving nature to the advantage of humankind. What else should I have learned in the period of suffering and loneliness other than a means to prevent such occurrences in future times. Time and again I have looked forward to a chance to advance into a field of active and idealistic service, even though knowing that I have to work at myself.

When I remember right, approximately 2 years ago I wrote into my diary a parable-like idea. Then I thought myself a gardener in human society caring and watching the growth of the good, the beautiful, and the useful. But first I'd need to equip myself with the tools. I'd have to clean up my own back yard before I was ready to go carrying for somebody's troubles.

It seems to me now that this was well aimed and full of noble intentions but without the fierce and fire of a man of action. How often am I told, "So is there anything you can't do?" Oh, they flatter me, of course; it is like sweet music that fosters emotion but does not encourage thought. If nobody else can see it, I know that I have to grow and/or that I have to change before I'm ready to dabble in greater affairs of humanity.

This question bothers my conscience now and then. I'm trying to explore myself, searching for a way to turn my better inside to a powerful dynamo that will propel my personality onto a level of Christian service. My studies of "civil" engineering, a profession that builds highways, railroads and bridges that connect distant places, that link city to city, shall become a similar means of connecting all people of good will, a way to open up and conquer the hearts of people everywhere.

Sometimes I have my doubts if this is any longer an engineering profession; nonetheless it is a fantastic engineering problem. It is the lack of an Army of peace seekers. Whenever I'm in distress, despair, I need only to walk under the nightly sky, to look at a colorful sunset or advance against a stiff wind that makes my hair fly, makes me feel a part of nature and a part in God's masterful plan.

October 13

I've had quite a busy day on my job. 189 cu. yds. were inspected and uncounted delivery tickets had to be written out for it. In the evening, H., J. and I went to the Cincinnati Gardens to see my first Ice-Hockey game. It was quite interesting and the skill of the participants admirable. Unfortunately, a few rough spots disturbed the all-over impression. Besides hockey, some hot-headed boys performed also wrestling and boxing.

October 19

Last Saturday I did not have to work for Nutting, so I offered Nancy to help cutting the hedges. Around noon I finished. Because I was so undecided, Nancy did go to a wedding and I went to see the football game. That means, only the latter part of it. N. and I looked at the floats which were shown as customarily at the home-coming game. Then we departed. On the way home I bought some sox and a shirt with the money Mr. K. gave me for the job. I wished he had not done it!

In the evening N. and I went to the homecoming banquet. I wore the new shirt, a red tie, brown slacks and H's gray checkered coat! The eats were excellent, fried chicken, potatoes, beans and salad. Also coffee and a piece of cake. Interesting games, some skids and dancing filled the evening. When I walked N. home it was past 12:00.

Sunday had its usual pattern, except that I had once more charge of the Wesley worship program. Bill Brayshaw and Paul Rhodes helped me to get things done successfully.

Mother is still held in Bremen. A disgustingly drawn out story.

Monday I worked only 'til 2:50 and Roland permitted to come to his house. There I did repair and patched some concrete work.

October 27

(Epicticus?)…Require not things to happen as you wish, but wish them to happen as they occur and be ready for them… What ever may happen to me I shall turn towards myself and inquire what facilities I have to make use of it. Sickness is a handicap to the body, but not to the free will of choice; lameness is a handicap to the ease of moving around, but again not to the faculty of choice.

I can say some such thing to everything that happens to me and I shall find it to be a handicap to something else but not to myself. Then I cannot lose, but only gain. Everything that is given unto me may be asked back. However while I possess it I must take care of it!

It is difficult, I reckon, to blend the choices of life but it is not impossible. If it were so, who in this world could be called happy? That all depends upon the definition of happiness. Is it the sunny geniality of fulfilled romance or some other fleeting emotions we call pleasures?

It seems to me, as I'm sure it was felt before, that these are only the visible happenings which take place on the surface of humanity. There is a deeper sense of happiness, as Aristotle puts it,….in the absence of that feeling of frustration and bewilderment that is so often felt in real life when one is face to face with an experience whose scope one cannot grasp nor comprehend…

To most men life is pretty much a set routine directed toward some more or less worthy first or preliminary goal. From then on it is in one's capacity of making choices to use the opportunities to raise his imagination above and beyond the walls that usually surround him. These dikes of habits, of repressions, of fear of the unknown, of prejudice and of ignorance.

Have we not set before us ideals and some of them manifested and demonstrated in the life of genial men? The patterns and meanings of life as they became evident to them are freely available to any man.

How many times has it been said that life is like a journey? Well, how do we act in such an occasion? Often we can decide what train to take, we may freely choose the pilot to fly us to our destination. Also we may be free to set the day of departure and the hour of a "good bye" to friends and relatives. That is probably all we can do.

Afterwards we are subject to a higher will. Our part is performed. The airplane may fall from the sky or the ship may sink. What can we do? Only that...to be ready to die. Without fear, without accusing God, for one should know that everything that is born must also die.

Life has been compared also with some social event. We are always reminded to behave aright. There will be things handed around. Then put on your hand and take a moderate part of it. Does it pass you by? Do not stop it. Has it not yet reached your place? Do not stretch your arms across the table to make your desires known.

How fitting is this to compare with in regard to children, to a wife, to public posts, to wealth!

Remember also that you are an actor in a comedy, maybe a drama, of such a kind as God, the author, pleases to make it. If short, of a short one; if long, of a long one. If it be his order you should play and act a poor man, a cripple, a governor, or a private person, see that you act naturally! For it is your business to act well the character assigned to you.

The true joy of a man is to do that which properly belongs onto a man. And that is first and foremost to be kindly affected towards his fellow man. Truly he will find himself most valuable to them when he tempers his usual emotions and appetites and disciplines himself to discern rightly all plausible fancies and imaginations, for he can contemplate the nature of the universe and the things in it.

November 2

Last Sunday I went to church to hear a very meaningful sermon which was delivered by a guest speaker from San Diego in California. He was a delegate to the Disciples of Christ convention that was held in Cincinnati. I was told and read about it in the paper that 10,000 people attended the final assembly at Cincinnati Gardens on Sunday afternoon. In a grand but silent and skillfully planned get-together of the many protestant denominations it was demonstrated where the different roads of the Protestant churches should terminate. The oneness of the destination is unmistakably best and quickest to attain in the combined efforts of the Christian brothers.

Nancy once was mentioning to me the interesting discussion which arose after a speaker had given his account of the pros and cons of the master plan of the City of Cincinnati. And then she meant under the heading, "master plan", an effectful worship at Asbury or Wesley may be elaborated. Whether she mentioned this to any other person as she intented to do at that time is of lesser importance than the trend of thoughts that have occurred to me in trying to explore the meanings and connections which would point out God's master plan in this world.

"Many a way leads to Rome" is an old saying but none the less readily to be applied anew and again. My job at the 6th Street viaduct extension is a part of the master plan of the city and the first construction of Auburn Ave. another.

Last night I saw Woodburn Ave. under construction and Ringold Ave. is nearly finished. Coming from the outside to enter the city one must travel over these highways and roads that demonstrate to him the necessity of the Master Plan.

How little difference does it make who designed the construction, what engineer gave his approval, who was in charge of the construction, or what contractor executed the work. These highways exist now and new and better ones are additionally thought of in the Public Improvement Plan of Cinti. They serve their purpose well regardless whether a viaduct is spanned across the valley in a daring arch or that it creeps along the hillside, only now and then trying a careful and short jump to be quickly resting upon deeply anchored foundations. So from East and West, North and South, from all diversions and directions highways lead into the city.

Many a road leads to Rome. This proverb has been thought of also in connection with the many different ways of life. There is no universal pattern after which one can build his life. Never the less everybody is a road builder and the obstacles in life are very easily comparable to the hills and valleys of the landscape. The individual intelligence and ingenuity is challenged to bridge the gaps and to rest upon foundations which are the experiences of forefathers and our own.

All our lives are more or less directed towards a preliminary goal, like a country road approaching a city. There is not much of a choice of direction except in two directions, the positive or the negative approach. Either way may eventually come to the same destination, for the earth is round. But one way is so much longer and the difficulties so much more frequently, that it generally remains an unfinished journey.

Some where along the road of life we are tempted to think that we have advanced far enough. We enjoy being on the middle of the hillside, overlook the valleys with contentment and suspect marvelous things to be seen from the mountain peak. We do not seriously attempt to go to the heights, daring the ways rarely trodden before by man. Our curiosity is well pleased and contented to marvel at these ideals of life and our heros rest upon elevated and decorated pedestals, like the gods in a Greek temple.

There may be times when we are well aware of being at the dead end of a street but that is soon smoothed out with a hellish invention we call the good conscience.

November 3

"You are an awful nice boy, but who in the hell needs a boy?" These words maliciously spoken by Les, the drunken crane operator at 6th Street caused me to stop and think. Even though I'm doubtful that he had any deeper meaning attached to it there is unmistakingly some glimpse of truth contained.

Today is my 26th birthday. Gray are the skys and a cold wind sweeps around the houses. 26 years old means surely not longer being a boy except for Mother. So I'm thinking of having reached the age of a young man. From now on to about 39 or 40 years are supposed to be the best years of life. What else can one wish for as being aware of his presence at the threshold of life's merits. Surely I will invest in this future everything I have and all that I believe.

One time ago Rev. Bright said, "Good is all that creates more good". And evil may be easily taken as the opposite of that. Therefore all a man does is good when he in turn uses his gains to the use of further improvement. That is, I understand, hardly valid in the business world, even though this principle will exercise a strong pull towards success therein too.

How much more is promised in the spiritual realm! In a sphere where values are measured by the intensity of appreciation, the desire to understand the need of its existence and the presence of love that forgives all.

The day before yesterday Dick Stevens and I went to the Bethlehem Methodist church to speak to a group of men about our Wesley Foundation. Dick wanted me to come along for two reasons. First, to give these people the view of a student and also, secondly, to meet the men of that church which have largely a German background.

In fact it was a pleasure to be with them. After some business of theirs was taken care of Rev. Dankgrift introduced Dick. Again and again I have to marvel at Dick's ease when talking to a group. He stepped forward with a winning smile, opened his jacket to indicate how much he felt at home, and put the hands leisurely into the pockets. And then his voice, pleasant and full; distinctly in his speech and never losing a moments time what to say next. His mind must work ahead; trusting his unfailing mechanism of speech he gave a fine account of the work done at Wesley.

By no means can I compare my appearance to his, because I can't hear myself talking and more so it is impossible for me to see my mimic, the most valuable assistant of an effectful speaker. First I thanked Dick for his fine introduction and the people there for their kind invitation and reception.

The Halloween time reminded me on the occasion long ago that "Fastnachts" experience many years ago when a friend of mine and I dressed like an old couple. The enthusiasm, of begging children here in America has so much in common with the attitude we displaced when we peddled from house to house and from store to store. Georg, the friend, and I had musical instruments in our unskilled hands. I'll bet there was no harmony in our performances. But what a thrilling experience to be remembered so vividly after nearly 20 years.

So I told them how much I was in the very same situation, except that the fiddle I was asked to play was the English language. They sure thought it to be a good joke and maybe there is no need on my part to be so modest. Only a very few times I ran out of words. In between I wondered at myself that I was talking so fluently.

November 9

And now back to school again. This morning I registered and paid my health fee which is not included in the tuition fees. The classes start tomorrow. My desk is crowded like never before. Tools, books, letters and various other things are displaced. Hardly that there is enough space to write this latest account.

A wonderful weekend lays behind me. It was a very opportune time to see the nature's fantastic and magnificent change. A long stretch of road extents between Cincinnati and Kent in Northern Ohio, where the Ohio Methodist Student Moverment Conference was held. Five of us drove up there to be joined by a sixth member, Bob Cody. The others were Micki, Rose, Paul Rhodes, Don Ankeman , the driver, and myself

Friday afternoon we left Cincinnati after we had gathered under delaying circumstances. Don is a "bum" of the road. We had to hold the breath at times when opposing cars, telephone posts and other obstacles seem to be not willing to clear the road for the speedy blue '42 model Plymouth. To the praise of the driver's superb ability it has to be said that no accidents occurred. In fact a heavy snow storm made his task even more difficult. In 6 hours and 10 min. we reached our destination

Even though we had traveled a considerable distance in one direction our knowledge of the English language was still valid. Well, I must remember that I'm no longer in Europe; probably the knowledge of 3 languages would have been necessary. In fact, there seemed to have been no detectable change in the habits of the people.

I can hardly wait to tell you what else takes place at a Methodist student conference. Just imagine there are many more young people that think like you do, talk like you wish you could, but also encourage you to voice your opinions and in small discussion groups there are heart to heart talk between hardboiled and hot headed idealists.

The Saturday program was opened by a silent meditation period. First Meth. Church of Kent served as assembly place splendidly. The sanctuary and all the other facilities were open for the purposes of the conference. The meals and refreshments were prepared by the people of that church and served in the basement there. They have a big church and plenty of space.

The highlights of that conference were doubtless the challenging addresses by D. Haggard, Professor of Religion at Ill. Wesleyan University. Because we were not able to attent the opening sessions on Friday afternoon, we missed the first of Dr. Haggard's addresses.

After breakfast Saturday morning we sang together in the auditorium. Triumphantly the voices were joined in singing religious songs; the high pitched of the girls well balanced by the boys contributions in the lower scales. Praise ye the Lord! While these melodies were still sweetly ringing in our hearts there came Dr. H's sermon, heavy and laden, challenging like an impending thunderstorm

Proof to me that there is a God! Don't try it like one can proof the binominal theorem. God is not an elective. No, He exists and He surrounds us with the inexorable laws of the Universe,

How, then, can one proof the existence of God? That there is a God need not to be proven. The world was created not by accidental birth and evolution. The universe is in its essentials a magnificent thought rather than the demonstration of a marvelous mechanism.

Then, we may raise the question, "What characteristics does the God have who created heaven and earth? What God is in this world and what is our relationship to him? And where can we meet him?"

First, it was pointed out the Bible is the means of direct communication between man and God, the reference for us how God met people like Moses all the prophets, and how He selects them. Like Isaiah hearing the voice in his heart while praying in the temple and his humble answer, "Here am I, sent me!" And Paul at the road to Damascus submitted himself to God saying, "What do you want me to do Lord?"

That is the God whom we can't escape. But God in the impartial order of the universe is also impartial to the individuals. He gives no favors and we hardly can conceive him as the God of Love, a lover loving you, your family and your nation more than some other people.

If the fish had a God, they would imagine their God as the biggest fish they could think of. And had the lions in the wilderness a God, they did think him the biggest and strongest lion. Why then wonder that our God is the highest and noblest being that we can imagine. The God who created all men equal cannot be thought of as giving favors. What God do we have in our minds? One as selfish as we are? Such a God does not exist.

Coming to college is for all young people a challenge in their religious thinking. And that in mind, how can one say, "I have lost my faith in God." Rather, it should be, "I have lost faith in my God who then was not the God whom we meet in the most highest and noblest ideals"

We cannot escape the laws of the universe, neither the moral laws, because they work themselves out. Besides these things there is also the inescapable challenge of the right. Have you ever heard someone say, "This is wrong"? What do we understand as right and wrong other than the standards that are conditioned by the society in which we live?

Why not say," This is not customary"? because the environmental condition changes from one place to another? Our common sense of right and wrong is a social attribute and not inborn. Then, according to that, there is no absolute right and no absolute wrong?

The inescapable phenomenon in human life is a moral sense; conscience, the means that brings us face to face with ultimate moral truths. May it have been well understood, up to now, that the God of the universe and the God of the moral laws is not an elective: He is, period

We need to grow and to mature in the evolution and understanding of the world around and about us. We have to think God's thoughts after him. God comes to individuals at the point of their deepest concern. God speaks to the individuals in the highest and noblest ideals. God speaks to us through the needs of the world. Do we listen, do we understand? Do we go to the temple and think the problems over. Deep concern-deepest thought. What want thou me to do, oh Lord? Here I am, sent me! We have to elect him in giving way for these deep concerns.

We need to- but do we want to? Here is the point of the most crucial decision we can make! What do we make out of the high ideals we pocess? What are our deepest concerns?

Are we so selfish as to just wish for a good time? What do we talk about, and what do we work for and study for? A money making profession, a home, a wife, security for the dear ones? Getting through school but still having fun all the time? No! These are not our deepest concerns, not that. The need of the world is the voice of God! Then we must choose our life carrier according to the world's need!

How can you offend your conscience? You cannot escape other than to walk willingly with your eyes pasted to your own security. Then the highest God, the God of your soul calls in vain and He seems to cry, "Whom can I send to fill the need?"

November 26

Thanksgiving went over a little different than I planned. I intented to study all day to catch up with my school work. While I was writing my reports for school, Mrs. Wurster from the Clifton Church called and invited me for dinner. Even though I had declined Dick's and also Mrs. Dolbey's invitation I agreed to come and had an enjoyable afternoon.

Her daughter with her inlaws and the two children were plenty of entertainment. A 24 lb. turkey was filling its dish completely. Hm. That was a meal! And yet it seems to me that for too many people in the world, "Thanksgiving" is just another holiday in the calendar. Around here it is often the day of the biggest turkey and the biggest football game of the season.

Much to my own surprise my instructor in surveying took time out to remind us that this should not be so but as it was intented by the colonists, a special occasion set aside to thank God for all the good He has provided for them.

There is something neglected in the course of studies at the University. For more than a year, I'm listening to highly scientific and intellectual talks; the high skill of Mathematics, Chemistry or Physics have been the argument. Were it not for Wesley and Clifton church I sure would have forgotten that there is all above God, the father.

But how many students go to church? I'm afraid it is not too high a percentage! And yet there is conspicuously a tendency toward religious thinking among American youth. However the time that I'm aware of it is mainly off campus! In fact, this young instructor of mine ranges first in my memory in finding religious thoughts an appropriate classroom discussion.

Uncle Hans was asking repeatedly whether or not my curriculum contained lectures in the philosophical and psychological fields. To my own distress we do not have them. Whoever wants to acquire some knowledge in these fields has to go about it himself. This explains why I ascribe to Wesley such an important function that it seems necessary to invest both time and talent in its activities.

In front of me lies a pamphlet telling about the Urbana Conference which will take place on Dec. 27 thru Jan 1st. Even though it seems a little expensive for a fellow like me who lives practically from the hand to his mouth this point of view becomes rather important when I think of the inspiration that will come forth out of this experience. It may become an asset in my life from which I can draw dividends again and again.

It is evident that I'm quite aflame and my enthusiasm will carry me over the long hours of labor in which I earn the means for its accomplishment. Often it is said that the ends justify the means but I say that the means applied predetermine the ends; and in that case I should benefit greatly because I'm going to apply myself in the most efficient way that I'm able of.

I wish and pray that my mother has the faith and the understanding that will help her to endure the time of her involuntary captivity. May Christel-boy be the cheer of her day and the thoughts of her far away sons the consolation of the night and a means by which we are near to one another whenever we desire to be so. In all my activities it is a wonderful assurance to have the trust and the confidence of a dear soul. Once I wrote a poem, headed by "Adios Home" that contained the lines, "…never will I even though far from home, go astray".

Then I was making a voyage in the land of dreams. Now a vast and deep ocean lies between here and the shores I spent my childhood. Sometimes I think that I was born in Frankfurt but my home is wherever God wants me to be.

November 27

Saturday once more I spent at Dick's house. I was working at the cleaning of his mother's place. Cleaning rugs, washing walls and floor, painting and varnishing woodwork was an appropriate continuance of my Friday occupation when I was whitewashing Roland's basement and caulking windows besides doing lesser jobs here and there. And always upon returning home I find so many things that should be taken care of that I get disgustet at times.

Friday evening I went to church to prepare the poster, washed my sox upon return and then sat down to work some problems for school. On Thanksgiving Day I worked 'til 1:30 a.m., Friday 'til just about the same time, writing a letter to mother and studying physics and yesterday it was already 10:20 when I got home from Indian Hills. And so it goes.

December 7

Heinz left tonight to meet mother and the other members of our family in New York where they are due to arrive on Dec. 9. I wish that Mother and my sisters are well. I'm anxious to meet the little nephew of mine. What will the reactions be? Are they honestly supporting my intention to attain a college degree? It may however also mean an unwelcome abridgement.

December 16

So then, yesterday Mother, my sisters and the little nephew of mine arrived here. After a stormy voyage and a tiring journey from New York to Cincinnati..

Mrs. Dalzell and Ray with his family were also at the station. It was more exciting to see the incident happen than the incident itself. That is not supposed a contradiction. But again the women of my church cooperated wonderfully. Rev. Bright and his amiable wife were the actors or executives of the most generous attitudes one can imagine. Blankets and bedding, dishes and a ready prepared meal were the expressions of their generosity.

Christel has developed into a likeable boy, probably slightly spoiled because he has been for quite a while under the strict (?) supervision of women. Nevertheless, it is most conspicuous that he knows what to do and when to obey orders. He now sleeps on the Hollywood-style bed in my study.

Heinz has gone to school. Mother and the girls excepted an invitation to go to Ray and Velma. Ray came after them in the meantime. So I'm alone with my thoughts and some schoolwork to do. It's also true that my Christmas mail should be written immediately. In school seems my efficiency to undergo a serious drop. There is no other explanation than I do not apply myself in the same fashion I was able to do in my freshman year. Any excuse is more or less invalid for there is, in deed, no excuse for one's own inefficietncy.

Talking to Mrs. Dolbey, Mrs. Dalzell, and to Roland and his wife is, again and again, giving me the feeling of having friends in them. My thoughts also are with Nancy and I hope to hear from her. Christel and I went to Wesley last night. He liked the cheese sandwiches they had served there. On the way home he thought that the streetcars are not too much different from the tram at home, the trolley busses are much faster, according to him.

The "Profile" is a publication of our campus here in Cincinnati. James Castello with whom I have worked for a while, is the editor of it. So he thought to print a profile of me. Bernd Forster, a student from Holland, was interviewing me on Sunday afternoon. They also want me to submit some written matter of my own. What would be fitted, I ask myself? Something original of myself does probably not exist! And again I'm mentally not at the most productive side at the time. I hope to be able to present something worth of being publicized.

December 25

Christmas is again. And with mother, too! Exactly two weeks ago, on Dec. 11, mother, Gretel, Helga and Christel came to town after a tiresome and stormy journey. Mother is still "the tireless worker", Christel a hard headed and somewhat spoiled child, even though not without abilities. Here too, time will tell.

Meantime another semester in school came to an end. It wasn't the easiest one either and in fact until the last day I was uncertain whether or not I passed the course in surveying. However, at the time when I turned in my field book, Mr. Howe, the instructor, announced the grade of the last quiz that turned out to be my unexpected salvation. A 93% boosted my floundering avg. of 55% so close to a "C" that Mr. H. felt provoked to give me that grade for the course.

Friday I introduced myself in the City Hall to my new "chief". My next co-op job will be with the City of Cincinnati in the Topographical Surveying Office. There I start on January the 3rd.

Also, meantime, it has been decided that I'll go to Urbana even though it seemed questionable since my financial situation came to a distinct "low". The generosity and the co-operation of Rev. Bright made it possible to eliminate the expense factor. Now I'm all set to start Tuesday morning when Rev. B. will pick me up.

Another meeting with Bernd has not yielded any definite or distinct advancement in his conception of my "profile". The picture was taken one day last week. In fact, the photographer whom I met at the Candle-light Carol Service in the 7th Presbyterian Church told me that the shot was well done.

Speaking of the candle-light service, never before have I seen so many candles together. It was a most impressing service to which Mrs. Dalzell had invited. Johnny came to provide the transportation. The church itself is a very beautiful building. An excellent choir framed the sermon with wonderful choral performances.

Today Ray, Velma and Garry came to be our guests. Amiable as ever, they also brought splendid gifts, a colorful tie with a dog's head makes me quite proud to wear it. Plenty of food, candies and other holyday snick-snack was at hand "Old time games" were enjoyed not only by us but also by Ray and Velma.

Later on I went for a walk, first to the church in Clifton and then to the

Mt. Storm Park because no-one was at the church. My thoughts were also with Nancy. Hope that she had a nice and a homesickless Xmas. Returning from Mt. Storm I felt urged to pass Warren Ave. As on so many other streets the joyous expression of Xmas spirit was conspicuously displaced at house front decorations and the heartwarming illuminations of the windows. How dark and removed from this inviting charm stood N's house amidst! Only Pep, the dog, inhabited the basement in all probability.

Clifton Church displaced two illuminated trees at her stairway, one on either side. It looked quite attractive. But also there in spite of the announcements on the Bulletin Board, neither Wesley nor the Asbury Fellowship met and darkness reigned.

The dormitory C on W. University seemed as evacuated as the campus itself. In a note to Bernd I asked him whether or not our date could be rearranged to meet at an earlier time.

December 26

Tonight I hope to meet L.S. Met her at Wesley and like her for some reason. When I awakened this morning it was close to 10 o'clock. Shame on me. In fact, I don't remember to have had such a lazy time for ages. This, of course, gave ample opportunity to roam the beautified realm of the past. Many a friend and contemporary occurred to my visions as the presumptious congregation in absentia.

Especially Rico reappeared quite vividly in demanding a sign from P.M. Kreusslers indeed ranked next and I should be ashamed not having remembered them on Xmas. Plenty of greetings arrived here to welcome the Mayer family. Outstanding was the fruit basket presented by the Student Committee of the Council of Churches Women.

Christel received numerous toys among which the automobiles outnumbered any other variety. Mother had an excellent wood carving for me.

A newspaper committee took notice of our reunion in Cincinnati. The C. Post carried it.

Lately I've encountered to read "The Prophet" by Kahlil Gibran, an Arabian poet. How wonderful, when he speaks to the people of Orphaeus. I liked to call it the city of everywhere. Anwering the questions concerning the basic attitudes in life the poet paints a beautiful picture both in style and in content.

December 27

And now in Urbana as a delegate of Wesley. Rev. Bright brought us up here in record breaking time. At occasion the speedometer indicated 80 mph.

As I was hoping for the financial difficulties did not outweigh the good will and the cooperation of Wesley and the individual delegates.

There are a number of things I'd wish to get out of this conference. First I pray for to be as open minded and receptive to the issues of the conference a possible. To return from here with a clear conception about the future path in thought and in action I shall pursue. It is more than a privilege to be here and I feel it is also the birth place or hour of a new sense of obligation.

May I learn how to live Christianity instead of talking about it and may I receive enough strength to act idealistic without bragging over it. Religion must express its virtues in the life and work and in all phases of it. And only through action can one be known truly to live up the standard that he is laying claim on.

To feed 2300 people is surely not the least difficult assignment. The facilities at hand and the most essential willingness of all partaking made it well done. And a good meal was it too, I must say.

What a thrill to meet people from my own country! Gerhard and Heiko are two fellows from Germany studying here in the States. Later on this evening I met a girl from Austria, a young man from Greece and another from Chechoslowakei (Prague)

The auditorium was filled quickly with delegates. In fact, more and more delegates who arrived late were pouring in. Softly an organ was played. Yet there seemed not to be a deeper sense of worship among the students. All over one could hear some wisper and damped conversation.

Only when the lights were dimmed down and a narrating voice was heard through the loudspeaker, silence loomed over the congregation: "In the beginning, there was darkness….And God said, 'Let there be light and there was light'" In a very ingenious way spotlights and floodlights were illuminating a giant miniature design of the solar system which was placed in the middle of the stage. In front of it was the dominating cross that seemed to extend itself through the universe.

Again through the P.A. system the messages from many student secretaries from many countries across the world were read, India, Burma, England, France and many others. In fact even Germany extended their greetings. Mrs. Roosevelt's commentary was also read and her regrets were expressed that she was not able to attend. Impressing messages by members of the student body wound up the welcome

The song , "O God Our Help in Ages Past": was recided together and after a final prayer we were dismissed, The conference under the heading, "The Christian Use of Power in a Secular World": had started.

On the way out, Ivan Dorion, our state president, ran across the way and we rejoiced in seeing one another. Multitudes of young people were crowding the exits. Everyone was trying to get the final formalities out of the way In the overcrowded lobby of the Wesley foundation, which pocess a beautiful building here, popular songs and Wesley traditionals were sung.

After we, Bob, Micki and I, had assured ourselves that Bev had arrived safely we disparted to look up our accomodations and call it a day. The first day at Urbana had ended.

December 28

The second day at Urbana. Mother's last birthday present to me was a very useful alarm clock, contained in a leather ettui for traveling purposes. Because I had set it for 6 o'clock it sure did not have any consideration for a sleepy fellow- 'til I got to the bathroom it was around 6:30, I imagine. A very good breakfast was served at the coffee house.

The day's program opened once more in the great auditorium. The students from all the colleges and universities filled seat by seat, so that the capacity was exhausted.

The excellent organist, Louis S. Hilbert Jr., presented Bach's Tocatta and Fugue in D. Minor. The impressive stage features from last night were still preserved and gave a good visual background. A voice over the loud speaker called to worship

A special edition of hymnals had been prepared for the conference. Each song was printed in three languages, among them German, too. At the side of Rev. B. I sang alternately in both tongues.

Immediately followed a declaration of faith: "I believe in God the Creator of heaven and Earth, Lord of all power and might:.....After this directed prayer, led by a girl in a very impressing fashion, the Lord's Prayer came from the lips of 2300 concerned students like the mighty murmur of the ocean or the roaring of a retained storm.

A litany was arranged and read by the leader and the congregation. The closing vesion of the Messiah, the Halleluia Chorus, was greatly performed.

From the final act preceding meditation on power, I remember vividly a few parts of expressions. Like…A man without God is a bubble in the sea and a single grain of sand in an infinite beach. And God without man is a being without mind, hands, feet, and fingers.

An able moderator introduced the platform speakers of the morning session. The motif was "The Christian use of Power in a Secular World". Dr. Harry Rubin gave a very good reading about the power dilemma in the 20th Century.

What is power in the understanding of the individual? Typically the many interpretations as obvious in the various messages to the conference from many places of this continent and the world. Hope and fear, well wishings and warnings dominated the context of the statements that were recommended as guide posts throughout the conference.

As Dr. Rubin pointed out, a great sense of insecurity has become the nightmare to the majority of the people! Men have been in such situations before our days and yet we think it harder and our imagination exaggerates.

January 1

Letters to Nancy, notes to Lois, Rose, Mrs. Dolbey and Dick were sent off. Also the Council of Church Women. Once more the pointer of time has moved to another year, 1950. A Happy New Year!

Once more the wondrous story of the birth of the Savior has been told again. That grandeur, manifestation of God's love to all men in the life of Christ, has its strongest attraction around the manger of Bethlehem. "God so loved the world" has been said for a thousand and more times. And yet, these words were repeated- and with unnumbering repetition- like a magic formula.

From there it is only an enticing step to see in Him the great magician, the one who performed the miracles to show his God-given powers; one of identical strength with the God of the book of Jonah...and subject to the same fallacious misinterpretations.

Wise and foolish men have met Jesus ever since He crossed the face of the earth. Somehow, the Gospel of Jesus, so important ever since, has not always ever since experienced the emphasis of its proper importance.

St. Matthew tells us how the Wise Men came with all their treasures to present them to Jesus, (Chap 2:12) And being warned of God in a dream not to return to Herod, they departed into their own country another way.

Whether or not a historical actuality, the history shows that whenever wise men experienced the presence of Christ, submitting to Him all they had, they....returned or departed "another way".

God's richest blessings will rest upon your work when your contacts among students result in....that they may return "another way".

January 9

Working in City Hall. Yesterday have been in charge of service of Sunday School, and again in evening at Wesley. In afternoon I played football with James Story and it was a burn. Today I'm all sore. Dick asked me last night if I was willing to run for president? Next Sunday is election at W. Don A. is the other candidate and probably the winning one. Walked home with Lois S.

January 30

Gretel's birthday

Meantime I was elected President of the W.F. Was quite an experience;

however, in the operation of the group lies the success.

My job is going O.K. Nancy sent me a nice letter- going to sent off a Valentine card to Lahore.

April 22

Should someone ever attempt to balance his actions as to what he performed and what he could have done and yet arrive at an unusually positive result- he most certainly will have my greatest admiration or my profound skepticism.

Benjamin Franklin's saying, "Be at war with your vices, at peace with your neighbors and let every year find you a better man" contains a good measure of truth and wisdom. To combine this with the strong point of emphasis that Prof. Cromback's excellent mind made in the cell, "Much of the trouble of our time", he said, "lies in the competitive spirit of our time; we need to cooperate in the adventure of peace."

One who ceases to strive against others and employs his will in the transmutation and development of his own mind preserves much of his energy. By exercising lawful authority over one's own mind by capturing the significance of Christ's teachings, the incomparable guidance for one's thought and action in a virtuous way to peace and enlightenment, one may also be able to lead others by consideration and love.

I'm but a student commencing at the lowest steps working toward such supreme accomplishment promised as the key to complete emancipation. For three years I was an apprentice to learn the trade as a locksmith. Now I'm engaged to acquire some scientific knowledge. But above all there are no limits set to the acquisition of wisdom and the right way of conduct.

Being chosen President of W.F. is an outward evidence of recognition, but more so it is an assurance of friendship, an encouragement to pursue towards the mastery of the mind until there is shaped out and wrought out of immaturity the clear profile of my deepest concern.

May 1

Saturday Fred and I spent 2 hours at the library to get some music that could help to entertain the girls and the boys at the International Weekend. After telling Mr. Kellogg of my absence, calling Jackie to say good-bye and bringing some letters to W.F., I found myself on the way to this Y sponsored weekend. Fred is the General Chairman and Vern is the responsible Y man, of course. Last night I spent quite some time discussing the meaning of God, prayer and rel. at large with Mason, the boy from Siam whose beliefs center around Buddah.

Earlier in the evening the group spend some leisure time at a camp fire, singing, telling stories from many corners of the world and holding one another warm because it was rather cool. The stars were fully assembled, some frocks gave their daily contribution to a concert that filled the air peacefully and sweet.

August 14

Once more an attempt to continue my diary. It seems almost inevitably a repetition that after a certain period of time I feel compelled to start all over.

Now after two years of ambitious striving in the University I have a fairly good standing on record. Should the last term's grades be good for the Dean's List recognition than a 83%. Dean's List is something to be almost proud of.

Could that meekly looking locksmith apprentice ever have had such lofty dreams? And yet I suppose that only through the means of mental preparation I've found both the knowledge and the courage to undertake this task. Graciously I acknowledge the invaluable assistance of all my friends across the ocean as well as the many pals here whose trust and confidence is more worth than gold and laurels or soon forgotten

The afternoon I spent visiting with Rose T. Heaven knows what we all talk about but is there anything this strangely mature mind does not approach objectively. Maybe not so much objectively than idealistically. That reminds me of Rico who once commented that there is not such a thing like an idealist. I also have heard it saying that one cannot live by principles alone but one must have them nevertheless.

September 21

Yesterday I stayed home from work at the City Hall. An extensive rest did help me to recuperate from long working hours and continuous nervous tension. Helga's birthday party was attented by numerous friends. Gretel, Clara, Erwin, Velma and Garry besides ourselves made the available space look somewhat insufficient and crowded.

No doubt there is nothing in this world that would substitute for kindness, love and affection. A love stranger is he who suffers from negligence, a darn fool who neglects. Now I bow humbly to God's gracious guidance, Jesus' incomparable comradeship, and hope from both the strength and the insight that will lift me up to the lofty pathway to virtue.

Appendix A
From Heinz Mayer's Memoirs

Toward the end of the war, Paul and I were to join other unfortunate people who were put into labor camps. By that time, we salvaged what we could and thanks to Gretel, found a small apartment in Wüstems in the Taunus Mountains. The town mayor, not an overly educated person, misunderstood on the phone when the orders came for Paul and myself to report to the main railroad station in Frankfurt, a certain day, a certain time. Well, when we got there, the transport had left without us. We had to report to the Gestapo based headquarters to find out what they had in mind. They must have had a party the night before, for there were many empty wine bottles lined up against the walls. I can't say they mistreated us, but simply told us the next time they would summon us, to bring warm clothes, good shoes, etc. Good advice from the hated and despised Gestapo.

When Paul and I finally left Frankfurt to be put into a forced labor camp, we did not know where they would take us. They put us in a camp called Blankenburg in the Harz Mountains. There, they were going to separate us for Paul and me to be in different camps. Paul was already being shipped out to Derenburg, not too far away. So I asked for permission to join him so we would be together again. Permission granted, and I was on my way, hiking all by myself to Derenburg to the camp where Paul had been sent.

There we were together again. The forced labor camp was one of many by the Organization Todt. One of the guards saw the ring I wore, my mother had given me. He wanted it, saying where I was going I wouldn't be needing that ring. Easy to figure out what he meant. So I told him where I was going, that ring would go also.

At the camp, we worked twelve hour a day shifts, digging big holes to store fuel tanks for the war effort. Needless to say, they were never put to use.

At the camp there were many imported laborers from other countries. We made friends with a family from Ukraine, whose daughter let us use her guitar for a few days at camp. To this day, I am thankful. I returned it to her family before we risked our lives and planned somehow to escape.

The night before we planned to run for our lives, I went to the Ukrainian family, who consisted of a young married couple (the son and daughter-in-law), the daughter, Lida, and their mother. They had invited us to a very special Easter dinner, for they had more privileges than we did. I went to tell them of our plans and gave them an address in Wüstems where they could get in touch with us if possible. Needless to say, that never happened.

Well, that next night, just before the collapse, the war almost finished, we succeeded and took what few belongings we had and ran for our lives. The night was pitch dark and one could not see a thing. A cart rumbled toward us. We did not have enough sense to hide in a ditch. So we met those people only to learn they did exactly what we did, escaped somehow.

There were four of us, Paul and I and two other brothers. We were debating which way to go since we were smack between the advancing Russian troops to the east and the advancing Americans to the west. Since we all wanted to go west toward Frankfurt, we decided to go that route. Somewhere we "confiscated" a small wagon for Paul to sit on, since he had an infected leg (a boil) and had great difficulties to walk. We walked as far as Goslar, when it was apparent that the Germans and the Americans were about to meet among gunfire etc.

American tanks were already in the town square and started shooting toward us. We hid our heads up on a hill behind a mound of dirt. What we did not know was that the Germans were behind us, not too far away. So we were caught in a cross-fire between the retreating Germans and the advancing Americans.

Somewhere along the way, a Red Cross Army nurse had joined us. She took her life into her own hands and waved a white towel or whatever it was (Paul said she took off her slip) and ran toward the American troops. One of the two brothers with us spoke English and managed to explain to the Americans we were not soldiers, but escaped from a forced labor camp. So they let us go.

We walked and walked until we came to a town called Huenfeld. There, the allies started to repatriate German women and children and we were fortunate enough to be put on a truck that was to take us to Frankfurt.

Meanwhile, our mother had a small room she lived in, since she had to work in Frankfurt. But when she came to Wüstems on weekends, we were told much later, she went down to the creek and cried. She thought she would never see Paul and me again alive. We were allowed to mail one card from the camp, but she never received it.

There was a curfew in Frankfurt, but we took a chance and walked to my mother's little furnished room the same night. Just what took place, I don't remember. I don't know whether we met in Frankfurt or Wüstems. The main thing was, we were united again.

Going back to the forced labor camp, several times I could have escaped by myself, but did not for fear they might harm Paul, possibly kill him.

Appendix B
Christmas 1946 - Letter to Gretel Mayer
Written by Betty Floding

This letter was written to Gretel after the Mayer family had already been in the United States for some time. Betty Floding (later to be Betty Morgan) was stationed as a WAC in postwar Germany and there she became friends with the Mayers, whom she had gotten to know when Heinz, who was working at the army base, took her to meet his mother. She and the Mayers remained in touch, and when Paul Mayer and his family moved to her home city of Atlanta in 1959, she became their beloved "Aunt Betty."

Christmas Eve

Never shall I forget, Gretel, that it was you who first said to me, "Nothing would please my mother more than for you to spend Christmas with us." Certainly nothing could have pleased me more!

Christmas Eve as I walk through the streets of Frankfurt, the cathedral bells, spared from being made into weaponry at the beginning of the war, rang out. On reaching the Mayers' home, Chris peers through the front door, all curls and Christmas excitement. I don't see how the German children lasted till Christmas. Every day Chris has been carrying two little pieces of paper around from the Christmas advent calendars- one given by the family and one from me. For days he has not been allowed into the front room where the tree has been prepared. One of the "boys" (was it Heinz or Paul?) fell while decorating the tree but he soon recovered.

Finally, we all entered the front room. It was darkened except for the lights on the tree. The Germans could in 1946 still use lighted candles. They were not dangerous because people put them out before leaving the room. Wax was carefully preserved from many previous celebrations.

Chris sits quietly in his grandmother's lap and sings all the Christmas songs he has learned in kindergarten before clambering down to inspect the toys and books, including a huge book of fairy tales with "Little Red Riding Hood" in German.

I go to the WAC (Women's Auxiliary Corps) detachment to take the WAC bus to Stuttgart where we sing the Messiah to a small group in a big auditorium so cold you could see your breath; and when we rose to sing a number and sat down again the seats were so cold you could feel it through your big WAC overcoat.

On returning to Frankfurt quite a bit late we find Alice and Heinz waiting where we'd agreed to meet but so cold Alice had said, "If they don't come soon, we'll have to go home."

We attended midnight service. Heinz shouldered a big box of things I'd bought at the PX (Post Exchange). The Germans couldn't get these things as their money at the time was worthless. In the large box were also my issue of G.I.. long underwear which I thought I would not need if I could get by without them until Christmas. On top of the huge carton was a green bough, which someone found to give an extra Christmas touch to the occasion.

Through the snow to the Mayers' where we gather in a cozy group around the little round black stove. I am given the couch near the tree to sleep on after Helga, with an all-embracing gesture, points to the table on which she already placed meat pies and said, "If you have hunger?"

One of the advent wreaths in church and in the home looked like a cart wheel with candles like a chandelier

Christmas Day

Morning Paul is off to a soccer game. The three women hostesses cooking. Heinz and I talk about Germany, past and present.

The feast; little sausages given by a butcher neighbor 'for the children', vegetables beautifully prepared from what Paul had been allowed to plant along a stretch of railroad tracks because he worked for the railroad.

Afternoon- We are joined by another WAC afraid to ask to spend the night with Germans. I did not ask. I simply signed out to your address. Alice says, "Now we have a good game", and it was. As we passed rapidly to singing, a bar of chocolate tied up with string and tried to open it with a fork as it passed us in a circle. The award for the winner who opened it was the chocolate bar.

Two Weeks Later

Chris, fixed with long curls and wide eyes, was in his little white bed with a cold or too much Christmas. He looked like a little Prince. His grandmother had put away many Christmas things and is now bringing them out one at a time, saying "It was too much for one little boy at one time!"

Can you see, after these reminiscences how much it meant to a lonely WAC in a foreign land to be included in your family Christmas, one of the best Christmases in her life.

If you have Chris's address, please send it to me. His grandmother said, "He has been such a good little boy." She was sure he would grow into a worthwhile person.

Appendix C
Lest We Forget

By Dr. Paul G. Mayer
Regents Professor
School of Civil Engineering
Georgia Institute of Technology

Written for the Georgia Tech Whistle
April 1985

Immediately after World War II, the news commentators were telling us not to forget Auschwitz, Belsen and Buchenwald. Recent viewing of the Holocaust documentary may have left many with an utter incomprehension of the events of only two scores ago. Auschwitz , Belsen and Buchenwald; the sight of charred bodies piled high convey ghastly impressions of incredible inhumanity, all buried in our memories as in our chronicles. More ponderous impressions of inflation, unemployment and other domestic and international crises, family matters and Reaganomics may now claim our attention to the fullest. Yet we should not forget.

I have other reasons to remember Hitler and the furnaces of Auschwitz. Once I was one of five children of one German-Jewish and one French-Protestant parent and Hitler ruled Germany. It was 1933 and I remember the fact that my teacher had to replace the morning prayers with stiff-armed salutes. Heil Hitler! Brown-shirted Nazis marched in front of my father's store and ruined the economic base of my family. Deprivation and economic collapse followed.

In 1938, a German official was murdered in Paris and in apparent retribution my father and thousands of others were taken to the Buchenwald concentration camp, only to return months later beaten and broken. In 1942, my sister died because of insufficient medical attention and delayed hospital admission. In 1943, German Jews were herded in cattle cars and railroaded into oblivion. My father, too, was led away by the Gestapo – this time never to return. He died in Auschwitz.

Not all misfortune came to us as a consequence of maniacal regime. In January of 1944, our house was bombed, victimized during an air attack by the U.S. Air Force on Frankfurt am Main.

Exactly a year later, the Gestapo incarcerated my brother and me in a labor camp in the Harz Mountains. As we were rounded up as forced laborers for the Organization Todt and as the Allied Armies surged across Europe and into Germany, we somehow screwed up our courage and made good our escape into the mountains and thence back home to our waiting and worried family. We were lucky – we survived!

Millions of others have witnessed the events of my youth – few can know the individual tragedies, the innocent and not so innocent victims of a world deprived of civility and decency. Pat stories about heroism under the boot of uncaring authorities may well commence with an electrifying episode. I have no such recollections. Out of the banked fire of my memories arose other realities. With my particular set of eyes from my particular circumstances, I was able to look ahead – without hating but without forgetting. Surely, how anyone can respond to life's tribulations and to its opportunities depends on the measure of truth to which one can achieve. What anyone can do about a predicament depends in an even larger measure on the society of which one is a part. Thus, the horrible story of the Holocaust could not repeat itself among a people that care for one another. Lest we forget.

Appendix D
Remarks at Yom Hashoah
Holocaust Memorial Service

Beth El Temple, Durham, North Carolina
April 28, 2009
By Dr. Frederick Mayer

My grandfather was Friedrich Mayer, born December 21, 1888 in Freiburg, Germany, who moved as a young man to Strasbourg in Alsace, where his father established a clothing store. There he married Alice Waeldin, a young Christian woman who worked as a clerk in the Mayer family shop.

Friedrich served in the German Army in World War I and when Alsace was returned to France after the war, he and Alice moved to Frankfurt am Main, where he opened a linens store. Alice and Friedrich, or "Fritz" as he was known to his family and friends, had five children—Marianne, Gretel, Helga, Paul and Heinz—and lived comfortably in a suburb of Frankfurt.

That life changed dramatically in 1938. On Kristallnacht, Friedrich's store was destroyed and he was one of those taken to Buchenwald, where he was badly beaten. Perhaps because he was a German veteran, or perhaps because my grandmother was so persistent, he was released several months later, and returned home, but he never recovered.

The years that followed were a terrible struggle for the family. Friedrich was unable to find any other work except manual labor. The children, categorized as "halb Juden" were prevented from attending school, and found what work they could. My father, Paul, 15 when Friedrich was first arrested, managed to secure an apprenticeship with a locksmith. In 1942, the eldest child, Marianne, became ill and, because the Nazis refused her medical care, she died.

In 1943, as Hitler began the "final solution", Friedrich was taken again by the Gestapo, along with the other remaining Jews of Frankfurt, and shipped to Auschwitz-Birkenau. My grandmother received at least one postcard from him. In a faltering hand he wrote that he was well and requested that they send him food, cigarettes, and paper. A scribbled post-script asked that they send money. They did.

Less than three months later my grandmother received a letter notifying her that "Your husband, Fritz Israel Mayer, died of heart failure on August 8, 1943 at 9:30 in camp Auschwitz." Family legend has it that his pocket watch was also returned. I cannot verify that, but I have his watch in my pocket tonight.

In 1945, my father and his brother were in a forced labor camp in the Hartz Mountains. As the Americans advanced across Germany, the two brothers decided to escape, and managed to cross the lines, but not before coming under fire. My father was hit by an American bullet but it was stopped by a book in the satchel he was carrying. We still have the book with a hole halfway through it.

In 1947, my father and his brother emigrated to the United States, and settled in Cincinnati. My father arrived in America without a high school education, speaking only a few words of English, but with a determination that God had spared him for a purpose. Within two years, he had talked his way into the University of Cincinnati, telling the officials there that his high school records would be "difficult to obtain." After receiving his degree in civil engineering, he went to graduate school at Cornell University, where he met and married my mother, Virginia Wagner, of Pennsylvania. In 1957, ten years after arriving in America, my father received his PhD.

My father never spoke with me of his childhood or of my grandfather, but I know that he never forgot. When his first child was born, he named him Frederick, and from birth, I was "Fritz".

Writing in his journal June 26, 1945, my father reflected on what he had lived through. He was then 21

"I sit at my writing desk in Frankfurt and write, think, and reflect.

Times have really changed. And you, Father, and you, my sister, you are sacrificial victims of an age which whirls over the West like a punishment of God.

Who and what will survive, what will pass, and what is yet to come? What is the way and the will of God?

What particularly comes to mind is the Pentecost sermon of the pastor of Breitenbach, and particularly its conclusion. God builds his temple out of ruins."

I light this candle tonight in honor of my namesake, Friedrich Mayer and in memory of my father, Paul Mayer, and as testimony to the transformative power of their memories.

Postscript

At the time of his death in 1985, Paul Mayer was 61 years old and a Regents Professor at the Georgia Institute of Technology in Atlanta, Georgia.

Under the auspices of the American Committee for Christian Refugees, Paul and his brother, Heinz, had come to the United States in 1947 as displaced persons. They were settled in Cincinnati, Ohio, where there were many German-speaking people and where they were sponsored by the Clifton United Methodist Church.

Both soon found work and attended evening school to learn English. During this time the young men were also able to save enough money to bring their mother, Alice, their two sisters, Helga and Gretel, and their nephew, Christian, to Cincinnati. Heinz completed his high school diploma in evening school and went on to achieve success in his chosen field of tool and die maker.

When Paul learned that the School of Engineering of the University of Cincinnati had a co-op program whereby working alternate quarters, he would be able to finance a college education, he applied. Asked about his high school records, Paul simply said that school records from Germany would be difficult to get. So despite his lack of a formal high school education, Paul was accepted at the University of Cincinnati where he majored in Civil Engineering. At Cincinnati, he was very active in the Wesley Fellowship of the Methodist Church and in the YMCA and he found time both to play soccer and to coach the Cincinnati Soccer Club team.

As time approached for graduation, Paul was faced with a decision. Should he follow his technical or his more philosophical interests? Should he go to graduate school in engineering or to theology school? After much soul searching, he decided on engineering, pursuing a special interest in hydraulics.

Paul was accepted into the graduate program at Cornell University and there he earned both Masters and Doctoral degrees. It was in Ithaca also that we met and that our first two children, Frederick and Marianne, were born. After finishing his graduate studies, Paul was offered a position as Assistant Professor in the School of Engineering.

For two years, Paul taught at Cornell. Then he was asked to come to the Georgia Institute of Technology as an Associate Professor. He was to teach at Georgia Tech for twenty-seven years. Two more children, Laura and Donald, born in Atlanta, completed the family.

Paul saw Civil Engineering as a way of serving humanity and for many years in his office there hung a banner, "Civil Engineering, A People Serving Profession." At Georgia Tech, Paul was active not only in teaching and doing research in his chosen field of hydraulics, but also in faculty and student affairs. He was quickly promoted to the rank of Full Professor and ultimately to Regents Professor. At Tech, he was to earn awards for both his teaching and his involvement in student affairs. At the time of his death in 1985, Paul was serving as Co-Chair of Georgia Tech's One Hundredth Anniversary Celebration.

On Paul's death, Georgia Tech President, Joseph M. Pettit, said of him:

"Paul Mayer was a remarkable professor. He taught civil engineering with skill and rigor, and was promoted in successive stages to the honored rank of Regents Professor. But among our many professors, he was perhaps our most humane. He was always working with students, always available, always serving as advisor to one of their societies. He valued social relationships within the faculty, and single-handedly advocated, and then managed the Faculty Lounge, that delightful gathering placed for food and fellowship at lunchtime. Finally, as Co-Chairman of our Centennial preparations, he provided vision and enthusiasm. I wish he could have been with us to share the results."

Paul's memorial service closed with the singing of "America the Beautiful" in honor of the love he had for the country he adopted and which adopted him when he emigrated from Germany in 1947

On the Georgia Tech campus, there is a permanent memorial to Paul, a meditation garden, planned and designed by the students. On a bust of Paul at the entrance to the garden are these words:

"For twenty-seven years, Paul Mayer, Regents Professor of Civil Engineering, enriched Georgia Tech. He loved knowledge and cared deeply for all members of the campus family. His spirit endures through the lives he touched."

Paul's spirit endures also in his family, in his four children for whom he had a deep and abiding love. He was proud of each of them and of their accomplishments. His spirit endures in his ten grandchildren, all born after his death and whom he would have enjoyed so much. May they be inspired by his determination to make a better life for himself and to make a significant contribution to the society in which he lived.

Paul's spirit has been also very much with me as I have edited these diaries and thus have reached a deeper understanding of him through his writing.

Virginia Mayer

2020